Renegades

RENEGADES
Digital Dance Cultures from Dubsmash to TikTok

Trevor Boffone

OXFORD
UNIVERSITY PRESS

OXFORD
UNIVERSITY PRESS

Published in the United States of America by Oxford University Press
198 Madison Avenue, New York, NY 10016, United States of America.

Library of Congress Cataloging-in-Publication Data
Names: Boffone, Trevor, author.
Title: Renegades : digital dance cultures from Dubsmash to TikTok / Trevor Boffone.
Description: New York, NY : Oxford University Press, [2021] |
Includes bibliographical references and index.
Identifiers: LCCN 2021001235 (print) | LCCN 2021001236 (ebook) |
ISBN 9780197577677 (hardback) | ISBN 9780197577684 (paperback) |
ISBN 9780197577707 (epub) | ISBN 9780197577714
Subjects: LCSH: Dubsmash (Electronic resource) | Hip-hop dance—Social aspects—
United States. | Dance and race—United States. | Dance and the Internet—
United States. | Social media—United States. | Generation Z—United States—
Social conditions. | Identity (Psychology) in adolescence—United States. | Cultural
appropriation—United States.
Classification: LCC GV1796.H57 B64 2021 (print) |
LCC GV1796.H57 (ebook) | DDC 792.8/0973—dc23
LC record available at https://lccn.loc.gov/2021001235
LC ebook record available at https://lccn.loc.gov/2021001236

DOI: 10.1093/oso/9780197577677.001.0001

9 8 7 6 5 4 3 2

Paperback printed by Marquis, Canada
Hardback printed by Bridgeport National Bindery, Inc., United States of America

To my father, Terry Boffone, who passed away on my first day at Bellaire High School, and to my students at Bellaire who asked me to dance with them and changed the course of my life forever.

CONTENTS

LIST OF FIGURES

PREFACE

The first time I tried to learn the Renegade, a dance challenge that was making the rounds on the video-sharing app Dubsmash, I was immediately obsessed. Who wouldn't be? It was set to a sick beat, had a catchy hook, and the lyrics were easy to remember ("wait," "renegade," and "go"). The dance was both familiar and unrecognizable. Sure, I had seen most of these moves before in other viral dances, but never in this way and certainly never at this quick speed. Now, I can usually learn a dance challenge with ease, but Renegade intimidated me. A lot. This dance was something else.

Two of my high school students, Reagan and Rian, introduced me to Renegade on Saturday, November 2, 2019. That day was one of those special days that reminded me why I got into education in the first place. We had met at Discovery Green in Downtown Houston to attend LEGO's Rebuild the World event. We spent the morning making LEGO creations, being interviewed for the official LEGO YouTube channel, and, as we did whenever we were together, dancing. It was a gorgeous fall day, the kind of day that Houstonians don't take for granted, but there was one problem: I was in pain. The previous day I woke up with a bad crick in my neck and I could barely turn my head. At. All. Any slight movement sent a shooting pain from my head down my shoulder through my back.

This was my new life. I had a dancing injury. It wasn't my first, and it wouldn't be my last. During the previous week, some students in my second period class and I had practiced the iconic dance to "Thriller" by Michael Jackson, which, as you might recall, features a very specific neck snap. You simply can't do the dance without snapping your neck to the side on beat while serving zombie face. We rehearsed the dance all week before filming a video of us in our Halloween costumes. Some of my students were actual zombies. Some just put on face paint. And me, I was Harry Potter (wand and all). The boy who lived—but all of a sudden, I felt as though I was going to die a premature death.

Reagan and Rian were patient with me, but I couldn't do the Renegade dance. The dance is hard enough with an able body, but the crick in my neck made it quite literally impossible to do half the movements. I also couldn't dance with any sort of speed or urgency. I could have possibly done a highly modified Macarena and been fine. I could have done the Electric Slide or the Hustle all day long. I was in great shape from the torso down, but Renegade? Forget about it! This dance wasn't in the cards for me. And, it would be fine in the greater scheme of things. Like any other Dubsmash dance challenge, Renegade would be popular for a week or two and then everyone would move on to the next dance challenge. I'd be dancing to Megan Thee Stallion, City Girls, or DaBaby again in no time.

I couldn't have been more wrong. Months later, the Renegade dance would become the world's most popular dance and something I'd be able to do in my sleep. Once I was back to full health and mobility a few weeks later, my students taught me the dance. It wasn't easy. I normally can learn a dance challenge in under fifteen minutes, but this one took weeks. I couldn't get past the complicated beginning. If I would successfully do the dance's initial choreography, I'd inevitably forget one of the following parts, the same moves that I had seemingly already become a certified expert on. Such is the experience of learning a dance challenge in the age of social media. Every day my students would teach me the dance for a few minutes here and there that would normally lead to a mix of frustration, encouragement, and lots of laughter. Because one thing was certain, my students and I always enjoyed the process of collaborating while we learned a dance and made a Dubsmash video, or a Dub as Dubsmashers call it.

When I started working at Bellaire High School in Houston, Texas, in 2018, I was immediately immersed in the diverse cultures of a large, urban, Title I public school.[1] At Bellaire, I was surrounded by an ethnically, racially, and socioeconomically diverse community where my own Whiteness was anything but the norm. The students began teaching me about their interests—especially the music they listened to and their style of dancing. Every day, I would learn something new from my student experts. The artists came first—City Girls, Blueface, NBA Youngboy, DaBaby, Roddy Ricch,

Jhené Aiko, and Michelle K, among others. And with the music came dances like the Woah, which has come to define Generation Z. Little by little, my students taught me how to hit the Woah. I'd put my hands in a fist and diagonally cross both of my arms on beat. From there, my students began teaching me variations of the signature Gen Z dance move, and before I knew it, I was drippin' sauce. Soon, we started using Dubsmash to make short dance videos, 10–15 seconds in length, after the week's work was done. As a result, we built community and developed stronger teacher/student bonds, which created a more engaging classroom atmosphere that enhanced student learning. Not to mention, we had a lot of fun in the process.

After months of dancing, in February 2019 my students encouraged me to create an Instagram account to post our dance videos. I was reluctant at first, but I ultimately saw a digital community as a beneficial extension of my classroom teaching. Almost immediately, my account—@dr_boffone—went viral, amassing over 300,000 followers (as of March 2021). During the last week of the 2018–2019 school year, my students and I were featured locally in Houston on ABC13 news and live on *Good Morning America* (*GMA*) before appearances on national television and social media platforms such as *Inside Edition*, *Access Hollywood*, *Localish*, and *The Shade Room*. As Figure 0.1 reveals, we began to engage in a different type of student-teacher relationship, one that came with clothing sponsors and photo shoots.

Figure 0.1 Bellaire High School students and author during a photo shoot for Sauce Avenue. Photo by Luke Parker.

Renegades is born from these experiences. It's the result of seeing first-hand the power that music and dance hold when it comes to identity formation among young people and, specifically, youth of color. It's the result of me becoming a Dubsmasher myself and going viral with my students. And it's the result of me desperately trying to make sense of how someone who looks like me could become a prominent figure in a movement that otherwise comprises teens of color. My Whiteness plays a pivotal role in my story.[2] Would I have gone viral if I weren't White? I think it's far less likely.

I went viral by posting a series of Dubs with two of my students—Black, identical twin girls Takia and Talia Palmer—on Instagram. Race is a key factor in how viewers receive these videos. Takia and Talia are hip. They are fashionable. They are insanely talented dancers. They can do backflips. And they've got that drip. Behind them is me—White (SPF 80 100 White), Jimmy Neutron hair, wearing a teacher lanyard, pretty nerdy ("white and nerdy" as Weird Al Yankovic would say), very stiff, can't properly hit the Woah, an average dancer but clearly having the time of my life. By any means, we don't go together, yet there we were, creating dance micro-performances to post on Instagram where millions of people would view them. Out of nowhere, this had become my new normal.

There is a rich history of White people navigating—for better or for worse—hip hop culture.[3] You can't paint a full portrait of hip hop without considering the contributions of White artists including the Beastie Boys, Weird Al, Kid Rock, Eminem, Macklemore, Post Malone, and Paul Wall. Neither can you understand hip hop without considering how the majority of people with ownership stakes in this historically Black and Brown form are White, from those who run labels to those who license music. White people have been involved in hip hop since soon after it began. With this in mind, hip hop studies scholar Imani Perry proposes, "When white performers sincerely adopt hip hop, and become adored by hip hop audiences, it takes place in part because of their embrace of both the aesthetic and political location of blackness and their sharing spaces with black bodies, such that their racial privilege becomes at least somewhat obfuscated."[4] While I respect Perry's assertions, I do acknowledge that my White privilege allows me certain access I otherwise wouldn't have. While I may be "down" with the Dubsmash community, I am still seen as an accessible White person to other teachers and the media. When they see me, they don't necessarily see the Blackness of the aesthetic forms I interface with in a given video. They see a White man, which, riffing on Perry, actually obfuscates the Blackness of the aesthetics. In twenty-first-century US culture, this changes the opportunities I receive. Yet, if I have learned anything from working with communities of color and studying critical race theory, feminist theory, and queer theory, it is that privilege isn't necessarily a bad thing and can indeed be a vector of change.

Renegades speaks to the various ways that, by acknowledging my privilege, I work against what bell hooks describes as the "white supremacist capitalist patriarchy": "the interlocking political systems that are the foundation of our nation's politics" and that play out in the digital dance world.[5] Apps such as Dubsmash and TikTok are powerful outlets that both push against and support existing systems of power that subjugate people of color in the United States. As media scholars Safiya Umoja Noble and Ruha Benjamin explore (in *Algorithms of Oppression* and *Race after Technology*, respectively), the algorithms that dictate new digital media often reinforce White supremacy and further subjugate people of color.[6] Race, therefore, forms the backbone of this analysis. I interrogate Whiteness in digital spaces, in my classroom, and, subsequently, in my writing. My position in the Dubsmash community is present throughout this book, but the chapters that focus on my teaching—that is, on me *and* my students—go further in depth into how Whiteness and my White male privilege operate in this work. Just as Blackness informs the Dubsmash world, so too does my Whiteness affect my role in the community and as the writer of this book. Accordingly, my identity is not something that I push aside in my work but is something that I am always mindful of.

Now, while the digital dance community was a new experience for me, the task of navigating my Whiteness in spaces predominantly composed of people of color was not foreign to me. First and foremost, I am a Latinx cultural studies scholar. My doctorate is in Latinx theater and literature, and I've spent the bulk of my career studying exactly that. For the better part of a decade, I have been working to understand what my place is in a community where I don't easily fit. Sure, I have a certain level of street cred because I speak Spanish, but ultimately I'm a White ally in the Latinx community. My work is informed by Latina feminist theorist María Lugones's notion of "world"-traveling. This decolonial feminist framework functions as a path toward coalition-building: people learn to love one another by traveling to others' worlds.[7] Moreover, my work engages the "loving eye," a term introduced by feminist theorist Marilyn Frye. "The loving eye" is a radical way of seeing the world that relies on conversation with people outside of one's own identity markers: "to know the seen, one must consult something other than one's own will and interests and fears and imagination."[8] Language access is integral to this type of work. For that reason, *Renegades* privileges storytelling rather than theoretical analysis. On every page, my goal is to create something engaging and relatable to the young people who encompass this research.

At Bellaire High School, I have carried the practice of this anti-racist theory with me into the classroom as I became a White ally for a community of students from a variety of racial and ethnic backgrounds. And, when I went viral as a Dubsmasher, I became a White ally in a definitively Black, decisively hip hop space. Throughout these experiences, I have been openly embraced and thoroughly included at every turn, which, I argue, is a testament to the inclusive, community-centered focus of both Dubsmash and hip hop. Even so, I do not see this work through rose-colored glasses. While I may not have been met with resistance to my face, there are still cultural codes and cues that I can't be attuned to. In a similar vein, there are conversations that happen beyond my immediate attention. My practice relies on the feminist practice of holding open space for how allyship has its limits.

This preface positions this work ethically by making space in the core of the book for the voices we need to listen to—those of Black youth. As much as this book is informed by my story, and by my own path from the academy to a high school classroom to Dubsmash and *GMA*, I am not the focus here. Yet, to exclude myself from the narrative would be to paint an abstract portrait of something that is anything but abstract. My position is thus that of insider-outsider: I'm part of the community that is the subject of *Renegades*, and being a Dubsmasher myself enables me to better understand the dynamics and ever-changing nature of the Dubsmash community. I'm part of the Dubsmash community but I am not a Renegade; I am an outsider by virtue of my age, social, cultural, and racial background, and because of my academic credentials. This outsider status contributes to my goal of objectivity. This type of collaboration has long been a core tenet of transnational feminist scholarship, research that is intrinsically devoted to building relationships.[9] Literary theorist and filmmaker Trinh Minh-ha describes the insider-outsider position as a "not quite the same, not quite the other space of being. The moment the insider steps out from the inside she's no longer a mere insider. She necessarily looks in from the outside while also looking out from the inside . . . she stands in that undetermined threshold place where she constantly drifts in and out."[10] Throughout *Renegades*, I weave firsthand accounts and behind-the-scenes anecdotes with an objective eye. According to cultural studies scholar Rachel Afi Quinn, by participating in this type of research, "getting so close as to be seen as familiar and recognizable in the context of Otherness, [the researcher] actively disrupts a binary of insider/outsider."[11] Indeed, this work occupies a gray zone.

The arguments made in this book are rooted in ethnographic work realized while I was teaching high school full time for two academic school years from 2018 to 2020. As such, my students are key players in this book. All students who appear in *Renegades*—as well as their parents—support my research. I have also shared drafts of this work with them. While the names of students in various anecdotes throughout the book are anonymized, the names of my Dubsmasher students are not. Although atypical, my choice to use their real names reflects their stature in the social dance community. The students that are named in relation to dancing have thousands—tens of thousands, in some cases—of followers on various social media platforms. They have been on local and national television using their real names, and, as such, *Renegades* just extends a type of exposure that is already present, if typically uncommon for high school students. While much of this fieldwork transpired in my classroom and the halls of my school, the work is also informed by my observations and engagement with youth on Instagram, Dubsmash, and TikTok. This work has seen me shift between digital and offline spaces to observe, document, and speak with youth about their social media use, identity performances, and the ways that viral dances affect their lived experiences.

Almost every artist in this book belongs to Generation Z. Also known as Zoomers, members of Gen Z were born from the mid-to-late 1990s to the early 2010s. As so-called digital natives, they have lived their entire lives with social media being not just relevant but thoroughly ingrained in their socialization. And although most of the subjects in what follows are Black girls, the digital dance community is not exclusively composed of this demographic. Rather, this community is a true cross-section of urban youth identities and experiences that speak to differences in race, ethnicity, gender, sexuality, religion, and socioeconomic class.

Renegades centers Blackness. It centers hip hop culture. It centers Generation Z. It centers artists. It centers dancers and musicians. It centers a community that has thus far been excluded from the scholarly record. But, as the Renegades in this book demonstrate, they won't be excluded any longer.

Introduction

A Tale of Two Teens; or, How the Renegade Was Born

As 2019 ended, seemingly every young person in the United States on social media was doing the Renegade. Writing for the *New York Times*, social media journalist Taylor Lorenz claims, "There's basically nothing bigger
right now. Teenagers are doing the dance in the halls of high schools, at pep
rallies and across the internet."[1] That was the case at Bellaire High School,
where suddenly it looked like we were in the film *Fame*. Every day at school
I would see students Renegading. On the way to the bathroom—Renegade.
While doing their work—Renegade. While talking to friends—Renegade.
They would walk to sharpen their pencil while miming the movements.
They would have five minutes before the bell rang and crowd together near
the window to film a video of them doing the dance with good lighting.
I would creep up behind them and dance bomb them—especially during
the breath section ("ha, ha"). Renegade was everywhere.

The fifteen-second dance challenge to rapper K-Camp's song "Lottery"
became one of the most iconic viral dance challenges on TikTok, the most
popular social media app for teens across the world. The dance quickly rose
to fame in October 2019 when TikTok influencer Charli D'Amelio, a White
teenage girl in Massachusetts (then only fifteen years old), "hit" the challenge and her ninety million followers soon followed suit. Overnight, the
highly complicated Renegade dance and K-Camp's catchy beats were the
new decade's first viral trend. Within five months, TikTokers generated
thirty-four million videos to "Lottery," which were viewed over three billion times. Kourtney Kardashian did the dance. So did David Dobrik.

Renegades. Trevor Boffone, Oxford University Press. © Oxford University Press 2021.
DOI: 10.1093/oso/9780197577677.003.0001

Members of the K-pop group Stray Kids Renegaded. Alex Rodriguez made his TikTok debut doing the dance. Lizzo hit the challenge with her squad, complete with matching bathrobes and towels on their heads. Although these celebrities undoubtedly increased the popularity of Renegade, the dance was a global phenomenon *before* it became the norm for celebrities to even be on TikTok. The acclaim of Renegade lies in teenage influencers like D'Amelio and other famous Gen Z TikTokers such as Addison Rae Easterling and Chase Hudson (aka Lil Huddy).

As the dance challenge's popularity grew, so did that of K-Camp's song. "Lottery" was released in April 2019.[2] From the beginning, the song was key to expanding the rapper's audience. According to Patrick Ross, the senior vice president of digital strategy at Music Ally, a music digital strategy and marketing company, "K Camp had a lot of great songs in the bag, and we knew each one was a building block to getting him back on top. We just had to keep moving forward, dropping albums, mixtapes, and singles, until we got to the right track. This happened to be 'Lottery.'"[3] The song took a few weeks to catch on, and soon teens across the United States were making freestyle dance videos and uploading them on various social media networks, principally Instagram, YouTube, and Dubsmash. The #LotteryChallenge then trended on Instagram in spring 2019, which led to the song's promoters engaging with the teenage dancers who had made the song a hit. Music Ally aggregated the best videos into a YouTube compilation to help promote the song and the work of these young dancers. Moreover, in what has become a common practice, K-Camp enlisted dozens of these dancers to be involved in the song's music video shoot in June 2019, an act that speaks to the symbiotic relationship between hip hop artists and teenage dancers. While musicians may be creating the music, social media dancers are creating the choreography that makes these songs popular and cements them into US popular culture. Just ask Lil Nas X, Megan Thee Stallion, Blueface, Doja Cat, and Brockhampton. Nearly every recording artist who is popular with Generation Z owes part of their fame to dance apps such as TikTok, Dubsmash, Triller, and Funimate.

The most popular figure in dance app culture, and perhaps the most well-known member of Generation Z in general, is Charli D'Amelio, the so-called reigning queen of TikTok. You simply can't discuss TikTok and not talk about what I call the "D'Amelio Effect." Virtually anything she posts will go viral. Her actions dictate the actions of millions of TikTok users and, by extension, an entire generation of young people on and off the app. Although D'Amelio was relatively late to the TikTok game, joining in summer 2019, it took her only ten months to become the app's most-followed account, overtaking singer and influencer Loren Gray in March 2020.[4] And with that high follower count comes something every aspiring TikToker wants— clout.[5] In the world of social media, clout is everything. Clout is the difference between your nephew posting a video on TikTok of him dancing to "The Boy Is Mine" and being excited because the video got 800 views, and Charli D'Amelio posting a video of her hitting the #DistanceDance during the COVID-19 pandemic and getting a casual 187 million views. In the first two months of 2020 alone, she appeared in a Super Bowl commercial, collaborated with Jennifer Lopez on a viral challenge ("J Lo Super Bowl Challenge"), was featured during the NBA All-Star Weekend, and signed a lucrative contract with United Talent Agency (UTA). This is clout. And after she hit the #RenegadeChallenge, millions of people hit the dance challenge, ensuring its proliferation and extended life.[6]

But while D'Amelio was rising to legitimate worldwide status, another teenage dancer was having a radically different experience. Jalaiah Harmon, a Black fourteen-year-old girl from Fayetteville, Georgia (seen in Figure 0.2), had created the world-famous Renegade dance but hadn't received any of the credit. On September 29, 2019, Harmon got home from school just like any other day. She asked Kaliyah Davis, a friend she had met through Instagram, if she wanted to collaborate on what would become Renegade. Harmon choreographed the challenging dance sequence with typical viral dance moves such as the Woah and the Wave alongside

Figure 0.2 Jalaiah Harmon. Photo courtesy Jalaiah Harmon; photo by Thiree Pinnock and Ty "Creed" Smith.

"throwback" moves like the Dab. She posted the video on the dance app Funimate and then cross-posted the side-by-side collaboration with Kaliyah on Instagram, where the video would inevitably get more traction from her 20,000 followers. The initial Instagram post got about 13,000 views, and soon her social media circle was attempting the dance. In October, dancer Global.jones (@0g.global) migrated the dance to TikTok. He changed some of the dance's more complicated moves, effectively simplifying it and making it easier for the masses. Soon thereafter, D'Amelio posted a video of herself doing the dance. Other TikTok influencers such as Addison Rae and Lil Huddy followed suit, and before the world could catch up, the D'Amelio Effect was in motion and TikTok had its most viral dance.

Naturally, the song's popularity grew as well, reaching new peaks each week, even months after its release.[7] But there were two catches—Harmon had danced to the beginning of the song as opposed to the song's chorus, which the producing team had been pushing beforehand. Moreover, Harmon changed the course of the song's history when she gave her challenge a name: the #RenegadeChallenge (aka the Renegade Dance). Harmon's seemingly simple act of selecting the word "renegade" had clear cultural capital, leading to the track's official title being changed from "Lottery" to "Lottery (Renegade)." As K-Camp's manager Naveed Hassan notes, the name was changed because "that's what kids were Google searching for."[8]

But as Renegade helped propel the careers of K-Camp and D'Amelio and drive up TikTok's popularity with Gen Z, little changed for Harmon.[9] She had created the iconic viral dance; the world had "discovered" her, yet no one knew that she was the original Renegade. Harmon's story, it seemed, followed a familiar legacy: as dance scholar Anthea Kraut acknowledges, the history of dance in the United States is a history of White "borrowing" from racially marginalized communities, "almost always without credit or compensation."[10] In the February 2020 *New York Times* profile that broke the story of Renegade's creatorship,[11] Harmon admits, "I was happy when I saw my dance all over, but I wanted credit for it."[12] Taylor Lorenz's interview with Harmon speaks to the roadblocks that Black teen content creators face when trying to receive credit for their work. The more popular the dance, the further it gets away from its creator, and, thus, the more difficult it is to trace back. Harmon, it appears, had missed her moment as White teens used her dance to continue amassing millions of followers across various social media platforms.

While Harmon was eventually credited as the dance's creator and featured on *The Ellen DeGeneres Show* and the NBA All-Star Game, her story speaks to a growing youth subculture of Dubsmashers. These artists—namely D1 Nayah, Jalaiah Harmon, TisaKorean, Brooklyn Queen, Kayla

Nicole Jones, and, of course, my high school students—have become key agents in culture creation and dissemination in the age of social media dance and music. These Black artists are some of today's most influential content creators, even if they lack widespread name recognition and, in some cases, the coveted blue check on Instagram that marks verification and "celebrity" status. Their work and influence are far-reaching, beginning on Dubsmash and spreading like wildfire on more popular apps such as Instagram and TikTok. They write the lyrics that your niece sings in between servings of turkey at Thanksgiving dinner. Their beats are the earworms that you just can't shake throughout the day. They choreograph the dances that college roommates hit during late-night study sessions. Their dance moves have come to define a generation. And yet, up until this point, the majority of influential Dubsmashers have not been recognized for their contributions to US popular culture. This book tells their stories.

Renegades: Digital Dance Cultures from Dubsmash to TikTok interrogates the roles that Dubsmash, social media, and hip hop music and dance play in youth identity formation in the United States. I explore why Zoomers use social media dance apps to connect, how they use them to build relationships, how race and other factors of identity play out through these apps, how social media dance shapes a wider cultural context, and how community is formed in the same way that it might be in a club. But this book isn't about the trends themselves. It's about the impact of the trends and an acknowledgment that—like the Charleston, Lindy, jazz dance, and Motown that predated them—these dances are a Black art and form of cultural expression that has been appropriated and made popular by White folks.

Dubsmashers privilege their cultural and individual identities using performance strategies that reinforce notions of community and social media interconnectedness in the digital age. Their identity and community inform—and are informed by—hip hop culture. Hip hop is now thoroughly ingrained in mainstream cultures across the globe, and as the culture has grown, so has the myriad ways that young people consume it.[13] Live performances in the park may have been people's primary access to hip hop in the 1970s and 1980s, but today's Zoomers get their hip hop fix from their phones. Indeed, apps such as Instagram and YouTube have all but replaced pop-up performances live on your block. Dubsmash lets users record short dance challenge videos before cross-sharing them on social media apps such as Instagram and Snapchat. In the chapters that follow, I will explore in more depth the apps themselves. The more than 200 million monthly Dubsmash users have created over 1.7 billion videos. To say there is critical mass on Dubsmash and that it is worth our scholarly attention would be an understatement. While the app might not be the most popular dance app (and while it might not have the name brand recognition that TikTok enjoys), its cultural capital is significant. In many ways, this book builds on Harmony Bench's work in *Perpetual Motion*, which examines how digital technologies "have thoroughly saturated the practices, creation, distribution, and viewers' experience of dance."[14] While Bench surveys a wider temporal field, 1996–2016, *Renegades* is firmly dedicated to unpacking the power of later developments in digital dance cultures, homing in on the period 2018–2020. As this book proposes, there is power in Dubsmash. Now is the time to unpack this phenomenon.

In *Renegades*, I explore how hip hop culture—principally music and dance—is used to construct and perform identity and maintain a growing urban youth subculture. As hip hop scholar Gwendolyn D. Pough recognizes, hip hop "is a youth movement, a culture, and a way of life. Hip-Hop is the culture; rap is the music."[15] And, as I reveal in this book, the way that young people are both shaping and engaging with hip hop culture is shifting. African American studies scholar Marcyliena Morgan notes that the work of top hip hop artists facilitates "representation, honesty—*keeping it real*—and leadership." Hip hop has become a bedrock of urban youth culture; young people engage with it to "confront complex and powerful institutions and practices to improve their world."[16] The work of Zoomers in hip hop, therefore, merits our critical attention.

Consequently, we must investigate the digital spaces where Zoomers congregate and where this work materializes. Dubsmash is a fundamental space to fashion contemporary youth identity, both of the individual and of the group. As dance scholar Katrina Hazzard-Gordon advocates, the "highly functional system of symbols" of hip hop dance shapes "individual identity development, peer-group status, and intergroup dynamics and conflict."[17] And, the Black body, as Jasmine Johnson writes, is a "technology: it knows, remembers, and utters. The black body in choreographic motion—when amplified by viral circulation—only heightens this intelligence."[18] Dubsmashers take up visual and sonic space on social media apps to self-fashion identity, form supportive digital communities, and exert agency. Indeed, they take up digital space in a rebellious way that pushes against mainstream notions of agency and identity. It is in recognition of this rebellion that I reappropriate the term "Renegades" to denote these culture producers.

The cultural work of Renegades is very much in progress. Theirs is a constantly shifting—and growing—place of culture formation and cultural inquiry. While Dubsmash and dance apps are still relatively recent, becoming a part of mainstream US culture only in 2018, these new forms of cultural engagement hark back to what scholar Emmett George Price III posits as one of hip hop's greatest strengths: the ability to launch "conversation around the development of new cultural aesthetics and renewed approaches to the formation and expression of artistic endeavors as a culture."[19] These cultural aesthetics represent what cultural theorist Raymond Williams labels "formal innovation," or emerging practices that challenge mainstream culture. Since these cultural forms are still in their early stages, they are often disregarded by the scholarly record. Williams suggests, "It is then easy to miss one of the key elements in cultural production: innovation as it is happening; innovation in process."[20] As *Renegades* demonstrates, we are in the middle of a major cultural moment in which Zoomers are stirring change through social media performance. This book is a testament to how focusing on culture as it emerges and develops is a fundamental component of explaining said culture.

Although the Dubsmash community is ethnically and racially diverse, all the Renegades in this book are Black. As I discuss in this book's first chapter, Dubsmash is by its nature a Black space, much as hip hop—as African American studies scholar Imani Perry writes—"is black American music. Even with its hybridity: the consistent contributions from nonblack artists, and the borrowings from cultural forms of other communities, it is nevertheless black American music."[21] My approach does not essentialize or simplify the Dubsmash community. Rather, it acknowledges the unique multiracial aspect of the community while amplifying the work of Black content creators. Dubsmash estimates that 25 percent of Black teens in the United States use the app on at least a monthly basis.[22] By focusing on the collective power and cultural influence of Black Dubsmashers, this work recognizes how perhaps the most marginalized racial community in the United States has consistently been responsible for much mainstream US popular culture. As the story of the Renegade dance exposes, a Black girl was responsible for the country's biggest viral sensation in the TikTok Age—even if this viral dance was largely credited to a White girl.

Most of the Renegades in this book are not just Black teenagers such as Jalaiah Harmon (Figure 0.3); they are Black teenage girls. Although there are plenty of well-known male Dubsmashers such as the Glo Twinz, Chris Gone Crazy, Debo, and Jay Go Crazy, young women are the trendsetters in this movement, and I privilege their narratives. Moreover, Dubsmash's data reveal that 70 percent of the app's users are female and 76 percent of users belong to Gen Z.[23] As the role and impact of (young) women in hip hop tends to be marginalized both in the academy and in the community, we must address the inadequacies of the often-told narrative. Accordingly, *Renegades* follows a lineage of scholarship that recognizes how women influence hip hop, affirming the creative and intellectual potential

Figure 0.3 Jalaiah Harmon. Photo courtesy Jalaiah Harmon; photo by Thiree Pinnock and Ty "Creed" Smith.

of Black girls.[24] As Hazzard-Donald claims, "Women are talkin' the talk of hip hop."[25] A form of Black girl play materializes on Dubsmash that is reminiscent of the musicality of hand-games and double Dutch that Kyra D. Gaunt discusses in her foundational *The Games Black Girls Play*.[26] By foregrounding play, joy, and labor, these women's artistic and cultural expression encompasses a complex spectrum of Black womanhood and youth experiences.[27] Just like Jalaiah Harmon, the Black female Renegades in the pages that follow are creating the dances—and in some cases the music—that push the art form in new directions and shape the way that US teens of all races and ethnicities experience social media and its reverberating effects. Their work, as African American studies scholar Stephanie Leigh Batiste proposes, "opens a space" for "transformations of knowledge and experience of race, self, and community."[28] And yet, Black teenage girls have received little, if any, recognition for this work.

While *Renegades* focuses most strongly on social media performance against a framework of hip hop studies, it also draws from theater and performance studies, gender and sexuality studies, hip hop education (#HipHopEd), and sound studies. Research from these fields has informed my approach to contextualizing how young people use social media as a fundamental site of performance, identity formation, and community building, writing themselves into the narrative and challenging the status quo and corresponding Whiteness of places such as TikTok. That being so, the present book centers Blackness. It centers Dubsmash. *Renegades* offers a timely intervention into our collective understanding of hip hop culture as it relates to its next generation of leadership and culture creation. The work is already being done. Now is the time to pay attention.

SOCIAL MEDIA: ZOOMERS CALL IT HOME

This book focuses on members of Generation Z or so-called Zoomers. Born in the mid-to-late 1990s to the early 2010s, members of this generation are accustomed to a quick pace of life, marked by rapid advances in technology that have led to an unprecedented global interconnectivity. The combination of high-speed internet, smartphones, and social media has shaped Zoomers' lives. While some scholars see the rise of digital technologies as a site of potential danger or as something that fuels an unhealthy obsession with fame (or clout),[29] I propose that the artists in this book engage with digital spaces to enable personal growth and community building. That is, social media is a fundamental site of youth identity formation today.

Youth identity formation has long been a field of scholarly inquiry. Yet, few—if any—book-length studies are exclusively dedicated to exploring Zoomer culture. It's simply too new. But we must begin this work. Young people occupy a unique position in the world: they are in the thick of discovering it while also attempting to negotiate it. They are actively forming new cultures and subcultures, new identities, genders, and sexualities that might not have been possible for previous generations.[30] And, the digital activity of today's young people—especially girls—is far more nuanced and culturally relevant than casual observers (read: adults) typically imagine.[31]

In the twenty-first century, social media is where many coming-of-age experiences take place. As so-called digital natives, Zoomers have only known a digital world. Ask them what a VHS is—or a landline phone—and you might get a confused look. Tell them about dial-up internet (make the classic AOL sounds, too!), and they will be mortified. This isn't the world they know. The world they know is all about access and speed. And it all happens directly from their phones. They use their phones for *everything*.

Their phones are used to keep in touch with family and friends. They use them to do their schoolwork. They use them to order food. They use them to watch Netflix. And, of course, they use them to connect with their friends via a plethora of constantly shifting social media apps. Scholars Howard Gardner and Katie Davis use the term the "app generation" to refer to this group of young people, who, they argue, "think of the world as an ensemble of apps, . . . see their lives as a string of ordered apps, or perhaps, in many cases, a single, extended, cradle-to-grave app."[32] The apps in *Renegades*—namely, Instagram, Snapchat, TikTok, and Dubsmash—are crucial spaces for identity formation and group bonding. They are as fundamental to the lives of young people today as arcades, malls, and roller rinks might have been for Millennials and Generation X. And it would be foolish of me to ignore the fact that by the time this book comes out, Zoomers might have moved on to the next best thing. Snapchat and TikTok might be a flash in the pan. Dubsmash might have been bought out by Facebook. Or, Zoomers might have migrated to another space. Gen Z culture shifts quickly and is nearly impossible to predict. As Zoomers so quickly move on to "the next best thing," what you are about to read may already be dated. But this is also why it is so exciting.

The formation of youth identity in relation to social media and the internet is not a new phenomenon, even if the names continue to change and the possibilities evolve. I distinctly remember being in the fifth grade, learning about AOL from a friend who had *everything* years before I did. I would go to his house after school, and we would use dial-up internet to explore what felt like an endless world. Little did eleven-year-old me know that AOL and dial-up internet were just the tip of the iceberg. As I grew up, so did the sophistication of what we now call social media. By middle school, everyone was on AOL Instant Messenger (AIM). By my junior year of high school, all my friends had a Xanga or LiveJournal where we would post a mixture of traditional journal material, daily accounts, listicles, and, of course, passive-aggressive missives. By the end of my freshman year of college, Facebook occupied every waking hour. Twitter and Instagram would follow. And before anyone could catch up to the rapid clip that technology had advanced, we were all on our sofas at night, scrolling endlessly. Since the dawn of the internet, social media has nearly always been a core facet of our lives, even if we didn't have a name for it. Young people, then and now, view social media as a critical place to construct their identities and form distinct youth subcultures. This is why if you were to walk into nearly any high school across the country and quote a popular line from the Rosa Cinematic Universe, students would immediately laugh or respond with the next line.[33] Someone from the Boogie Down Bronx could visit

Fargo, North Dakota, and do the Renegade or Say So dance with complete strangers on the street. These memes, songs, and dances are entrenched in Zoomer culture. This new technology is what unites youth today. And the saturation of social media for Generation Z is precisely why a book such as *Renegades* is possible.

In the age of social media, apps become a key site of identity performances. Teens use profile pics, likes, favorites, story posts, feed posts, and the like to present or conceal different parts of their identities.[34] Social media profiles are an indispensable component of how teens develop a sense of self and community. While social media profiles in the early days of MySpace and LiveJournal may have been opportunities for people to try on new masks and develop alternate identities, teens in the social media dance world use apps to paint a more accurate picture of their lives. Moreover, profiles on apps such as Instagram serve as a public-facing record detailing social events and shared experiences. Indeed, we must recognize the social aspect of social media. According to media studies scholar Kirsten Drotner, youth producers of digital culture get on social media not because they are interested in the technology but because they seek connection and entertainment.[35] Because nearly everyone else has social media, youth engage with it to belong and keep up with social ties. Not engaging would mean being left behind.

As the social media landscape has expanded rapidly, so too has the way that youth engage in leisure-time social media practices. In fact, youth today have increased opportunities to develop a hyper-personalized digital experience that more accurately echoes their individual priorities.[36] According to scholar Alicia Corts, "by entering new virtual spaces of performance, we experience ways of performing that steps outside the boundaries of the physical world, giving the illusion that virtual performance is unlimited."[37] Performing identity online offers new possibilities for young people to legitimize themselves *and* their community. Social media apps grant young people a site "to work out identity and status, make sense of cultural cues, and negotiate public life."[38] Whereas apps give Zoomers various identity blueprints, they also give them space to shape their identities, resulting in a more unique, stronger sense of self.[39] This book is about how the latter influences the former. As such, the digital realm mirrors the ways that teens experience the nondigital world, albeit with endless possibilities for self-expression. This results in a sense of belonging that is shared among influencers and casual users alike. That is, belonging to a community culture is essential to social media dance networks.

Digital spaces such as Dubsmash and TikTok allow Zoomers—and especially teens of color—to produce cultural content that, in turn, facilitates young people's participation in an increasingly inclusive and democratized media culture.[40] Although it is easy to disregard social media as pure entertainment, pleasure, and escapism, the apps in this book are all integral to shaping our collective cultural identity in the United States. Indeed, as S. Craig Watkins claims, "The popular media productions created by black youth represent a distinct sphere of cultural production."[41] Digital spaces add equity to dated socialization practices, allowing previously marginalized individuals the opportunity to recognize the import and value of their identities; they are no longer automatically excluded for not being the mainstream.[42] Much of this power lies in social media's facilitation of virality, which, as African American studies scholar Ashleigh Wade proposes, subverts traditional power dynamics. As a "mode of freedom" that holds "transformative power," social media use among Black youth pushes against the ongoing state surveillance and control of Black US Americans.[43] Moreover, as scholar André Brock Jr. reveals in *Distributed Blackness*, digital spaces such as Twitter are home to integral community conversations and information sharing, the result of which amplifies Blackness and places it at the center of digital media.[44] Unsurprisingly, Black joy is central to this digital cultural work and is itself a source of power and transformation.[45]

To fully understand Zoomer culture, then, we must understand how Black Zoomers produce digital content and thereby influence the way that non-Black teens engage with social media. Here again, Black girls are doing much of this work, even if their "experiences remain invisible and undertheorized."[46] Social media apps give Black girls more opportunities to develop supportive communities and draw on their agency in ways that aren't always readily accessible to them at school and at home.[47] As African American studies scholar Kyesha Jennings recognizes, digital media grants Black women spaces "to evoke politics of disrespectability, promote gender expansive performance and reverse traditional sexual dynamics," shifting their agency "as they construct their personas in digital spaces."[48]

Writing in 2008, a decade before Dubsmash's re-launch, social media scholar Danah Boyd posed the following questions about MySpace and Facebook: "Why do teenagers flock to these sites? What are they expressing on them? How do these sites fit into their lives? What are they learning from their participation? Are these online activities like face-to-face friendships or are they different, or complementary?"[49] Writing twelve years later, Kyesha Jennings questions "what [the song and corresponding mantra] 'hot girl summer' tells us about significant changes in the ways that black women cultivate community in digital spaces": "How are black women constructing their identities within systems of controlling images and more importantly, how do they grapple with respectability politics?"[50] *Renegades* considers how these questions speak to Instagram, Dubsmash, and TikTok with regard to dance subcultures among Zoomers. How do Black Zoomers promote an unspoken, shared set of cultural values on social media? What strategies do teens use to build and maintain digital communities? How do teens use social media dance apps such as Dubsmash to create identities as hip hop artists? What are the ways that unison dancing on social media factors into building community? Can dancing on Dubsmash lead to a transformative hip hop pedagogy? How do outsiders (read: White adults) perceive social media dance cultures, and how do Black teens push against any subsequent marginalization at the hands of White supremacy?

TOWARD A THEORY OF RENEGADES

As Renegades, the artists in this book such as Brooklyn Queen (Figure 0.4) embody the nuanced ways that Dubsmash users push against mainstream notions of civility and identity. While the term "renegade" can refer to a person who deserts and betrays an organization, country, or set of principles—someone who has treacherously changed allegiance—I refer to the word's alternate definition: a person who behaves in a rebelliously unconventional manner. As I argue, Renegades use digital platforms and hip hop culture to push again the pervasive Whiteness, and corresponding White supremacy, of mainstream US pop culture as evidenced on apps such as TikTok. Renegades take up visual and sonic space on social media apps to self-fashion identity, form supportive digital communities, and exert agency. The cultivation, performance, and theatricalization of urban youth identity is a radical act of Zoomer politics that writes Dubsmashers into a narrative that has thus far excluded their voices. Just as hip hop culture emerged from the core values of the civil rights movements of the 1960s and 1970s, the work of Renegades on Dubsmash emerges from a place of determination, self-actualization, and artistry that far predates the dance app. It reflects a cultural pride that was a mainstay of the hip hop community even before Sugar Hill Gang's wildly popular crossover hit "Rapper's Delight" went mainstream in 1979.[51]

Renegades are Generation Z's b-boys and b-girls, hip hop's original break dancers.[52] As I propose, Dubsmash—like break dancing before it—is "a public showcase for the flamboyant triumph of virility, wit, and skill. In short, of style."[53] B-boying, according to hip hop scholar Joseph G. Schloss, is a "profoundly spiritual discipline . . . as much a vehicle for self-realization as a series of movements."[54] Dubsmashing is no different. Through Dubsmash, Renegades create the disruption that shifts culture right before

Figure 0.4 Brooklyn Queen. Photo by Dove Clark.

our eyes. As Gwendolyn D. Pough argues in her groundbreaking *Check It While I Wreck It*, "When Black bodies and Black voices lay claim to public spaces previously denied to them, that space necessarily changes on some level due to their very presence."[55] This is precisely the cultural work of Zoomers in hip hop. They bring the wreck—a hip hop term that implies skill, recreation, boasting, fighting, or violence.

Pough posits, "The Hip-Hop concept of wreck sheds new light on the things Blacks have had to do in order to obtain and maintain a presence in the larger public sphere, namely, fight hard and bring attention to their skill and right to be in the public sphere."[56] Dance historian Sally Banes similarly recognizes breaking as "a way of claiming the streets with physical presence, using your body to publicly inscribe your identity on the surfaces of the city, to flaunt a unique personal style within a conventional format."[57] Pioneering hip hop studies scholar Tricia Rose notes how Black cultural work is "about a carving out of more social space, more identity space. This is critical to political organizing. It's critical to political consciousness."[58] Renegades, by way of social media's unparalleled cultural impact, "now enjoy a form of publicity once denied to them."[59] In this world, social media has replaced many physical urban spaces. Identity is not merely inscribed around the city but is instead played out in fifteen-second dance clips on cell phones. Thus, Renegades carve their identities out in a public sphere that is everywhere and nowhere at once—social media platforms as experienced on our cell phones.

With this genealogy in mind, I theorize a typology of Renegade identity that enables processes of disidentification and community building. According to José Esteban Muñoz, disidentification describes "the survival strategies [of] the minority subject."[60] It is an identity-in-difference: racial outsiders navigate mainstream culture by reconstructing it to benefit themselves as opposed to complying with "acceptable" forms of racial identity. By disidentifying, Renegades position themselves both inside and outside of the dominant culture's thoughts on how identity should be formed and performed. This process of constructing an identity that pushes against the mainstream while simultaneously *becoming the mainstream* is indicative of Renegade culture. To this end, dance is a powerful act in both identity politics and community building. As Thomas F. DeFrantz proposes, "Power is what is seen in the form, and power is what these dancers mean to channel by their performances."[61] Renegades find this power in their insider-outsider position, which allows them to develop a form of double consciousness to navigate the digital world of social media and beyond.

Judith Butler asks about "the possibilities of politicizing disidentification" in her book *Bodies That Matter*, calling attention to "this experience of misrecognition, this uneasy sense of standing under a sign to which one does and does not belong."[62] Although Butler is specifically referring to the ways that women navigate the patriarchy, her words also illuminate how Dubsmashers challenge the dominant system while actively participating in the very power dynamics that they critique. Disidentification is both seeing and failing to see viable identifications. This is precisely what Renegades do: they identify and disidentify to (re)claim a plurality of identifications.

Disidentification relies on recovering what's old and making it new again. It depends on deciphering what Muñoz calls the "encoded meaning" of cultural texts, a meaning that is inherently "universalizing and exclusionary." Muñoz theorizes: "disidentification is a step further than cracking open the code of the majority; it proceeds to use this code as raw material for representing a disempowered politics or positionality that has been rendered unthinkable by the dominant culture."[63] Renegades simultaneously identify with mainstream dance app culture and push against the ubiquitous Whiteness of apps such as TikTok in order to redress dated racial scripts. That Renegades do this through the strategic use of hip hop culture is noteworthy, and—as is the case with Jalaiah Harmon—the ways that Black youth culture permeates into mainstream (White) culture should not be lost on audiences. While Renegade identities are at times shaped in response to the cultural forces of White supremacy, sexism, and homophobia, these performance practices are dedicated to imagining and mobilizing a new cultural norm. That is, as Muñoz argues, "These new social relations would be the blueprint for minoritarian counterpublic spheres."[64]

My theory of Renegades also draws from Chicana feminist scholar Chela Sandoval's theory of differential consciousness, which describes a fluid, "mobile identity" that develops in response to the experience of multiple oppressions. As she writes, "Entrance into this new order [of differential consciousness] requires an emotional commitment within which one experiences the violent shattering of the unitary sense of self, as the skill that allows a mobile identity to form takes hold."[65] To maintain a differential consciousness, the subject must work within systems of power while simultaneously developing strategies of resistance.[66] A differential consciousness rebels against the rigid binaries that the mainstream tries to impose on marginalized peoples. It demands that the individual occupy the hazy gray area.

Accordingly, Renegades must learn to navigate (un)familiar networks by means of developing an oppositional consciousness that allows them to exist as an insider-within. They are much like what Chicana queer theorist Gloria Anzaldúa has described as the New Mestiza, a border dweller who must construct a world *without* borders. In *Borderlands/La Frontera*, Anzaldúa explains that navigating the physical and metaphorical borderlands as a space of rupture enables a new form of oppositional consciousness to develop. This process is freeing because it troubles and, eventually, removes the borders that limit identity and experience. Anzaldúa's border crossers are "the squint-eyed, the perverse, the queer, the troublesome, the mongrel, the mulatto, the half-breed, the half dead; in short, those who cross over, pass over, or go through the confines of the 'normal.'"[67] They thrive in a space that is full of ambiguity and contradictions.[68] Given these premises, I position Dubsmash as a third space and Renegades as digitally dwelling border crossers. Renegades use Dubsmash to push against traditional confines of identity construction and position themselves as the future voices of a more inclusive world. From this in-between space, from the liminality between the digital and the analog, Renegades journey on "the path of a two-way movement—a going deep into the self and an expanding out into the world, a simultaneous recreation of the self and a reconstruction of society."[69] Subsequently, Renegades hold the potential to transform the world around them, the same world that may have previously labeled them as unimportant outsiders.

The identity performances I archive in the pages that follow all speak to these theories of insider-outsiderness. Renegades maneuver the mainstream while simultaneously contributing to youth subculture. They construct their digital personas and performances in such a way as to signal a powerful future in which community is the focus and previously marginalized identities are the mainstream.

CHAPTER ORGANIZATION

Renegades is divided into six chapters that each respond to a different aspect of how Renegades use Dubsmash and other social media dance apps to build community, fashion generational and individual identities, and take control of space that has been denied to them in other facets of their lives. In chapter 1, "Digital Communities: From Dubsmash to TikTok," I explore these related but divergent social media apps. While providing a critical overview of the apps that facilitates the analysis that follows, this chapter examines their racial divide, arguing that Dubsmash is a Black space and that TikTok is a White space. An understanding of the racial politics of the social media dance world is essential to painting a full picture of how Zoomers of color navigate digital spaces to create content that then becomes the mainstream and to push against systems of White Supremacy, misogyny, homophobia, and the like.

The book's second chapter, "This Bridge Called Dubsmash: Renegades Call It Home," analyzes the varied ways that Renegades build digital communities using Dubsmash and Instagram. As I argue, online communities hold the potential to democratize access and reject coastal biases typically seen in popular US culture. The traditional entertainment centers of Los Angeles and New York City, while still important, are relegated to second-tier status behind cities such as Dallas, Houston, and Atlanta, in addition to less-populated areas across the American South. By taking up digital space on an inclusive platform, Renegades recenter traditional scripts of community building, effectively demonstrating the necessity for culturally responsive communities. These Dubsmashers search for what is familiar and lay the groundwork for equity and inclusion from there, promoting a shared sense of values that enables a plurality of voices to rise to the top. I use the official Dubsmash Instagram account as a case study, unpacking the nuanced ways that Dubsmash promotes the work of its most well-known influencers alongside a growing set of Renegades who show brand loyalty by regularly engaging with the app and who promote this subset of hip hop culture through their micro-performances on Dubsmash. Specifically, I explore the different ways that Dubsmash has used dance challenge and games to bring people together and further a sense of connection during the COVID-19 pandemic of 2020.

In chapter 3, "The Original Renegade: Dubsmash, Hip Hop Culture, and Sharing Values in a Digital Space," I provide a critical framework for understanding the symbiotic relationship between hip hop and Dubsmash. Influenced by scholarship in critical race theory, gender studies, and hip hop, this chapter explores how Renegades have forged an inclusive digital community through Dubsmash. My argument is that Dubsmash's culture of giving credit is the nexus from which a shared sense of values grows, one that encourages Dubsmashers to recognize the work of *other* artists. To demonstrate this, I use Jalaiah Harmon, the "Original Renegade," as a case study. Harmon's origin story from anonymous viral dance creator to full-blown celebrity status demonstrates how hip hop values operate in the Dubsmash community.

Chapter 4, "Gone Viral: Creating an Identity as a Hip Hop Artist," examines how Dubsmash and other music-based apps can become fundamental digital spaces for hip hop artists not only to shape a distinct identity but also to establish their careers, even as the apps also threaten to render these artists invisible in moments of virality that divorce content from creator. By closely reading the digital presence of Renegades TisaKorean, Brooklyn Queen, and Kayla Nicole Jones, I explore how musicians position themselves as both music and dance content creators on Dubsmash to gain a following. The case of TisaKorean, the rapper who introduced the world to the now-iconic dance move the Mop, speaks to the power of going viral in the digital age. Likewise, hip hop artist Brooklyn Queen and comedian and rapper Kayla Nicole Jones have been able to leverage their popularity on Dubsmash, TikTok, Instagram, and YouTube to cement their music careers.

In chapter 5, "Moving as One: Unison Dancing, Muscular Bonding, and Hip Hop Pedagogy," I explore how dancing in unison helps Renegades create stronger relationships and a more formidable sense of community. I use my own classroom experiences with my students as a case study in community-focused pedagogy. Building on research on Broadway chorus lines and military formations/drills, this chapter analyzes the role of unison movement and muscular bonding in making Dubsmash videos. I argue that dancing in unison with students on Dubsmash creates an affective response that helps build stronger relationships between students and teachers. As such, this chapter is a testament as to how Dubsmash can be used as a tool of hip hop education and culturally responsive teaching. To further demonstrate how Renegades materialize in the high school classroom, this chapter also features interviews with other dancing teachers. Dubsmash pushes against the barriers typically seen between teachers and students in public education, effectively becoming a tool of anti-racist community building.

Chapter 6, "When Karen Slides Into Your DMs: Race, Language, and Dubsmash," uses my experiences as both a Dubsmasher and a teacher to unpack the role that language plays in identity formation. Specifically, I analyze outsiders' perceptions of Renegades in tandem with the linguistic and theatrical ways that Renegades push against the dominant narrative. My argument is that the relationship between language, race, and power influences how Dubsmashers such as my students construct their identities through music as well as how others criticize those same identity formations. I again use my classroom as a case study, here focusing on what I refer to as "a tale of four messages," or a one-hour period in January 2020 in which I posted a Dub of my students and me dancing to "COOKIE SHOP" by ZaeHD & CEO and then immediately received four messages—one hypercritical message from a White follower and three supportive messages from Black followers. This case study offers a point of departure to unpack the ways that White outsiders attempt to police language and, by extension, the cultures of my students and other Renegades.

Renegades concludes with an outro, "The Revolution Will Be Dubsmashed," in which I explore how the Renegades throughout this book used their social media platforms and clout to further social justice messages during the height of the renewed Black Lives Matter movement following the murder of George Floyd in summer 2020. As I explain, Renegade Zoomers played a significant role in celebrating Blackness and made many of these "moves" on social media. Whether it was through attending marches, creating viral dance challenges, or producing new music, Renegades positioned their creativity, joy, and labor as central to the movement for Black lives. Their work forced onlookers, moreover, to recognize the labor of Black girls in our social movements. Renegades reveal, ultimately, that the revolution will be digital.

CHAPTER 1

Digital Communities

From Dubsmash to TikTok

When Jimmy Fallon took over for Jay Leno as the host of *The Tonight Show* in 2014, he brought his quirky off-the-wall, happy-go-lucky style to Studio 6-B at 30 Rockefeller Plaza in New York City. During Fallon's tenure behind the desk, videos of his antics with guests have shown a knack for going viral. Segments with him dancing in tight pants with Jennifer Lopez; demonstrating the evolution of mom dancing (Michelle Obama), end zone dancing (Justin Timberlake), hip hop dancing (Will Smith), and dad dancing (Chris Christie); performing hit songs such as "All I Want for Christmas Is You," "Santa Claus Is Coming to Town," and "Let It Go" using only classroom instruments; and lip sync battles with celebrities like Emma Stone have all enjoyed widespread digital circulation. Every few weeks Fallon has another segment that spreads across the internet, becoming a must-see for anyone interested in staying on top of the cultural zeitgeist.

The October 14, 2015, rendition of *The Tonight Show* would prove no different. Pop star Selena Gomez joined Fallon for another one of his recurring skits. The skit involved testing out new apps in the Apple Store. This week's app—Dubsmash. During the segment, Fallon and Gomez played with Dubsmash on an iPad. Fallon made Dubs of him dancing and singing to the "800-588-2300" jingle for floor and carpet company Empire Today and Dubbing over John Travolta's infamous "Adele Dazeem" moment in which he mangled Idina Menzel's name at the Academy Awards in 2014. Gomez acted out the opening lines of *The Lion King*'s "The Circle of Life" and the iconic line from the film *Taken*: "I will look for you, I will find you,

Renegades. Trevor Boffone, Oxford University Press. © Oxford University Press 2021.
DOI: 10.1093/oso/9780197577677.003.0002

and I will kill you." Fallon and Gomez didn't just make short videos, they used their full arsenal of facial expressions and charisma to work the iPad camera. Viewers watched them making Dubs in silence before the duo revealed their creations, much to the delight of the studio audience and those watching from home. The moment turned monumental for Dubsmash as millions of people watching from home downloaded the new app and its popularity skyrocketed overnight. Dubsmash, it seemed, was set to become the next big app, joining the likes of Instagram, Twitter, and YouTube. It seemed that wasn't in the cards, though, as TikTok gained in popularity.

Fast forward to March 10, 2020. Charli D'Amelio made her way to Studio 6-B to film a segment with Fallon—"Teaching a Dad 8 TikTok dances." As with anything D'Amelio does, the segment went viral, introducing a new, non-Zoomer audience to D'Amelio and TikTok dances. And what is the point of teaching someone how to dance if there isn't a final performance? To cap off the segment, D'Amelio and Fallon performed the "Oh Na Na" dance challenge to a soundtrack of audience cheers. Of course, *The Tonight Show* is more than a show simply featuring silly skits. During the interview portion of her performance, D'Amelio talked about her journey to fame, which only took about ninety minutes. She uploaded a video of her doing a dance challenge on the way to dance camp. Before she even arrived, she was TikTok famous—and not long after she was *famous*. By her one-year anniversary on TikTok, she had amassed over 58 million followers who have viewed her videos over 2 billion times. And, along the way, she helped shift the culture of TikTok from an app featuring virtually any type of video to one that is now firmly known as a dance app even though content on the platform is diverse. As D'Amelio goes, so does TikTok. As D'Amelio dances, so do millions of TikTokers.

While Dubsmash and TikTok began years apart, both emerging in foreign markets before making their way to the United States, each app has become synonymous with different corners of Gen Z culture. It is quite literally impossible to fully understand Zoomers today without first understanding the role that social media plays in their identity formation and their day-to-day lives. Although Jimmy Fallon might engage with apps as mindless entertainment for *The Tonight Show*'s audience, there is so much more to social media dance culture than these short segments reveal. Today's Zoomers, as part of what Howard Gardner and Katie Davis refer to as "the app generation," rely on social media sites as fundamental spaces to play with and perform identity.[1] Digital spaces are today's arcades and malls. They are the first place that young people go to feel connected. They are the spaces Zoomers go to learn about culture. They are the sites that Gen Z uses to form a collective sense of generational culture. That is, social media is more than just a place for escapism but is a critical space to theorize and actualize Zoomer culture.

This begs several questions. How did Dubsmash go from a user base defined by global celebrities to anonymous Black teens in the United States? How did Dubsmash become synonymous with hip hop culture? How did Dubsmash get co-opted by Generation Z? How did Dubsmash shift from an app for Dubbing over popular clips from TV and film to an app for dance challenges? And, of course there is the question that everyone always asks me: But what about TikTok? What does TikTok have that Dubsmash doesn't? What are the possibilities and limits of each space?

In this chapter, I provide an overview of both Dubsmash and TikTok, as these are the two most popular apps that Renegades use to create content and, as a result, are the two apps that are essential to the chapters that follow. Although both apps are still in their infancy, their histories and cultures reveal a racial divide that marks much of the analysis throughout this book. My work in this chapter is as simple as it is complicated. I argue that Dubsmash is a Black space and that TikTok is a White space, becoming Gen Z's answer to the differences between *American Bandstand* and *Soul Train*, which were critical sites for sharing dances, making dances more popular, and also dividing audiences, typically by race. Although both Dubsmash and TikTok feature racial diversity to varying degrees, the histories and cultures of both spaces speak to how Blackness and Whiteness operate in US popular culture, which ultimately affects the lived experiences of Zoomers and other people who engage with the apps. This chapter's primary aim is to lay the groundwork for the work that follows in *Renegades*. That is, to understand the cultural contributions of Renegades, one must first understand the dynamics of the digital spaces that they occupy.

DUBSMASH: FROM LIP-SYNCING TO DANCE CHALLENGES

While Dubsmash is known today as a popular app among Black teens in the United States, it was intended to be something quite different.[2] When the Berlin-based app originally launched in November 2014, it was primarily marketed as a lip sync app in which people would record videos of themselves mouthing sections of songs, films, and famous quotes. Dubsmash's initial success was the kind of thing that every app developer dreams of. Within seven days of launching, Dubsmash reached the number one spot in Germany, something they would soon achieve in twenty other countries, notably France, the Netherlands, and the United Kingdom. President and co-founder Suchit Dash credits much of the app's initial success to the conversational nature of the content.[3] The global success had 50 million downloads within the first six months.[4] At its height in 2015, Dubsmash had over 200 million users and 350 million installs.[5] Megastars such as Rihanna, Neymar, Stephen Curry, Hugh Jackman, Josh Groban, Jennifer Lopez, Selena Gomez, Reese Witherspoon, and Khloé Kardashian all made lip syncing videos.

Ultimately, Dubsmash's initial successes proved to be short-lived. While it was a veritable global sensation for much of 2015, most of its users stopped using the app after about thirty days.[6] And, to make matters worse, retention rates never got above 5 percent, which is not a recipe for long-term success.[7] As co-founders Suchit Dash, Jonas Drüppel, and Tim Specht recall, "We had to do something most startups never dream of. In the middle of what looked like a moment of huge success, we realized we had to tear our company down. If we hadn't, it wouldn't have had a future at all."[8] In a March 2020 essay in *Fast Company*, Dubsmash's founders give a firsthand account of how Dubsmash made the unexpected jump from lip-syncing to dancing, and from the likes of Selena Gomez and Rihanna to unknown Black teens across the United States.

The team decided to strip the company down to its core, move from Berlin to New York City, and make something that had been a flash in the pan into a long-term part of app culture. Josh Constine notes, "They spent a year coding a new version of Dubsmash centered around Following and Trending feeds."[9] CEO Jonas Drüppel acknowledges, "We realized to build a great product, we needed a depth of expertise that we just didn't have access to in Berlin. It was a risky move and we felt the weight of it acutely. But we also knew there was no other way forward, given the scale and pace of the other players in the market."[10] During this reflection and rebuilding phase, Dubsmash realized they didn't need to radically re-envision the app. At its heart, Dubsmash works because of "the quality content made by the very keenest few, combined with more fun or surprising content from other users—and that gave us an idea about the right way to rebuild the app and the company."[11] The team didn't stray far from its original idea. Instead, they shifted their focus to the users who were still engaging with the app. These users were largely teens of color in the United States who used Dubsmash in a way it was never intended to do—to share dance routines they had choreographed, sometimes set to their own original music. It was a safe space for Black teens to try out new dances and songs and grow an audience base of like-minded fans.

With this information in hand, in October 2018 Dubsmash rebranded as an app for making dance challenges and music videos. Constine proposes that Dubsmash's biggest competitor, TikTok, was also its savior.[12] As TikTok emerged in the United States in August 2018, teens across the country became increasingly interested in the micro-entertainment phenomenon. "Instead of haphazardly sharing auto-biographical Stories shot with little forethought, people began storyboarding skits and practicing dances. The resulting videos were denser and more compelling than content on Snapchat and Instagram."[13] Dubsmash's re-launch two months later was able to benefit from the market's newfound interest in micro-video digital content.

By focusing on users who were already dedicated to the app, Dubsmash made room for a community of mostly Black teens to forge a digital space of their own that was, in many ways, an affinity space. It was a safe space to create content, try out new dance moves, release new music, and build a brand alongside other teens of color. Users would then cross-share their content on other apps, a practice that remains common today. As such, Dubsmash 2.0 doesn't rely on celebrity appeal to attract new users. Rather, it relies on Zoomer content creators who have large followings on Instagram. These users—such as D1 Nayah (@thereald1.nayah), Chris Gone Crazy (@chris_gone_crazy), and Brooklyn Queen (@brooklynqueen03)— create content on Dubsmash, post it on Instagram, and, as a result, bring new users to the Dubsmash app and help keep user retention relatively high. By any measure, Dubsmash is doing well with its target audience. According to Dubsmash, about 40 percent of the app's users engage with the app daily.[14] Monthly and daily user counts have grown by 60 percent and 163 percent, respectively, since the October 2018 relaunch. By February 2019, Dubsmash was consistently ranking among the top ten entertainment applications in the iOS App Store. Dubsmash is unique in this regard, as it is one of the only apps to have begun in the top ten, plummeted to the bottom of the ranks, and the re-emerged back in the top ten.

As of 2020, Dubsmash has over 200 million users across 192 countries who have created over 1.7 billion videos. According to the app, people of color comprise around 95 percent of Dubsmash's user base, 76 percent of its users belong to Gen Z, and 70 percent identify as female. Moreover, the company also claims that about 25 percent of Black teens in America use the app on a regular basis.[15] In a month, Dubsmash has 3 million active creators on the app who post 8 million videos that are watched over 1 billion times—a whopping 40 percent of Dubsmash's daily users create content. The app comprises 27 percent of the United States' short-form video market share by installs. Not including TikTok, Dubsmash has 73 percent of the US market. As security risks surrounding TikTok grew in the media, surely thanks to US government officials frequently voicing concerns that the Chinese government was using the app to spy on people, Dubsmash saw a sharp rise in downloads during the last week of June 2020 that lasted through the summer.[16] Perhaps most impressive, Dubsmash experienced a growth of 400 percent in its first eighteen months following its relaunch, firmly situating the app in Zoomer culture by July 2020—and, critically, these users stick around. In December 2020, Dubsmash was acquired by Reddit. Notably, all Dubsmash operations will remain the same and the user experience will be untouched. Dubsmash, it is imperative to recognize, has achieved all of this without spending any money on marketing and advertising in its lifetime; the app has relied entirely on positive experiences from its users and subsequent word of mouth. This data reflects how Dubsmash has been openly received by its community and how the app has quickly cemented itself as a key site to create and experience Black Zoomer culture.

Part of the appeal of Dubsmash is the usability of the app. Compared to competitors such as TikTok, Dubsmash is simple to use and so it's less daunting to record a video. Users select a sound from the app's millions of Dubs and record their video selfie. The ease of use speaks to the creators' philosophy of keeping the app lean. That said, the bulk of the video sharing is done on other apps such as Instagram, YouTube, Twitter, and Snapchat, where there is considerably heavier traffic and engagement, which can require a level of tech savvy. Dubsmash's mobilization of popular music also draws considerable numbers of teens, and teens of color, in particular. While Dubsmash features sound bites of nearly every musical style, rap music proliferates on the app, dominating the Trending Dances and the Hot Dances pages, which helps draw in teens of color who want to stay ahead of the latest music and trends. Accordingly, Dubsmash's brief history reflects the various ways that rap music has been a key form of Black culture and expression in the United States. As rap has gained in popularity since its emergence in the 1970s, we have seen music play a pivotal role in how individual and communal identities are informed by music and dance. As Todd Boyd, aka The Notorious PhD, notes, "The recent proliferation of African American film and televisual representation, with rap music serving as a primary means of influence, has led to new definitions of African American popular culture in both the academic and the public domain."[17] Dubsmash is the next phase in understanding how rap music permeates and subsequently influences Black popular culture.

Rap sets the tone for the type of dances that Dubsmashers choreograph and push out to their followers. All it takes is the right combination of music and dance to trend on Dubsmash and then, perhaps, get picked up by an influencer on Instagram or TikTok, where the dance can then go viral.

The journey from fifteen-second clip to viral fame reveals the unique ways that Dubsmash is another example of how, as S. Craig Watkins explains, "the lively expressive cultures created by African Americans plays a lively role in patterning the racial and gender identities of youth as well as the general popular culture scene."[18] Moreover, as Dubsmash is in many ways a Black space, it enables its users to be playful and be met with community support in a way that isn't always the norm on other apps. Dance scholar Thomas F. DeFrantz proposes that "Hip hop dances also gain power from their subversive [black] stance outside the moral law of [white] America. The black body in America has long been legislated and controlled by political systems both legal and customary."[19] I suggest this is where the power of Dubsmash emerges. As a supportive, subversive space that contrasts many of the ways that (White) identities are forged on apps such as TikTok, Dubsmash has been well received by its target community, Black people, which has allowed it to grow in popularity and, as a result, penetrate US popular culture.

Moreover, Dubsmash has positioned itself at the forefront of Zoomer culture creation. While the Renegade dance challenge may be the most mainstream example of how Dubsmashers use the platform to play with identity and create content that goes viral on other social media apps, it is just one of many instances in which users test the waters on Dubsmash before taking content to other spaces. According to Suchit Dash, "The community that exists on Dubsmash is very much ground zero for a lot of trends around dance. We see a lot of instances where the core germ of an idea happens on Dubsmash first, and then starts to permeate elsewhere. To have access to and continue to grow that community is so critical."[20] Despite the success of Dubsmash 2.0, Dash, Jonas Drüppel, and Tim Specht still believe that they are only "maybe 1% of the way on our journey. There is still a long way to go."[21] Whether Dubsmash's journey is just beginning, at its peak, or coming to its close, one thing is certain—the app has had a tremendous influence on mainstream Generation Z culture even though credit is not always given to the app or to its Black content creators. As individual and collective Zoomer identities are still in the process of shifting and cementing themselves on the global stage, we must continue to pay attention to the digital spaces where this cultural work unfolds.

BUT WHAT ABOUT TIKTOK?

While every Renegade in this book is an active TikToker, TikTok is *not* their first stop on the road to creating culture and building community.

That said, to fully understand the story of Renegades, one must understand the racial dynamics at play on TikTok and how those differ from apps such as Dubsmash that are decisively safe(r) spaces for people of color. TikTok has emerged as one of the world's most essential platforms for youth expression, identity formation, and shaping a collective generational culture among Zoomers. It has done the unthinkable in passing Facebook, Instagram, Snapchat, and YouTube in monthly downloads in the Apple Store.[22] Yet, the platform is not without its critiques. The app was created in 2016 by Chinese conglomerate ByteDance and wasn't available in the United States until summer 2018.[23] Its growth paralleled the rise of Musical.ly, an app founded in Shanghai in 2014, which had relative success in the United States with 20 million users. In November 2017, ByteDance bought Musical.ly for around $1 billion and, in August 2018, merged the app with TikTok, which was already gaining popularity outside of China. By April 2020, the app had been downloaded over 2 billion times.[24] Like Dubsmash, the majority of TikTok users are young women; women ages eighteen to twenty-four comprise 22.6 percent of the app's users.[25] Although TikTok notoriously doesn't disclose user data or any real insider info, Vanessa Pappas, general manager of TikTok US, admits in April 2020, "We've seen an incredible surge in terms of both the level of creativity and diversity in the content and our users and what they're sharing."[26] This creativity and diversity of content are precisely what has led to praises and criticisms of the platform. For instance, TikTok has been under an increased amount of criticism for the ways that the platform privileges the work of White content creators and, as an extension, Whiteness.[27]

Although TikTok first entered the US market in summer 2018, it has already become a cultural force that defines Gen Z. Although there are no hard numbers that have been made public, experts believe that around 50 percent of users are between the ages of thirteen and twenty-four.[28] Spend any amount of time with teenagers today and you will quickly recognize the impact of the app. In my high school classes, students often deploy TikTok memes as humor (I, myself, am guilty of this too). TikTok memes such as the Rosa Cinematic Universe and "I'm in the ghetto" have become a significant part of the high school experience. And, while it might be difficult to gauge cultural impact through observations, the numbers don't lie. TikTok has around 500 million monthly users across the globe and has been downloaded over 2 billion times. The app was the most downloaded iPhone app during the first part of 2018, beating out mainstays Facebook, Instagram, and YouTube.[29] Moreover, during the beginning of the COVID-19 pandemic in March 2020, as much of the US population was quarantined in their homes, TikTok became an integral place for entertainment. And, since videos are made with cell phones, it became an equalizer. All of a sudden, global celebrities were using the same technology as teenagers in their bedrooms. The main difference? On TikTok, teenagers run the show. D'Amelio and the app's other big-name influencers are almost exclusively teenagers. So, when D'Amelio and Jennifer Lopez both end up quarantined at home, D'Amelio's audience was about 40 million followers larger than that of Lopez at the time, a disparity that has only grown over time. Contrast this to older apps such as Instagram, where Lopez had 120 million followers compared to D'Amelio's 19 million followers during the same period, and one can begin to comprehend how much cultural influence an app such as TikTok provides to Zoomers.

Like Instagram and Twitter, the algorithm dictates the TikTok experience. Writing for *The Hollywood Reporter*, Natalie Jarvey notes, "Fame comes fast and furious on TikTok, which uses a powerful algorithm to excavate someone from anonymity and turn them into an overnight sensation."[30] Such was the case for Charli D'Amelio, who has become the poster child for how big TikTok fame can become. D'Amelio, who was once your average teenager, now has a team of agents, managers, and lawyers working to support her brand and her potential to earn millions. D'Amelio's fame and influence all begin on the "For You Page," which is the default landing page when opening TikTok. This first content that users interact with is content that the *algorithm* considers popular. This is different from Instagram and Twitter, where the algorithm prioritizes content based on who users follow and engage with. While TikTok does have a feed dedicated to the accounts that users follow, studies show that less than a quarter of TikTokers engage with the feed, instead opting for popular videos on the For You Page (FYP).[31]

The FYP feed is exactly where users regularly confront TikTok's most famous influencers. Many of these influencers are members of the so-called Hype House, a collective of thirty of the app's biggest stars who hang out and film content at a Los Angeles mansion, otherwise known as a "collab house."[32] The Hype House is the December 2019 creation of Chase Hudson (Lil Huddy) and Thomas Petrou, who recognized the value of creating a place where TikTokers could more easily collaborate and grow their followings together. Jarvey sees the Hype House as another iteration of how young people would flock to Hollywood at the beginning of the 1900s: "The Hype Housers, really, are just carrying on a tradition that began nearly 100 years ago, when Hollywood studios first flung open their doors. Countless idealistic young people have made the trek to Los Angeles to bunk up, form networks, experience heartbreak, face rejection and—sometimes, just sometimes—find fame. The big difference is that these kids have a multimillion-follower head start."[33] In this way, TikTok reinforced coastal biases in which Los Angeles is still seen as *the* place to be. TikToker Gianluca Conte recognizes the power of Los Angeles: "You're just surrounded by influence. In L.A., if you talk to four people, one is probably going to have over 100,000 followers on Instagram. Even people that don't prioritize social media have 20,000 followers from just being here in L.A."[34] In a similar vein, in an interview with Tom Ward of *Forbes*, Petrou explains why the Hype House works: "When we moved in, Chase had 3,500,000 followers. If he went and got an apartment by himself, he might have 5 or 6 million now but not 9 million. Also, when you have a house, everyone wants to come over. No one wants to go to a two-bedroom apartment. Now, we can invite every big creator to the house."[35] By becoming a home to TikTokers such as Charli D'Amelio, Dixie D'Amelio, Addison Rae Easterling, Kouvr Annon, Nick Austin, Calvin Goldby, Avani Gregg, Patrick Huston, Daisy Keech, Ondreaz Lopez, Tony Lopez, Ryland Storms, Alex Warren, James Wright, Jack Wright, and Wyatt Xavier, the Hype House has not only helped grow each member's follower count and market appeal, but the collective has helped cement TikTok itself as the crown jewel of Gen Z culture creation.

Notably, this group is entirely comprised of White or White-passing young people who all fit within traditional Western beauty standards. Even Chase Hudson acknowledges the power of being attractive on TikTok: "You either have to be talented at something, or a weird funny mix, or extremely good looking."[36] Alex Warren adds, "If you have all three, you're a TikTok god."[37] The overwhelming Whiteness of both TikTok's upper echelon of influencers and the Hype House has not been lost on observers. Shortly after the Hype House took off, TikToker @uncle.tomm posted a video calling out the Hype House as being a place for White TikTokers and advocating for "The Melanin Mansion."[38] The public criticism of TikTok reached a tipping point of sorts in March 2020 when *The Intercept* published a story based on leaked internal documents it obtained. These documents detailed how TikTok told app moderators to suppress content created by anyone who was viewed as too unattractive, poor, or disabled. Their content was demoted on the app in favor of young people who fit into the Hype House aesthetic who would help increase the short-term new user retention rate.[39] Moderators were told to flag any content from users with: "abnormal body shape," "ugly facial looks," "dwarfism," and "obvious beer belly," "too many wrinkles," "eye disorders," and many other "low quality" traits.[40] The motivation, it appears, was to reinforce the notion that top-tier TikTok content should be aspirational to attract and retain new users. And, as these leaked documents convey, TikTok tech designers and leadership quite literally baked discrimination into the app itself while they publicly denied doing so.[41]

Aspirational content, as it seems in the TikTok world, revolves around Whiteness. On this account, TikTok's algorithm and politics reflect Safiya Umoja Noble's findings in *Algorithms of Oppression: How Search Engines Reinforce Racism*, in which she demonstrates how algorithms are potentially racist because they integrate the biases of their creators. Consequently, algorithms can reinforce systems of White supremacy, misogyny, heteronormativity, and the like. A key aspect of this is controlling what users see. According to Noble, "Search results reflect the values and norms of the search companies commercial partners and advertisers and often reflect our lowest and most demeaning beliefs, because these ideas circulate so freely and so often that they are normalized and extremely profitable."[42] On a similar note, in *Race after Technology: Abolitionist Tools for the New Jim Code*, Ruha Benjamin presents the concept of the "New Jim Code": "the employment of new technologies that reflect and reproduce existing inequities but that are promoted and perceived as more objective or progressive than the discriminatory systems of a previous era."[43] Benjamin argues that, although tech appears to be neutral regarding discrimination, it often works to "hide, speed up, and even deepen" it.[44] Noble and Benjamin's findings explain, therefore, how social media platforms can amplify existing racial hierarchies while claiming to be equitable spaces. Because of this, privileging Charli D'Amelio and other Hype House TikTokers is not just about maintaining a standard. Promoting the work of popular White TikTokers leads its influencers and TikTok itself to make money from systems of oppression, like racism, reinforcing what bell hooks describes as white supremacist capitalist patriarchy.

Responding to this, on May 19, 2020, Black TikTokers created the #ImBlackMovement, a digital protest on the platform that asked non-Black allies to change their profile picture to the raised Black power fist, unfollow at least one person who does not support Black creators, and follow at least one Black content creator.[45] #ImBlackMovement was spearheaded by Lex Scott, who also is the founder of Black Lives Matter Utah. According to Scott, "I did this because black creators are being silenced on TikTok and other social media platforms and I am fed up. Our videos are taken down and our accounts are banned when we speak against racism. I want TikTok to change their policies when it comes to black and brown creators. We should not be punished for speaking against racism. The accounts of actual racists should be taken down."[46] Similar to complaints against other social media networks, most notably Twitter, the #ImBlackMovement wants to hold the app accountable for how it proliferates problematic and harmful content that privileges White creators who fit within traditional Western beauty standards and, as a result, profits from racism. Moreover, the movement addresses the implicit biases and prejudices that many TikTokers harbor.

The ways that TikTok's White users engage with Blackness reinforces a problematic racial hierarchy. In "Tik Tok's Digital Blackface Problem," Tatiana Walk-Morris argues that videos made by White TikTokers that use Blackness as comedy "raise serious questions about how minorities are represented on TikTok and how such platforms disconnect songs and dances from their historical and cultural context, resulting in tone-deaf and offensive content."[47] It seems that it was inevitable that the prevalence of digital blackface seen on Facebook and Twitter would eventually make its way to TikTok where White teens do the Crip Walk and mouth/lip sync to sound clips of Black people for comedic effect. Videos using the hashtags #Ghetto, #InTheGhetto, and #NWordPass have become popularized on the platform. The bulk of these videos riff off stereotypes of the Black community. Thus, TikTok represents an evolution in the ways that White people have obsessed over Black culture and used Blackness as a site of entertainment since at least the 1820s when Blackface first appeared in minstrel shows throughout the United States.[48] From post–Civil War era "coon shows" to Jim Crow to digital blackface, White US American culture has consistently shown a fascination with Blackness.[49] Although many of these practices are not intended to be harmful, inevitably they are malicious and help foster a White supremacist ecosystem in the United States that sees Black people targeted in ways that White people will never understand. Although Gen Z is often considered to be the most "woke" generation compared to their predecessors, the actions of White teens across platforms such as TikTok reveal that anti-Black racism remains a significant roadblock on the road to social justice, equality, and inclusion.

This reached a tipping point in April 2020, when Georgia high school seniors Stephanie Freeman and Jeffery Hume posted a "parody" cooking show video, "How to Make N****rs."[50] The video riffed on a popular TikTok challenge in which users create a "dish" by pouring cups of water representing different ingredients together into a sink where the name of the concocted dish is written on a piece of paper. These videos can be quite funny, but Freeman and Hume's was anything but that. The video saw the White couple casually using the N-word, while adding ingredients such as fried chicken, watermelon, not having a dad, making poor life decisions, robbing White people, and going to jail. After the video went viral, Freeman and Hume were expelled from school and college offers were rescinded. While Freeman at first issued an apology, she soon changed her tune as the negative repercussions of her racist actions began to take place. Reacting to the negative feedback, Freeman wrote, "'Black' people ruined my life. They can't function in a society so they took my future. They're mad me and my boyfriend proved a point. All they know how to do is act ghetto and racist and low class. WHITE POWER. I DO NOT CARE ANYMORE," effectively doubling down on the White supremacy seen in the original video.[51]

While some point to Freeman and Hume's age as an excuse for their actions, others see the process of posting a video online as an opportunity to filter out potentially problematic content. For example, Mustafa Gatollari posits, "Before they hit upload, you know they've had a chance to review their actions, yet they still elect to forge ahead and let the entire world know how they're absolutely awful human beings."[52] Notably, Freeman and Hume's TikTok was fifty seconds—long by TikTok standards—and featured many edits, meaning that the process to create the video took a significant amount of time. Even if the couple rushed through the process, they still had to come up with the idea, gather their props, and inevitably film multiple takes to get it "just right." There are always multiple chances to reconsider one's actions before a video is posted. The couple claimed it was a joke, but it ignited a renewed conversation on the app about how White teens get to be "just teenagers" while Black teens aren't given such opportunities.

Per usual in the digital age, much of the dialogue surrounding Freeman and Hume's video took place on Twitter, which is geared toward conversation. Twitter user @JamilaGonzale14 posted, "Crazy how they get to be 'just teenagers' but black people never get that."[53] @gmayo28 added, "Also, 'stupid teenager stuff' is stuff like underage drinking or climbing onto the roof of your school, not making an incredibly racist video."[54] In response to the video, TikTok said, "We are committed to promoting a safe and positive app environment for our community . . . we do not permit hate speech. The behavior in question is a violation of our guidelines, and we remove any such reported content."[55] Although Freeman and Hume's video has been perhaps the most egregious example of overt racism on TikTok, their video did not emerge from a vacuum. That is, TikTok has a culture that signals to White teens that content that uses Blackness for comedic—and often racist—fodder is acceptable. And not only is it acceptable but it holds the potential to go viral which can lead to legitimate monetary gains.

It should come as no surprise that most teens on TikTok are not there to engage in critical conversations about racism or issues of homophobia or sexism. According to Kyra D. Gaunt, engaging in critical conversations on apps such as TikTok ruins the joke: "The whole system is about gamifying our humiliation, laughter, embarrassment, shame, crying. . . . It's all about monetizing and gaming that stuff for attention. But there is no critical reflection, downtime."[56] According to artist and critic Mandy Harris Williams, the lack of critical reflection is particularly detrimental to race relations, on- and offline, especially in a moment when Black culture is penetrating the mainstream in a way that we haven't seen before. Harris Williams notes, "Technology makes it so that you don't have to actually be around Black people to pick up Black culture: Many white kids would be horrified to learn a real history of Black social life in America, much less social dance; and they insist that their Black cultural vocabulary, movement, lilts, and tilts are actually 'internet culture.'"[57] TikTok, then, is another example of how the contributions of Black artists are undervalued in the United States, as White content creators profit off the work of Black creators—rationalizing this violent process of consumption and appropriation as merely the effect, product, and exemplar of "internet culture." White TikTokers gain "street cred" by being able to navigate Blackness on the app while simultaneously, whether consciously or not, minimizing the work of Black TikTokers. As Lauren M. Jackson, author of *White Negros: When Cornrows Were in Vogue . . . and Other Thoughts on Cultural Appropriation*, notes, "Blackness is undermined for the ease of its manipulation—but then again, that's been true for much longer than there was ever such a thing as TikTok."[58] It seems, therefore, that while TikTok is a space that can become a source of empowerment and agency for some, it is also an app that is plagued with many of the material issues of racialized identity that are hallmarks of social life in the United States. To that end, TikTok is not necessarily (digital) escapism because there is no escaping what bell hooks refers to as an imperialist, White supremacist, capitalist patriarchy.[59] Digital platforms do not always offer a reprieve from anti-Blackness and sexism, for example, but are inherently systems that replicate the issues at hand in the face-to-face, non-digital world.

Despite the problematic racial dynamics of the app, TikTok doesn't appear to be going away anytime soon. In fact, during the summer of 2020, TikTok became even more of a household name as Donald Trump frequently spoke of the potential security concerns of the app. Curiously, much of Trump's criticism of TikTok came on the heels of the app becoming *the* de facto organizing tool for Zoomers during the Black Lives Matter movement. Young people used the app to share footage of police brutality and organizing information during the George Floyd marches. Later in June, Zoomers used the app to overwhelm Donald Trump's website, booking over one million tickets to his infamous Tulsa rally on June 20, 2020, which saw a sparse crowd attending what the Trump administration promised would be a packed rally with a substantial overflow crowd.

Throughout the summer, Zoomers continued to use TikTok to quickly spread information while their actions demonstrated how advertising and targeted marketing don't work on the app in the same way that they do on Facebook and Twitter. In short, Zoomers controlled the narrative on TikTok and there was nothing that Trump could do to stop it unless he got rid of the platform altogether—which he tried, unsuccessfully, to do.[60]

TikTok did, in fact, see a ban, albeit on the other side of the globe. In June 2020, India banned TikTok and other Chinese-owned apps for security reasons, an action that saw Dubsmash jump to 610,000 installs, or an increase of 321 percent, over the same month.[61] The results suggest that, should TikTok disappear in the US market, other short-form video apps like Dubsmash are uniquely positioned to fill the gap. While Trump's criticism only fueled interest in TikTok as well as its competitors such as Dubsmash, it did reveal the many ways that youth culture influences mainstream US popular culture. Quite literally, short-form video apps and social media dance community run the show. Their users are setting the tone for life in the contemporary United States.

Since its entry into the United States in summer 2018, and despite its rollercoaster summer of 2020, TikTok has only grown in popularity, going from a space almost entirely composed of teenagers to an app that virtually every celebrity *must* be on. It would seem that anybody who is anybody is on TikTok. Yet, as *Renegades* presents, much of TikTok's dance culture emerges from Dubsmashers. Accordingly, my work in this book focuses on Dubsmash while paying close attention to how TikTok allows Dubsmashers to go viral and, in turn, influence the larger US popular culture.

CONCLUSION

On April 21, 2020, music legend Babyface did something that Zoomers do all the time: he got onto Instagram Live. Surrounded by a dramatic landscape of white candles on black pedestals, a floral arrangement, and two Grammy Awards, Babyface was soon joined by Teddy Riley of new jack swing fame. The duo took to Instagram for the third installment of what had become one of the most talked about events in the hip hop community during the COVID-19 pandemic—Instagram Live rap battles branded as Verzuz. The two went back and forth with banger after banger, sprinkling the battle with tales of discovering Toni Braxton and phone calls from Michael Jackson wanting to be hooked up with Halle Berry. Writing for *Essence*, Joi-Marie McKenzie claims, "It felt like the end of every party or the beginning of every relationship. It felt like high school parties in the gym, or late car rides home, listening to the Quiet Storm. It felt like a cookout at auntie's house or listening to the playlist your boo made for you."[62] At one point, Snoop Dogg commented on the live stream: "I love being Black." Comments from Brandy, Uzo Aduba, Ashanti, Nelly, Tyrese, Chris Tucker, and Jermaine Dupri filled the scrolling chat and furthered the notion that this was a must-see cultural moment. Not to mention that the two-hour battle had over 500,000 viewers at one point. To say Babyface vs. Teddy Riley had it all would be an understatement. The hip hop community took notice and soon Verzuz battles were the weekly must-see entertainment in spring 2020. Babyface vs. Teddy Riley led to Nelly vs. Ludacris, Erykah Badu vs. Jill Scott, and T-Pain and Lil Jon. Instagram—and social media in general—took on new meanings while people suddenly found themselves stuck inside their homes in quarantine.

During the COVID-19 pandemic, social media apps became critical sites for entertainment and socialization. But, funnily enough, older generations who had previously disregarded the ways that Gen Z engages with digital cultures were suddenly relying on these same platforms to pass the time and stay connected with their community. While the Renegades in this book all regularly use Instagram Live to interact with fans, for global celebrities such as Drake, Rihanna, Janet Jackson, Ava DuVernay, Oprah Winfrey, Michelle Obama, and the like, "going live" is uncommon. In the *New York Times,* Jon Caramanica lingers on hip hop's old guard's newfound interest in digital media: "What's unfolded in the weeks since is a wholesale reshuffling of the nature of celebrity. Without the usual systems of amplification and distribution, the very tools of fame are changing—benevolent magnanimity is out, relatability is in; polish is out, transparency is in."[63] Caramanica writes that hip hop has been at the forefront of this trend, evolving and adapting to digital media with a flexibility that has been characteristic of hip hop since its origins. While Caramanica's standpoint is certainly true, it also disregards the cultural work of hip hop's youngest generation—Zoomers. As *Renegades* demonstrates, going live on Instagram, using TikTok to push out artistic content, and the like are not tools that suddenly became popular during the coronavirus pandemic. Rather, Zoomers in hip hop have been using these platforms to strategically interact with fans, cultivate careers in the arts, build communities, disseminate widespread cultural practices, and create a shared sense of generational identity. As legendary hip hop icons took to social media en masse, it became more apparent that Gen Z is establishing cultural norms and practices that are then emulated. Instagram's music partnerships manager Fadia Kader admits, "Hip-hop as a genre is willing to take risks. It's the influencer that influences influencers."[64] And, as the work that follows in this book demonstrates, Zoomers are these influencers. What they are doing today becomes the norm tomorrow. The music they are dancing to on Dubsmash and TikTok today becomes the soundtrack to Verzuz rap battles of the future. Their dance moves become the dance moves that define a generation. Now is the time to pay attention. If not, we might get left in the dust.

CHAPTER 2

This Bridge Called Dubsmash

Renegades Call It Home

By March 16, 2020, it became all too apparent that the COVID-19 pandemic was only just beginning. A few days prior, my school district had canceled all in-person classes for a few weeks, which would soon end in remote learning for the remainder of the school year and well into the following school year. Virtual became the new normal. As I sat in my apartment eating endless meals of pasta (not to mention my renewed interest in cake and cereal), I missed my students. So much of my creativity stems from being around and learning from them. While I may be the teacher in charge of their education, I often feel like *I am the student*. I show up to class and they teach me about music, fashion, slang, and, of course, dancing. Being around highly motivated young people who have their pulse on the shifting cultural zeitgeist is one of my favorite parts about being a teacher. My classroom, like any other space that they occupy, is a critical site where their culture and subsequent community building materialize. Yet, there I was, stuck inside my apartment with no real hope of reconnecting with my students. When Governor Greg Abbott officially announced on April 16 that Texas schools would finish the school year with remote learning, many of us had to reconsider the ways we connect with other people. We were charged with rethinking how we build and maintain community. And, perhaps most significant, we were forced to question and re-envision the very makeup of community and how are needs as community members are met.

So, I turned to the digital. I turned to my Dubsmash community. One night, I came up with the "Quarantine Collab" to bring people together and

Renegades. Trevor Boffone, Oxford University Press. © Oxford University Press 2021.
DOI: 10.1093/oso/9780197577677.003.0003

take our minds off things for a bit. My vision for the Quarantine Collab, short for collaboration, was simple enough—gather a collection of the biggest Dubsmashers into one big dancing collage.[1] Collabs are common on Dubsmash, where Dubsmashers use the app PicPlayPost to create video collages where they dance "alongside" other dancers, most commonly in side-by-side duets. Since I had lost the opportunity to physically work side by side with my student Renegades, I wanted to expand how we use social media to create collaborations, especially during times of crisis. I thought that having as many people as possible collaborating would send a big message to the Dubsmash community. I began messaging other well-known Dubsmashers. Although I had met some of them in person and had regularly interacted with them online, others were simply dancers I followed and who followed me. We had never interacted in a meaningful way. This was the chance to fix that. I gave everyone the invitation and directions to send me a Dubsmash video of them doing the "Out West Challenge" to the song "Out West" by JACKBOYS and Travis Scott, featuring Young Thug. By this point, the #OutWestChallenge was enormously popular and it was nearly impossible to find a popular digital dancer who had *not* hit the challenge.[2] Compared to other dance challenges, Out West is remarkably simple, unlike Renegade; the movements are slow and there are only a few dance moves. Lean forward, then to the right, then cross and drop your arms before repeating the same sequence to your left. After that, you alternately raise and jut your right elbow right, then left elbow left before raising your right arm up, left arm up. Hold them up. Sway, sway, sway. Hit the Woah. That's it. Since the dance was well known and easy to execute, I knew that I could compile nine videos together with everyone moving in perfect unison, which is exactly what happened.

After some enthusiastic behind the scenes efforts, the Quarantine Collab went public on March 19, 2020. The video featured Jay Go Crazy, Jalaiah Harmon, Brooklyn Queen, La La So Lit, Barrie Segal, Laii, D1 Nayah, Diamond, @baybewil__, Eisha, and me, all dancing from the comfort of our homes at the beginning of what would become a very long quarantine.[3] All the Quarantine Collaborators shared the video on their personal Instagram pages and the conversation began—how can we take advantage of and leverage digital spaces to build and support community? Although a ten-second dance collab may seem like a relatively minimal act, disregarding the power of social dance to bring people together simplifies something that is actually incredibly complex. The Quarantine Collab, as a piece of hip hop collaborative culture, enabled both the featured performers and the Dubsmash community an opportunity to find themselves in the art and relate to each other. It became a way to simultaneously perform personal and collective identity. And, perhaps most significant, it became a blue-print for how we might use social media dance to ease anxieties during the pandemic.

On the heels of the Quarantine Collab, the official Dubsmash Instagram account began to further cement its role as a trendsetting communal space. The account hosted Instagram Live shows with popular Dubsmashers that allowed for deep conversations on any number of topics that were rele-vant to the community and the global moment. For example, Barrie Segal interviewed Diamond (@0fficialdvamondx) on March 20, 2020, about her work as a nurse working amid the novel coronavirus. The Live sent a key message to the Dubsmash community that the app was for more than dance challenges. This was a culturally responsive, socially engaged com-munity that was not going to simply ignore the hardships facing many of its followers. Dubsmash was instead going to use their platform to provide for its community and enact social change. As quarantine continued, so did this work evolve. Some of this work was educational, but much of it was focused on using entertainment to maintain the connectedness that makes the community click. Dubsmash released several Instagram Story templates for users to interact with and learn more about each other. They also initiated #dsxquarantine, a series of challenges carried out over two weeks that saw Dubsmashers competing to be each day's winner (aka the person who slapped the hardest).

In this chapter, I focus on the different ways that Dubsmash uses the Dubsmash and Instagram apps to build digital homes for Renegades. I argue that online communities hold the potential to reject coastal biases typically seen in US popular culture and the entertainment industry and to thus democratize access. *Renegades* positions Dubsmash as a subversive, even rebellious, space that has successfully targeted and supported Zoomers, facilitating their abilities to permeate larger US popular culture. By taking up digital space on an inclusive platform, Renegades effectively demon-strate the necessity for culturally responsive communities. Dubsmashers search for what is familiar in popular culture and lay the groundwork for equity and inclusion from there, promoting a shared sense of values that enables a plurality of voices to rise to the top. Consequently, the cultural work happening on Dubsmash is not relegated only to dancers with high follower accounts. Dubsmash privileges a democratized model that fosters a spectrum from veritable celebrities such as Kayla Nicole Jones and The Wicker Twinz with millions of followers to virtual unknowns who are en-gaging with the app for the first time. I believe Dubsmash's accessibility makes such egalitarianism possible. Dubsmash users feel comfortable re-cording videos and posting them. And they know that, by and large, their work will be met with positive feedback in a way that is uncommon on other social media platforms.

To unpack the power of digital communities as it relates to the cultural work of Renegades, this chapter focuses on how community is modeled on both the Dubsmash app and the official Dubsmash Instagram account. I focus on the creative ways that Dubsmash promotes the work of its most well-known influencers alongside a growing set of Renegades who show brand loyalty by regularly engaging with the app and who advance this subset of hip hop culture through their micro-performances. These Renegades comprise a distinctly Black youth subculture on- and off-line. Through its promotional system, Dubsmash fashions equity that is then re-enacted by its community. The result is a proliferation of community values and practices that can be seen across social media.

THIS BRIDGE WE CALL DUBSMASH

Dubsmash's role as a site of Black digital community building hasn't emerged in a vacuum. Black digital communities have been a key corner of the internet since at least the 1980s.[4] And, as the internet has grown, so have the myriad ways that Blackness is experienced and theorized in digital spaces. In this way, to understand Black Zoomer cultures, one must also understand how digital spaces play a fundamental role in the everyday life of young people and, consequently, become sites where youth develop and cement collective and individual notions of identities. Digital spaces, then, have increased the opportunity to form kinships with a group of like-minded young people in ways that simply weren't as accessible even two decades ago.[5] Whether it is Black *Game of Thrones* fans using #DemThrones on Twitter, platforms like blackgirlnerds.com, or Black girls reclaiming their bodies via twerking videos that circulate online, digital spaces give people the chance to expand collective notions of Blackness while simultaneously enabling people to retain their individuality.[6]

My work situates social dances on Dubsmash—and viral dances, in general—as leading to community building. As a form of movement "rooted in the materiality of everyday life," social dance is, according to dance scholar Julie Malnig, "essentially vernacular in the sense that they spring from the lifeblood of communities and subcultures and are generally learned informally through cultural and social networks."[7] On this account, social dance spaces such as Dubsmash can have a profound influence on everyday life and, in particular, how we experience community and interact with others.[8] As dance scholar Katrina Hazzard-Gordon notes, community dance and social interaction "have been linked to the availability of different kinds of 'dance arenas,' including jooks, honky-tonks, and after-hours joints" that allow groups to form an aesthetic commonality.[9] Since dance spaces make socialization possible, I turn my attention to how Dubsmash serves as a digital dance space-turned-bridge to build community. Digital spaces are Zoomers' answer to the arcades, malls, and roller rinks that dominated the youth social scene in the pre-digital era.[10] Put simply, without the digital—and without Dubsmash—the Renegade community wouldn't exist. And, naturally, music is a fundamental part of this digital community. That is, music and dance provide shared experiences that more easily facilitate the formation of digital communities and, as a result, youth subcultures. This is hardly a new concept. Hip hop studies scholar M. Elizabeth Blair affirms that "youth subcultures have been often organized around music."[11] Dubsmash is no different. Music provides the basis from which all other aspects of the culture and community originate on the app. As such, social dance is "symbolic or expressive of a host or social and cultural values particular to their time, place, and historical context."[12] Social media dances such as Renegade, Donut Shop, and The Mop play a fundamental role in the generational identity formation of Gen Z, and Black Zoomers are at the forefront of this work.

As a Gen Z extension of the hip hop movement, Dubsmash was quite literally (re)built as an app to enable Black creativity, self-actualization, self-determination, and, of course, community building. According to digital media scholar S. Craig Watkins, "Hip hop enables its participants to imagine themselves as part of a larger community; thus, it produces a sense of collective identity and agency."[13] Thus, this movement-as-community benefits from the collective efforts of its constituents to generate a digital culture that doesn't reinforce the typical racist, sexist, and homophobic systems that impact larger US popular culture. With this in mind, I situate the Renegade community on Dubsmash within theorist Nancy Fraser's notion of a "subaltern counterpublic." Riffing off Gayatri Spivak's "subaltern" and Rita Felski's "counterpublic," "subaltern counterpublics" refer to the parallel spaces where marginalized communities create and share counter cultures. The result shapes an oppositional consciousness that better meets the community's needs.[14] This is to say that subaltern counterpublics, such as Dubsmash, are built on the premise of inclusion and parity among its participants and materialize as a result of being excluded by mainstream, dominant public spaces. Having spaces and places such as this are integral to hip hop. According to hip hop studies scholar Murray Forman, "Virtually all of the early descriptions of hip hop practices identify territory and the public sphere as significant factors, whether in the visible artistic expression and the appropriation of public space via graffiti or B-boying, the sonic impact of a pounding bass line, or the discursive articulation of urban geography in rap lyrics."[15]

Even though community building can take many forms, I find that social media dance performance allows this work to transpire in such a way as to blend the corporeal and the digital. According to Harmony Bench, dance in digital cultures can be transformative by repeating dances, "inviting users to have co-ownership in the creation of a dance experience, and enabling users to share the rendition of a work that results from their participation."[16] That is, when we reimagine dance for digital screens, we are able to form a community that relies on co-ownership. While I might watch Dubs on my living room sofa, I recognize the dance moves and, in many cases, I know the feeling of performing them. This allows the viewer to bond with someone who they may not necessarily know or have interacted with on social media. In the case of popular dance challenges such as Renegade and Out West, for example, the experience of watching others perform the dance often includes me performing the dance in my mind. For that reason, the body is a fundamental site of community building that allows a Renegade politic to emerge, reaffirming the notion proposed by Cherríe Moraga of the importance of the body and performance to generate sociopolitical activism: "Experience first generated through the body returns to the body in the flesh of the staged performance. In this sense, for me, it is as close to direct political activism as I can get as an artist, for theater requires the body to make testimony and requires other bodies to bear witness to it."[17] Although Moraga specifically theorizes live stage performances, I find that the work of Renegades testifies to the nuanced ways that digital dancers (re)envision and (re)appropriate dominant narratives and spaces around race, gender, ethnicity, and sexuality.

The performance itself is a crucial act in shaping the community in question. My understanding of this process recalls anthropologist Victor Turner's notion of "communitas," or community building that is made possible through the performance process. Communitas encompasses a shared feeling by a group of people when their lives begin to acquire wholeness and meaning. This process rejects hierarchies, effectively placing everyone on the same level via a commons-based approach to art-making. By situation community members as equal agents, communitas enables them to have a shared experience. Typically, this involves rites of passage. While Turner discusses rites of passage that traditionally involve coming-of-age, religious, military, academic, professional, or sports contexts, I claim that dance apps should be analyzed within a rite-of-passage lens that both recognizes how digital dancing affects its constituents—its community—and foregrounds how performance facilitates self-growth opportunities. As the personal accounts in *Renegades* reveal, Dubsmash is a rite of passage that has changed these people's lives in distinct (yet interconnecting) ways.

Dubsmash, as a vibrant self-selecting community, does not assimilate itself or its Dubsmashers. Like communitas, this community allows each person to maintain their individuality while becoming part of a shared community.[18] It is necessary that these individuals come together under the confines of a collective to construct a mode of belonging achieved through the concept of community. In *Black Noise: Rap Music and Black Culture in Contemporary America*, Tricia Rose furthers this point, noting how deploying a style—such as Renegade aesthetics, for instance—can become a tool of oppositional consciousness and serve as the glue that ties people together. Rose writes, "Developing a style nobody can deal with—a style that cannot be easily understood or erased, a style that has the reflexivity to create counter-dominant narratives against a mobile and shifting enemy—may be one of the most effective ways to fortify communities of resistance and *simultaneously* reserve the rights to communal pleasure."[19] This is precisely what Renegades do.

In this way, the Dubsmash community is not just one of location and belonging, but what José Muñoz calls dislocation and unbelonging.[20] This community is formed as much around what is common and what unites community members as it is about difference. While one could argue that other dance apps such as TikTok do the same thing, as I detail in other parts of this book, Dubsmash privileges identities that are marginalized on TikTok. For instance, Queer Black Renegades such as D1 Nayah, Laii, and the Glo Twinz are not only the norm on Dubsmash, they rule the roost and are the cultural tone setters.[21] Not to mention that 95 percent of the apps users are people of color. This is a stark contrast to the most influential TikTok users such as members of the Hype House who all reinforce notions of Whiteness and, as an extension, White supremacy.

Given Dubsmash's role in community building and collaboration, the app serves as a bridge for Zoomers and anyone else who engages with it. My analysis of Dubsmash as a bridge is informed by *This Bridge Called My Back: Writings by Radical Women of Color*, a landmark anthology of work by transnational feminists curated by Gloria Anzaldúa and Cherríe Moraga. The collective also sought to create a platform for conflict resolution. By building, resolving, and collaborating, women of color theorists position bridges as a "physical and psychic struggle. It is about intimacy, a desire for life between all of us, not settling for less than freedom even in the most private aspects of our lives. A total vision."[22] As a bridge, an integral part of Dubsmash—and the corresponding Renegade culture of dance challenges—revolves around cultivating and sustaining a supportive community, improving yourself, and educating others. Paying it forward is a key component to what makes this community work. It is all about collaboration, lifting others up, and giving artists credit for their music and choreography. As Dubsmasher Solomon Snowden tells Cherie Hu for *Forbes*, he will collaborate and dance with anyone who wants to: "It doesn't matter how many followers you have or any of that—it's all about the love of dance. If people need help learning moves, I'll even FaceTime with them and help them train and prepare properly. It's always important to give back to the scene and to the youth. If no one's helping them, then once everyone gets old, what kind of scene are we going to have?"[23] This is something I experienced firsthand. Before posting my first Dubsmash video I was riddled with the anxiety that people would roast me, which was the polar opposite of what I did experience—nearly unanimous positive support. It didn't take me long to recognize the community-first, collaborative nature of Dubsmash. This unique community is precisely what separates Dubsmash from its more mainstream rival, TikTok, and is the reason this book focuses so heavily on Dubsmashers.

Herein lies the power of Dubsmash as a tool for community building, especially in digital spaces. While Dubsmashers have an interest in hip hop music and dance in common, the app is what unites them. It's what makes Dubsmashers Dubsmashers. It demonstrates the nuanced ways that hip hop culture can create a sense of community and a sense of belonging, two things that young people are desperate to have even if they don't always give voice to those desires. Moreover, where there is community, there is obligation. As the Renegades in this book all attest, obligation is a key facet of the Dubsmash lifestyle. There is an obligation to the community. There is an obligation to uplift the work of others. There is an obligation to collaborate. There is an obligation to become a better version of yourself.

HOW DUBSMASH DOES IT

The first social networking sites such as Friends United, Friendster, MySpace, and Facebook were created to help people reconnect with old friends, make new friends, and perform friendship with everyday friends in a digital setting.[24] While the social media platforms in this book do not follow the same trajectories of those early social network sites, they nevertheless continue a lineage of digital spaces that are what Nicole Ellison and Danah Boyd call "networked publics."[25] According to Ellison and Boyd, networked publics have four key aspects: persistence, visibility, spreadability, and searchability.[26] As social media has become more sophisticated and an increased site of constant social interaction, so too have the nuanced ways that digital natives use app culture to forge and sustain new communities. Platforms such as Instagram, as Kyesha Jennings posits, are "hallmarked by pleasure politics broadly defined and communal engagement."[27] These new digital spaces "offer the necessary tools to create meaning that is far more visible and accessible than other spaces allow."[28] Therefore, digital platforms like Dubsmash and Instagram can do significant work to push against the marginalization that Black Zoomers face in other aspects of their lives and, unsurprisingly, this is marked by pleasure politics. That said, social media is not without its detractors. But while some studies on social media posit that social media leads to increased feelings of social isolation, I contend that the work of Dubsmash does quite the opposite.[29] Social media apps enable Zoomers to feel a higher level of connectedness than ever before and, as a result, social media can lead to meaningful interpersonal experiences for young people.[30] While some people see digital socialization as inferior to in-person interactions, overlooking the unique power that online interaction holds fails to acknowledge the unique social context of digital communities.[31] That is, this isn't a debate about which form of socialization is more effective—face-to-face or digital—so much as a conversation that recognizes the role of both in how Zoomers experience life.

It bears repeating that Dubsmash was re-created as a space to specifically serve the mostly Black teens who were still engaging with the app as it crashed and burned as a lip-sync app. According to Jonas Drüppel, "The old Dubsmash lip-syncing product was used very differently in different markets. We decided it would be easier for us to focus on one customer at a time, and then expand from there."[32] As a result, Dubsmash decided to privilege the teens who primarily used the app as a dance app. That is, the teenager Dubsmashers dictated the life span and future of the app. Without the young artists, there is no Dubsmash and, as an extension, there is no book about any of this. Drüppel adds, "Our biggest takeaway early on is that we didn't listen to our users. We would be in the clouds, thinking the new features we were building and rolling out were amazing, but then they just didn't work."[33] Dubsmash 2.0 has fixed this issue, staying in constant communication with its users on Instagram, oftentimes asking followers what they want to see from the app. That is, as opposed to Dubsmash 1.0, which featured a team working in an office trying to stay on top of future trends for the app, Dubsmash 2.0 instead allows its users to help shape the look and feel of the app. Notably, this is quite different than most social media platforms of a certain size. And, much of this work happens on Instagram where Dubsmash uses the more popular app to cultivate community.

The official Dubsmash Instagram account (@dubsmash) models community and socialization in myriad ways. With over 1.3 million followers, @dubsmash has considerable clout and, by extension, influence. Yet, its size, while impressive, allows it to retain a certain level of accessibility that is nearly impossible to attain on the official TikTok Instagram (@tiktok), for example. @tiktok has over 26 million followers, which dilutes any sort of community building that could potentially take place on the account. Moreover, @tiktok only shares content that is already popular on the TikTok app, reinforcing the necessity to go viral on the app before being invited into the fold. That is, TikTokers *must* have reached a certain level of engagement *before* they can be featured on the TikTok Instagram account. The Instagram account, therefore, is an extension of the power dynamics already at play on the TikTok app itself.

As a dance app, most of Dubsmash's Instagram posts are dedicated to showcasing dance challenges that its users choreograph on the Dubsmash app before other dancers mimic or riff off their choreography. As previously detailed, Dubsmash 2.0 was refashioned as an app for dance challenges and, thereby, was at the forefront of a larger trend happening across the country. As teens of color continued to use Dubsmash to forge digital space and a corresponding community dedicated to dance challenges after Dubsmash 1.0 went out of vogue, the mainstream United States was also gaining interest in short, viral dance challenges. Indeed, digital spaces have become key sites for hip hop interaction and these dance challenges began to serve as fundamental collective practices of this culture. At a certain point in 2018, it seemed that there was a new viral dance trend that anyone who was anyone had to hit. To remain culturally relevant and in the know, hitting dance challenges is essential. Writing for *Billboard*, Rania Aniftos named 2018 the "Year of the Dance Challenge."[34] Into 2021 so-called viral choreography continues to spread like wildfire on Instagram and Twitter, where teenagers recreate the dances, sometimes adding their own twists. They then post their version of the dance challenge, which encourages their friends and followers to then do the same viral dance. Users rely on hashtags to circulate their videos and further open up the circle (aka the community).[35] Dancers no longer have to physically hold space together; their phone now holds that power to connect them with fellow dancers across the world.[36] Most of these dances get little digital movement. Others, however, are certifiably viral. Drake's "In My Feelings" challenge and Beyoncé's "Before I Let Go" challenge are two that perfected how far a dance challenge can take a song.[37] As Dubsmash and TikTok grew in popularity over

2019 and 2020, a viral dance challenge could dramatically change a song's trajectory and an artist's career. Recording artists such as K-Camp, Doja Cat, Megan Thee Stallion, Roddy Rich, Krypto9095, Blueface, and ZaeHD & CEO have all capitalized off the dance challenge effect. And, perhaps, there is no better example of this than Lil Nas X, whose success with "Old Town Road" is largely connected to its viralness on Dubsmash and TikTok, something he rode all the way to number one on the Billboard Hot 100 and two Grammy Awards.[38]

Dubsmash's Instagram account regularly posts video compilations of trending dance challenges on Instagram TV (IGTV). As with any other content, these sometimes-lengthy posts feature users who at times have recently joined the app or have few followers, which is fundamental to fostering a sense of belonging. By being featured on Instagram, Dubsmashers also develop brand loyalty that can help increase user retention and the lifespan of an app. Just hit one of the trending dance challenges on the Dubsmash app and users can be featured on Instagram. It's as simple as that. There is no gate-keeping. There is no privileging of Dubsmash influencers. There is an open door policy that applies to anyone willing to become part of the culture of digital dance challenges. Much of this work revolves around maintaining the feeling of community and belonging. Since Dubsmashers are often at the forefront of cultural trends, giving them a digital space of their own is pivotal. Suchit Dash acknowledges the importance of community: "The community that exists on Dubsmash is very much ground zero for a lot of trends around dance. We see a lot of instances where the core germ of an idea happens on Dubsmash first, and then starts to permeate elsewhere. To have access to and continue to grow that community is so critical."[39] Dash reiterates the role of Dubsmash in shaping Gen Z culture, "Dubsmash is ground zero for culture creation in America—it's where the newest, most popular hip-hop and dance challenges on the internet originate. Members of the community are developing content that will make them the superstars of tomorrow."[40] Having access to this community and cultivating a home for hip hop influencers is integral to Dubsmash's long-term success going forward.

While Dubsmash has modeled its values and community-first approach since its relaunch in 2018, which is the subject of the following chapter, perhaps the app's work during the early weeks of the COVID-19 pandemic reveals what power a digital community holds, especially during times of crisis. As most of the United States—not to mention much of the world—went into quarantine in March 2020, a feeling of isolation loomed large. In my case, for example, I went from being around hundreds of young people daily at my high school to all-of-a-sudden *only* interacting with my partner and our cat. This abrupt change in both pace and lifestyle brought new challenges to my life even though I am one of the more privileged people in the country. For instance, I still got my regular paycheck and, as a result, I didn't have to worry about rent or food or health care. Despite this, however, I missed my community and, judging by my interactions with young people on Instagram, I wasn't alone. We all recognized that we needed a break from school, but quarantine was not what anyone had in mind.

While digital spaces can't 100 percent replicate in-person socialization practices, they can nevertheless do meaningful work to keep communities intact and connected. Such was the work of Dubsmash in the time of coronavirus. In addition to its regular slate of Instagram content, Dubsmash used two primary strategies to keep people connected and to help raise morale among its followers. The strategies—quarantine games and challenges—gave Dubsmashers a way to build upon relationships that had already been facilitated through the app while also giving the app's primarily youth audience meaningful dance challenges and collaborative opportunities to engage. These may seem like simple acts, but they demonstrate that Dubsmash is more than *just* a social media app or a place to watch short videos on Instagram. Rather, it is a site of youth identity formation and a collective experience.

As soon as quarantine was becoming a reality, Dubsmash began regularly using the Instagram Story function to post games to its followers. The Dubsmash Instagram account was far from the only account to create such games. Instagram doesn't have a designated games feature, but provides templates that can be "decorated" with text, emojis, and GIFs that transform the template into an interactive game that is then shared among a community of Instagrammers. Over the course of March and April 2020, Dubsmash released templates for games like #dsquizzes, This or That, My Fav Things in GIFS, and Inside of My Brain Be Like (in GIFS). While the content and scope of each of these was unique, they all asked users to tag three friends and Dubsmash upon completion. Tagging is twofold. Tagging friends gives users a chance to connect with their friends in a digital space, but it also alerts those friends and provides them an opportunity to learn something new, thus enhancing digital friendships. By tagging other users, Dubsmashers enable the games to forge a ripple effect in which the Dubsmash circle continued to expand. For example, My Fave Things in GIFS was a simple template that featured nine white circles with a prompt above each. Each prompt asked users to select one GIF that best represented their favorite food, animal, drink, color, TV show, hobby, season, place, and state. Once complete, Dubsmashers could tag their friends to continue the game. In addition, by tagging Dubsmash, @dubsmash could share the results as a story post, thus furthering the reach of the game and introducing the community to Dubsmashers they might not otherwise know about. This helped to create a community that went far beyond *just* dancing. While there is a set of community norms including music styles and clothing brands that dictate what Dubsmash aesthetics look like, Dubsmash games went a step further in giving Zoomers a platform to fashion a unique identity and to privilege individuality.[41] That is, Dubsmash's digital community fosters an emergent aesthetic that binds Dubsmashers together.

In addition to games, Dubsmash relied on its bread and butter—dance challenges—to keep people connected. A key component of feeling connected is that of staying "in the know" and staying on top of culture as it is shifting. While practicing social distancing, many people experienced feelings of isolation and disconnection from face-to-face communities. Although many young people get their social and cultural fixes at school, the switch to remote learning threw a wrench into the typical ways that students and other young people socialize and experience community. I argue that quarantine magnified the role that digital technology plays in our day-to-day lives. Even though in-person gatherings were few and far between, if they happened at all, digital gatherings became the de facto norm. Live-streaming, Instagram Live shows, Zoom game nights, and the like became the *only* safe way to socialize. Although this came as a shock at first, we soon collectively learned that digital socialization practices are not inherently inferior to face-to-face gatherings and, in fact, play a different role in how people socialize.

An essential part of socialization is that of staying in the know and finding out about things. This is precisely where Dubsmash intervened, by means of #dsxquarantine, a two-week series of challenges in April 2020 that featured a new dance challenge announced each morning. Challenges included: Savage Megan Thee Stallion, Jackson wang 100 WAYS, Usual like Kobe, Like that Doja Cat, hit the Woah, any throwback challenge, find an inanimate dance partner, Toosie slide, pajama day, #bussinxtremaine, Next caller, brooklynxair, Big Talk Tempo, need a freak need a freak, Who that at the door?, and RENEGADE PT. 2. These challenges ranged from simple to extremely difficult, giving dancers of all abilities the chance to win. Once Dubsmash posted the new challenge, Dubsmashers then had to make the appropriate Dub and post it by midnight using the hashtag. The following day, Dubsmash featured the winner in a feed post on Instagram. And, some winners got Dubsmash swag such as T-shirts and hoodies.

A hallmark of the Dubsmash Instagram page is that it features a diverse range of Dubsmashers who vary from well-known content creators to more up-and-coming dancers who may only have a few hundred followers. That is, the number of one's followers doesn't dictate access to the Dubsmash Instagram page. During #dsxquarantine, this was especially true as daily winners were almost entirely comprised of unknown Dubsmashers. Dubsmash doesn't reinforce the typical hierarchy in the social media world that only privileges those with high follower counts. For Dubsmash, things such as artistry, positive sense of self, good humor, and, of course, killer dance moves trump clout.

CONCLUSION

In *Dancing Communities: Performance, Difference, and Connection in the Global City*, dance scholar Judith Hamera reveals the various ways that dance provides the infrastructure to build communities. Although Hamera focuses on face-to-face dance communities in Los Angeles, her analysis of dance aesthetics and approaches that support building relationships, which is a fundamental aspect of creating and sustaining a sense of community, is pertinent.[42] There is little doubt that in-person social dance provides ways for community to develop in meaningful ways, but it would be unwise to disregard the value and power that digital dance communities such as Dubsmash hold. Suchit Dash recognizes the shifting role of social media for young people today. Dash claims, "The early years of social were about taking your offline friends and connecting more deeply online. Now, with Social 2.0, teens and younger millennials are connecting online first around shared interests, then becoming close enough friends to begin meeting offline as well."[43] Indeed, social media dance is not simply a digital space to forge a sense of community, but is a fundamental site that can have lasting repercussions IRL—that is, in real life. Renegades strategically use Dubsmash as a site to (re)imagine digital spaces in which identities that are often overlooked and underprivileged in mainstream spaces such as TikTok can not only find the space to exist, but, rather, these identities become the norm. In this community, Black Zoomers aren't marginalized. They are the ones who are recognized for their unique contributions to the larger US popular culture. And, the fact that Renegades can do this in a space like Dubsmash and the larger Dubsmash Instagram community speaks to the power that the digital has in community building for Generation Z.

CHAPTER 3

The Original Renegade

Dubsmash, Hip Hop Culture, and Sharing Values in a Digital Space

The film *Friday* was a bona fide hit when it debuted in 1995, quickly etching itself into US popular culture. The film was the brainchild of Ice Cube, who was already a household name from his 1991 acting debut in *Boyz in the Hood* and from his rap group NWA. *Boyz in the Hood* was a poignant coming-of-age drama and NWA's music frequently engaged in sociopolitical commentary about street life in South Central Los Angeles. Songs such as "Gangsta, Gangsta," "Fuck Tha Police," and "Express Yourself" became anthems that resonated with communities of color across the United States. *Friday*, then, it would seem, was a comedic departure for Ice Cube. The film showed the humor that can exist in places like South Los Angeles while also demonstrating how, much like his rap music, Ice Cube's comedy could be deployed as a tool of resistance. *Friday* follows Craig Jones, who is *always* unemployed, as he and his friends and family face a series of conflicts that so happen to take place on Friday. *Friday*—in addition to its two sequels *Next Friday* (2000) and *Friday after Next* (2002)—all attained cult status, becoming a popular reference point in the Black community.[1] While I had forgotten about the *Friday* film series for the most part, I had no choice but to acknowledge their staying power when I stepped foot into Bellaire High School in 2018. No matter where I looked, my Black Zoomer students were interacting with the film franchise, even if they weren't aware of it.

Renegades. Trevor Boffone, Oxford University Press. © Oxford University Press 2021.
DOI: 10.1093/oso/9780197577677.003.0004

Enter Blueface.[2] The Los Angeles rapper burst onto the scene in October 2018 just as Dubsmash relaunched. His song, "Respect My Cryppin" became a viral hit and his Benjamin Franklin face tattoo ensured that no one was going to forget who he was. He followed up with the mega popular 2019 remix of "Thotiana," featuring Cardi B and YG, which has been his most successful single, peaking at number eight on the Billboard Hot 100 chart. As his popularity grew, his music became part of the soundtrack of digital dance culture—not to mention that I couldn't go a day at Bellaire without hearing his music. Blueface was everywhere. And, like the other recording artists in this book, he is prolific. Building off of his viral success in 2018, he announced his debut studio album, *Find the Beat*, on October 11, 2019, an album that featured a single that would become the sound bite to Dubsmash and TikTok's next viral dance trend—"Holy Moly" featuring NLE Choppa.

"Holy Moly" begins with, of all things, *Friday after Next*.[3] Blueface samples the audio from the scene in which Craig and Day-Day (Ice Cube and Mike Epps, respectively) get jobs as security guards at a strip mall owned by Moly (Maz Jobrani), whose doughnut shop, Holy Moly Donut Shop, is the crown jewel of the shopping center. Despite the song having virtually nothing to do with Moly's shop, or *Friday after Next* for that matter, the scene offers Blueface an entry point into the song. "Holy Moly" starts: "This is the Holy Moly Donut Shop, ah? Say it with me, guys, 'Holy Moly Donut Shop.'"[4] The beat drops and Maz Jobrani's voice is replaced with that of Blueface, now rapping the line: "Holy Moly Donut Shop." Ultimately, Blueface uses donut as a metaphor for a gunshot wound: "Holy moly / .40 leave him like a donut (holy moly) / Pull up and shoot like Ginobili (Ginobili) / Can't wear the Rollie without the poly (Poly)."[5] While it's impossible to know how "Holy Moly" would have fared in an alternate universe devoid of dance apps, that's not the world in which the song was born. When Charli D'Amelio danced to the song on TikTok, the D'Amelio Effect was in place, and "Donut Shop" was inaugurated as the hot new viral dance challenge that every TikToker across the world would soon be hitting. But, like the story of the Renegade dance challenge that began this book, D'Amelio did not choreograph the dance. She merely copied choreography created by one of the most well-known and loved Dubsmashers, someone whom D'Amelio also happened to follow on TikTok at the time—Anaya Price, better known as D1 Nayah (@thereald1.nayah) among her 1.6 million followers. Ask anyone in the Dubsmash community and they will inevitably tell you that D1 Nayah is one of the platform's most influential and prolific content creators. As D1 Nayah's TikTok profile declares, she is the "Ceo of viral dances."[6] If you've made Dubs then you have probably danced to D1 Nayah's choreography. And, while she is intentional about creating hashtags for her dance challenges and Dubsmashers routinely use these hashtags to create a conversation around certain dances and to credit choreographers, D1 Nayah's Donut Shop dance got lost in the fold when D'Amelio didn't give her credit on TikTok.[7]

Alongside the fight to recognize Jalaiah Harmon as the Renegade creator, D1 Nayah's journey to being recognized for creating Donut Shop would mark the first quarter of 2020 as a period of time when the tensions over Dubsmash and TikTok would spill over into the mainstream, opening up conversations about artist credit and community values on various dance apps. While some argued that "it's just a dance" and "everyone is doing it," others saw Renegade and Donut Shop as two more examples of the ways that White creators appropriate and profit from the work of Black people while original creators linger in anonymity. To those who resisted the simple act of giving dancers credit, many Dubsmashers said, using a popular phrase from *Friday*, "bye, Felicia."[8]

This chapter examines things that are admittedly hazy—the cultural norms and values of dance apps. They can't be measured and there is no published roadmap of norms and values on apps such as Dubsmash. Even so, as *Renegades* manifests, there is a shared set of values that the Dubsmashers in this book embody. My argument is that these values come directly from the origins of hip hop itself. Using a theoretical framework influenced by scholarship in critical race theory, gender studies, and hip hop, I theorize a shared sense of values of the Dubsmash community that enables Renegades to build an inclusive digital community. I track how accountability, capitalism, and credit as a kind of reparations come together on and around social media platforms. This chapter questions—can a dance app have an unspoken shared set of values? And, more specifically, how do Renegades not only forge but maintain these values? My argument is that Dubsmash's culture of giving credit is the nexus from which a shared sense of values encourages Dubsmashers to recognize the work of *other* artists. In a sense, Dubsmash is built on a culture of paying it forward.

To demonstrate this, I focus on the issue of dancer credit and, by extension, copyright, especially as these terms reveal fissures in the ways that Dubsmashers and TikTokers approach conversations around artistry and social media. I tackle the question of crediting artists, with a specific focus on dancers whose work isn't always legible within the terms of copyright. Put simply, short clips of dancing posted to social media can't be copyrighted. Yet, Renegades have been working around this issue for years by developing a shared value system that relies on crediting content creators, be they the musicians writing the lyrics and beats that form the backdrop of Dubs or the people who hone their craft as dance app choreographers. As Jalaiah Harmon and D1 Nayah's stories demonstrate, receiving credit for creating viral dance challenges can be the difference between anonymity and clout. It can be the difference that monetizes something that so many people do for free—social media use. That is, money plays a significant factor in questions of credit and copyright. With this in mind, I return to Jalaiah Harmon as a case study. As "The Original Renegade," Harmon's origin story from anonymous viral dance creator to full-blown celebrity status demonstrates how hip hop values operate in the Dubsmash community. The story of how the Dubsmash community rallied around Harmon's erasure and pushed against systems of cultural appropriation and White supremacy informs the various ways that Renegades position themselves as the torchbearers of a communal culture built on many of the same values espoused by the larger hip hop movement.

HIP HOP VALUES ARE DUBSMASH VALUES, DUBSMASH VALUES ARE HIP HOP VALUES

Hip hop originated from the Bronx (aka The Block) in the thick of the civil rights movements of the 1960s and 1970s. Hip hop began in the streets, parks, community centers, and nightclubs of the Boogie Down Bronx and nearby Harlem. It slowly spread throughout New York City and the region before quickly becoming ingrained in communities across the entire country.[9] Hip hop, as an urban culture, was a strategy for addressing the systematic racism and socioeconomic marginalization that the Black and Latinx community were facing and continue to face. As a result, hip hop was a liberation movement that privileged the cultural influence of young Black and Brown people as it showcased their determination, self-actualization, artistry, and communal pride.[10] Using music and dance cultures—not to mention the visual practices of graffiti—as an entry point, hip hop became a crucial site to form a collective urban youth rebuttal to the racist and classist policies that marked the Reagan-Bush era, specifically its social and civic disregard of communities of color in the United States.[11] By 1979, with the successes of the Sugar Hill Gang, the country at large was taking notice of hip hop's contributions to larger US popular culture, and by the 1990s, what was once a grassroots culture was soon an international, multibillion dollar industry that has become an indisputable powerhouse in the worldwide music scene.

As hip hop scholar Joseph G. Schloss claims, "many academic observers of hip-hop assume that, just because hip-hop principles often go unstated, they therefore do not exist."[12] Yet, there are in fact a cohesive set of shared values that penetrate much of hip hop culture. Much of the values that still connote hip hop harken back to the person who institutionalized it—Afrika Bambaataa. Bambaataa founded the Universal Zulu Nation in 1973.[13] Taking up space at the Bronx River Center, the Universal Zulu Nation was not just a hip hop awareness group. Rather, it served as a crucial site to bring together the artists—DJs, MCs, b-boys/b-girls, and graffiti artists—who would cultivate the foundational aesthetics of hip hop.[14] As such, hip hop is definitively a culture that includes many aesthetics, genres, and ways of performing. While rap remains intrinsically connected to hip hop, the two are not mutually exclusive. Rather than simply rap, hip hop is, according to Gwendolyn D. Pough, a way of living and being, "a state of mind, as a way of life that is tied to a youth movement of change—a change movement that builds on a legacy of movements against oppression in this country. Hip-Hop culture didn't just spring up full-grown. It builds on a past. It has a legacy."[15] Therefore, by working with an understanding that hip hop is a culture, we can begin to unpack the role that Zoomers of color use Dubsmash as a strategic place to grow hip hop culture in new, digital directions. Indeed, Renegades operate using a distinct, unspoken set of cultural values that are embedded in the larger Dubsmash community.

While the casual eye might overlook the tight-knit structure of hip hop, the culture still adheres to a set of values that were a bedrock of the community when Bambaataa was key to organizing it. Espoused by Bambaataa and, as an extension, the Universal Zulu Nation, the core values of hip hop are peace, love, unity, and having fun. These four values were the focal point of Afrika Bambaataa and James Brown's 1984 song "Unity (Pt. 1—The Third Coming)," which also addresses socioeconomic and political issues relevant to communities of color. While frequently repeating "Peace! Unity! Love! And having fun!," Bambaataa and Brown also sing,

C'mon!,
Love power! (Got to have it!),
Unity power! (What we need!),
Funk power! (Got to have it!),
Fun power! (What we want!),
Peace and unity! (Got to have it!),
No drugs! (What we want!),
No crime! (Don't do no time!),

Give it to 'em!,
Children power! (What we need!),
Knowledge wisdom (Got to have it!),
A whole lotta understanding,
Fun power! (Bring 'em back to the fold!),
Education (What we want!),
Love and peace (Give it to 'em, give it to 'em!),
Unity! (What we need!),
Funk power! (Love your brother!),
Owww![16]

In tandem with the album's artwork featuring Bambaataa and Brown holding hands in a powerful act of solidarity, "Unity" speaks to the power that hip hop can bring.

While Bambaataa and Brown couldn't have possibly imagined the ways that the internet would overtake nearly every aspect of our lives, the core message of "Unity" has lived on through a new nation, one that is fueled by social media—Dubsmash. As an extension of hip hop culture, Dubsmash operates with an often unspoken value system that the Renegades in this book all encompass. This Dubsmash Nation relies on its community of Renegades to maintain a safe space that encourages a plurality of identities to emerge and (re)claim a collective sense of Zoomer culture. Just as Bambaataa proclaimed, this community is dedicated to peace, unity, love, and having fun. By embodying these values through social media performance, community members solidify the space as an integral part of Zoomer self-expression. This is to say, it is quite literally impossible to gain a full understanding of Generation Z without analyzing the impact of digital spaces such as Dubsmash.

Dubsmash's values are a fundamental reason why the app is so successful in the community it is trying to serve. Hip hop's four values, which undergird Dubsmash's values, animate Renegades' efforts to secure credit and copyright for their dance movements. Based on my ethnographic research, these values are transmitted through a feeling. It's a feeling that I've felt firsthand and it's something that every Dubsmasher I've spoken to has felt. These values are put in place by and for the community. So, yes, in the case of Dubsmash, an app can have values and those values can be exactly what makes the community a safe and welcoming place that lets someone like me share space with someone like D1 Nayah. In the end, we may be different in so many ways, but Dubsmash brings us together and that, folks, is a beautiful thing.

CAN A DANCE EVEN BE COPYRIGHTED?

The online discussion around values became a hot button issue in December 2019 and January 2020 when Jalaiah Harmon's Renegade and D1 Nayah's Donut Shop went viral on both Instagram and TikTok, yet the dancers themselves were left in the dark. Their stories reveal the possibilities and roadblocks that coincide with virality and dancer credit, while serving as case studies of how social media apps can maintain and reject communal values. The culture of giving credit to dancers for their choreography is a bedrock of Dubsmash and, subsequently, is a point of contention that separates the app from other social media dance spaces. As hip hop culture is "fundamentally concerned with the fair distribution of ownership rights and claiming control over the American cultural imagination,"[17] Renegade's trajectory sheds light on how disregarding dance credit is especially problematic; doing so replicates systems of White supremacy that have historically disenfranchised Black people and communities of color in the United States. According to dance scholar Anthea Kraut, dancers not only lose out on "economic and artistic capital but also status in a raced and gendered hierarchy" when their choreography is reproduced without their consent or name attached.[18] In *Perpetual Motion*, Harmony Bench builds on these thoughts, adding, "Imitation and replication lie at the heart of how dance travels. In considering how dance steps and dance practices circulate through digital media, fundamental questions regarding the nature of dance rise: can dances or steps be owned? How does one give or receive movement?"[19] While concepts such as imitation and replication may seem harmless, once we factor in the monetary value of being credited and going viral, we can begin to recognize the importance of artist credit. Accordingly, debates around dancer credit mark shifts in the community's collective understanding of ownership rights of creative properties, something that the mainstream TikTok world had been exclusively thinking of as musician credit, if at all.

It is no secret that going viral is no longer about becoming popular for a moment. Going viral is about clout and making money; therefore, "to be robbed of credit on TikTok is to be robbed of real opportunities."[20] Creators of viral dances often go viral themselves, quickly gaining large follower accounts across their social media platforms. As these content creators go from anonymity to fame, they become influencers and gain the perks that come with the title, namely sponsorship deals, brand deals, media opportunities, and, perhaps the most decisive thing, clout. Young people with significant follower counts are lucrative marketing spaces—effectively, hyper-specific social media billboards—that large companies have become increasingly interested in.[21] It can also lead to an increase in opportunities to network with other influential people in the arts and entertainment industry. As I have experienced, becoming an influencer means easier access to other influencers and celebrities. For example, in the Instagram direct message (DM) inbox, message requests are automatically filtered by the "Top Requests," which are from users with the highest follower accounts, meaning that a message from someone with 500,000 followers will appear before one from someone with 500 followers. Accordingly, people are more likely to open messages from users who are verified (indicated by a blue check following their account name) and with high follower accounts. Moreover, Instagram influencers regularly get sponsorship deals via DM requests. While much of this involves getting free swag, there are lucrative paid brand deals that begin from a simple DM request.[22] DMs are also where the majority of media requests I have received originated. And, it bears repeating, with a higher follower count comes more opportunities and clout. There is power in the blue check.

The issue of Black artists being unable to benefit financially from their work is familiar. This has been particularly salient in the dance community. In *Choreographing Copyright: Race, Gender, and Intellectual Property Rights in American Dance*, Kraut traces authorship and interrogates "the raced and gendered politics of ownership in dance in the United States from the late nineteenth century to the early twenty-first."[23] Because choreography is corporeal, choreographers' bodies are always "implicated in the circulation of their choreography. The threat of dance's circulation, therefore, is that it can enact a kind of bodily commodification, turning producers into products, subjects into things."[24] Removing Jalaiah Harmon from Renegade and D1 Nayah from Donut Shop commodifies the work of Black girls and reinforces the same problematic racial and gender hierarchies that have been pervasive throughout the history of the United States. The history of White people appropriating Black aesthetics has long been pervasive in popular musical styles such as blues, funk, gospel, jazz, rap, and soul, of which all find their origins in Black communities. As M. Elizabeth Blair notes, in the 1950 and 1960s, "most major record producers were interested in promoting only white artists, such as Elvis Presley, to perform rock and roll music that had previously been recorded by black artists. The white performer was instrumental in promoting the acceptance of the musical style among mainstream audiences."[25] Such cultural appropriation was normalized in a system devoted to financially profiting off of popularity. Musicologists Richard Peterson and David G. Berger explain how Black R&B artists "were most often the victims of the 'cover tactic,' where major 'white' companies would quickly record and market a version of a fast-selling song recorded by a smaller independent 'black' company."[26] This phenomenon is perfectly captured in the musical *Dreamgirls*. After Jimmy Early releases "Cadillac Car" as an explicitly Black song and subsequent ode to the Black community, the record is quite literally stolen by a White producer who then re-orchestrates the track to give it a distinctly "White" sound that is reminiscent of the Beach Boys. The White version of "Cadillac Car" becomes the hit and Jimmy Early is left in the dust despite being the original creator of the content.

The United States has a rich history of Black performers having their work appropriated by White people, a history extending into contemporary social dance in the digital sphere. Jalaiah Harmon's story demonstrates how receiving credit as a dancer can be a life-changing act. But even so, her story presents many of the challenges that are common to social media apps, namely, the lack of giving artists credit for their work on TikTok. While there is a growing practice of giving musicians credit when their work is posted to TikTok, made far easier given the prevalence of obtaining lyrics through a quick Google search, few TikTokers embrace a culture of crediting dancers for their choreography. The app doesn't have community norms around giving credit nor, before the Jalaiah Harmon story broke, did its top influencers engage in the practice. The practice of giving credit has historically been virtually impossible given the difficulty of tracking the genealogy of videos posted to TikTok. This is due in large part to the fact that the TikTok feed is not chronological, meaning there are no timestamps on videos, and to the fact that hashtags are sorted by popularity. As writer Rebecca Jennings notes, "if someone with more followers steals your dance, it's likely theirs will be the one that blows up."[27] Even if you developed a dance and created a hashtag for it, other users with more followers using the same hashtag will be promoted on the app. This means that content creators with few followers are easily obscured; on TikTok, they are obscured in favor of White users with many followers. As such, the TikTok search feature is another algorithm that supports a racist system.[28]

In the age of digital dancing, questions of credit and copyright are especially pertinent. Jennings affirms, "Dances are virtually impossible to legally claim as one's own."[29] Viral hip hop dances follow a legacy of other hip hop aesthetics such as sampling, for example, that do not fit neatly within the copyright parameters laid out in cultural and property law.[30] In *Parodies of Ownership: Hip-Hop Aesthetics and Intellectual Property Law*, Richard L. Schur explains that settled case law and legislation "never quite resolved the questions of property and cultural ownership that hip-hop aesthetes have put forward."[31] Apart from complications raised vis-à-vis hip hop, in particular, there are questions of whether dance can be copyrighted at all.

According to the Copyright Office's guidance, the answer is a definitive no: "individual movements or dance steps by themselves are not copyrightable."[32] Kraut recognizes that the US copyright law added choreography into the 1976 Copyright Act, where choreographic works were added to the list of protectable categories, but social dances were not included.[33] New digital technologies further complicate intellectual property law, as copyright laws do not catch up to quickly shifting cultures. This contributes to a culture of digital content that reveals copyright law as another tool of White supremacy. That is, existing copyright laws are complicit in reinforcing racial hierarchies and they do not appear to be an avenue for rectify the issue.[34]

Copyright conversations have been common in the online video game Fortnite, where several high-profile lawsuits have been filed by people like *The Fresh Prince of Bel-Air* actor Alfonso Ribeiro, who saw his infamous dance, "The Carlton," end up on Fortnite with the moniker "Fresh," and by rapper 2 Milly (Terrance Ferguson), who filed a lawsuit when he saw his popular Milly Rock dance show up on the game. In both cases, the dances were turned into visual assets with motion graphics meant to reward Fortnite users, encouraging them to engage with the platform more. Put simply, these dances helped increase Fortnite's popularity and capital while a racial divide similar to that on Dubsmash and TikTok seemed to surface. As Ferguson's lawsuit stated, Fortnite owner Epic is "exploiting African-American talent in particular in Fortnite by copying their dances and movements."[35,36]

Yet, other digital communities have found ways around the issues of crediting, in lieu of securing legal copyright remains an issue. For Dubsmashers and Instagram dancers, it's best practice to tag the accounts of both the musicians and the dance creators in any given video. Doing so increases searchability and digital connectedness, but dancers also use hashtags to help track a dance's history, a process that can more efficiently lead back to the dance's creator. On TikTok, however, the unstated cultural norm is for dancers to post a video and not tag anyone. This led Jennings to question, "When a popular TikTok celebrity does a dance, do they have the obligation to tag the less-famous person who invented it? . . . Do TikTok celebrities like Charli D'Amelio and Addison Rae, who post videos of themselves doing viral dances to millions of followers, have a responsibility to find the original creators—a task that can often be quite difficult and time-consuming—and give them credit?"[37] For Black content creators and their advocates, there is only one response to these questions: an emphatic yes.

TikTok is one of the biggest video apps in the world and, as can be expected, has changed the game for how we engage with social media. And while the app is a key site for developing culture and identity, many of its most viral dances—Renegade, Donut Shop, the Mmmxneil, and Cookie Shop, for instance—did not originate on TikTok; these dancers were created by Black content creators on smaller apps. These Dubsmashers post to Instagram to achieve a wider audience and, "if it's popular there, it's only a matter of time before the dance is co-opted by the TikTok masses."[38] In Lorenz's article, ultra-popular YouTube star Kayla Nicole Jones posits, "TikTok is like a mainstream Dubsmash. They take from Dubsmash and they run off with the sauce."[39] Music producer, songwriter, and rapper Polow da Don adds, "Dubsmash catches things at the roots when they're culturally relevant. TikTok is the suburban kids that take things on when it's already the style and bring it to their community."[40] Indeed, once the story of Harmon went viral, memes comparing Harmon and D'Amelio to the Rancho Carne High School Toros cheer squad and the Compton High Clovers of the 2000 teen film *Bring It On* began popping up across the internet. The memes riffed off one of the film's iconic exchanges, in which the Clovers confront the Toros for stealing their routines and winning nationals with them no less:

ISIS: Oh, you know what? She's right. So then we'd be doing them a favor. So then they can feel good about sending Raggedy Ann up here to jack us for our cheers.
TORRANCE: Raggedy Ann?
ISIS: Ugly red head with the video camera permanently attached to her hand. Y'all been coming up here for years trying to steal our routines.
LAVA: And we just love seeing them on ESPN.[41]

In this case, the Dubsmashers want to receive the credit for the content they create, but this simple act has often been met with controversy (not unlike in *Bring It On*). Many times, their calls for receiving credit have gone unnoticed or unaddressed by TikTokers. Moreover, it isn't unlike instances of audiences praising non-Black people such as Miley Cyrus for twerking while not giving the same treatment to Black people when they do it.[42] As Kyra D. Gaunt claims, "their practices are exploited because they exist in the public domain where the right to copyright and royalties are not assigned."[43] While social media content created by Black girls penetrates larger mainstream culture, their artistry remains a place of exploitation. Dubsmash just provides other examples for understanding cultural appropriation and the politics of social media production.

Given the Renegade Challenge's unparalleled popularity, Harmon became a central figure in the fight for a culture that credits dancers. But she was not alone—other well-known Dubsmashers were in the same boat. Namely D1 Nayah, whose Holy Moly Donut Shop dance became TikTok's next biggest thing, even though it originated on Dubsmash and was cross-posted to her more than 1 million followers on Instagram. In early January 2020, Barrie Segal, the head of content at Dubsmash, began a virtual movement to honor Harmon and D1 Nayah's artistic practice, and to raise awareness around crediting. On January 17, 2020, Segal posted a series of videos on her Instagram account (@barrrie) asking Charli D'Amelio to give credit to D1 Nayah for Donut Shop.

Segal's original post included three frames—one of D'Amelio and Addison Rae doing Donut Shop, one of D1 Nayah doing it, and a screenshot of the breaking news that the entire D'Amelio family had signed with United Talent Agency. Her caption read:

> Here's @charlidamelio doing a dance by @thereald1nayah. she doesn't give credit to the choreographers/creators of the dances she does, so most of her 18m followers (yes 18m) think it's her original choreography. Earlier this week she signed with one of the world's biggest talent agencies. @tiktok, @dubsmash, and @instagram don't have a 'dedicated' place to give credit to a choreographer, but like . . . c'mon . . . the @dubsmash community has been using tags, hashtags, and mentions to "work around" this issue for a while and give "vc" or "video credit" where it's due. should @charlidamelio let her followers know she's doing @thereald1.nayah's dances? is it the apps responsibility to track this? is choreography intellectual property? (if not why tf not? discuss. (this doesn't even get into the issue of how musician credit gets washed out in IG . . . tune by @ bluefacebleedem) [sic][44]

Segal's post started small, but soon gained steam. Segal's post was quickly picked up by the gossip account the TikTok Shaderoom on their Instagram page (@tiktokroom). What was initially a plea for respecting the work of dancers soon became a full-blown controversy that further demonstrated the racial and cultural divides between Dubsmash and TikTok. Segal's post received over 1,100 comments that revealed how divided people were on the issue. Much of the criticisms of Segal's post harkened back to the fact that millions of people hit viral dance trends and, as such, "it isn't a big deal." For example, Disney Channel actress Skai Jackson, who is Black, responded in an Instagram post: "Okay but millions of people have done the dance so your [sic] going to ask everyone for credit? You should be happy that millions of people are doing the dance lol."[45] As seen throughout this book, there was a cultural divide over how people viewed the issue. It wasn't only an issue of each user's race, but more so an issue of how individuals acknowledged or disregarded the racial dynamics at play. While some—mostly White teens—said that race had nothing to do with credit, for many Black teens on Dubsmash, race had *everything* to do with it. The lack of credit became, then, another instance of Black girls' artistic practice being exploited, and their larger contributions to US popular culture being ignored.[46]

Following Skai Jackson's post, Segal responded, "@skaijackson artistic credit is sooo important. It translates to massive opportunities for creators if the right people know who did it. And for artists in America it's not like it's easy to make ends meet. Their ability to get credit is what they rely on to ultimately make a living off their craft."[47] Segal reiterated these thoughts in an April 2020 *Teen Vogue* profile on Harmon: "I was kind of highlighting how important it is for the original creators to get credit because it can lead to real business opportunities."[48] In the age of social media, high follower counts result in opportunities, many of which come with monetary compensation. Rebecca Jennings offers Haley Sharpe, a sixteen-year-old in Huntsville, Alabama, as a case study.[49] Sharpe created the incredibly popular viral dance to "Say So" by Doja Cat, a dance that has become a part of Doja Cat's official choreography as seen in the music video and in concert. After creating the "Say So" dance, Sharpe amassed over 1.4 million followers on TikTok, which has led to an increase in networking opportunities and, ultimately, chances to get paid for her work. Speaking with Jennings, Sharpe highlights how credit begets credit: "But if they don't, then it just starts a big ripple effect of not crediting."[50]

The discussion soon reached a tipping point when, after pressure from Segal and other well-known Dubsmashers and their fans on Instagram, the media took notice. A *New York Times* profile on Harmon completely changed the game. Segal had been working behind the scenes to get the media to cover the story and, as usually happens with the media, all it took was one major profile for the dominos to fall. By the time the *New York Times* story was circulating, Harmon was being featured on nearly every major news outlet. The story, it seemed, had entered the mainstream. In the Dubsmash community, Harmon was already a Renegade. Anyone who was paying attention knew about her contributions and talent for viral choreography. To think that the effort to get Harmon exposure for Renegade was a solo effort by Segal would be to disregard the collective work of the community. While Segal did the heavy lifting, the journey to artistic credit needed the community support that saw users tagging Harmon and sharing her story and commenting on giving dancers credit. On popular posts on the TikTok Shaderoom's Instagram account about the issue, Renegades took to the comments section to voice their support. Most comments were from

White teens who didn't see any issue with Harmon being left out of the picture, but Renegades kept the story going long enough so that larger, more mainstream media outlets could pick it up. Throughout the journey, Dubsmash values were on full display.

Despite attention given to Harmon, other dancers like D1 Nayah never received widespread credit for their work. As the drama surrounding Renegade unfolded, Renegades continued to be lost in the fold and issues of the archive of viral dance trends were not adequately addressed. That said, the Renegade controversy did mark a cultural shift going forward. Dancers began to receive credit for their work on TikTok in addition to other platforms. Charli D'Amelio now gives dance credit on her TikToks, which is slowly changing the culture on that platform. For example, in March 2020, Keara Wilson created the dance challenge to Megan Thee Stallion's "Savage," which went viral and made the song a hit. By this point, giving dance credit was more the norm and, almost immediately, there were articles circulating the internet about Wilson. Within a few weeks, Wilson received the coveted blue check on Instagram. And, of course, Megan Thee Stallion's song became a major hit that was nearly impossible to avoid throughout 2020. Speaking with Darlene Aderoju for *People*, Megan Thee Stallion acknowledges the power of digital dance cultures: "The internet has always been my friend when it comes to my music catching on. My hotties are always so supportive. They usually just keep a lot of things going. One of my favorite hotties, Keke, came up with a dance to 'Savage.' . . . The hotties really keep the music alive for me."[51] While quarantined during the COVID-19 pandemic, Megan Thee Stallion hit the challenge, posting it on Instagram.[52] As has become customary with viral dance trends, the musicians engage with the dance as much as the casual Dubsmasher or TikToker does, revealing the key role that Zoomer digital choreographers play in impacting popular culture at large. Kyesha Jennings recognizes, "Black women artists have taken advantage of this creative outlet to engage with their fans, expand the reach of their music and overall monetize their brand."[53] Renegades do not create dance trends that merely circulate on social media. They becomes an integral aspect of the life and success of a song as well.

As Keara Wilson's story reveals, the culture around dance credits is shifting. D'Amelio and other members of the Hype House will now give dance credits and tag content creators in their captions. While the practice is still not widespread, it is becoming more of the norm. Per usual, this is common practice for Dubsmashers such as Yoni Wicker of TheWickerTwinz: "We have 1.7 million followers and we always give credit whether the person has zero followers or not. We know how important it is. That person who made that dance, they might be a fan of ours. Us tagging them makes their day."[54] On Dubsmash, values dictate behavior, and these values dictate that artist credit isn't an option, but a necessity.

Since joining the Dubsmash team in 2018, Barrie Segal has been working behind the scenes to support the work of Dubsmashers who recognize the tremendous earning potential that is possible on Instagram but, due to their inexperience, don't always understand how to capitalize from it. Segal works to secure professional (i.e., paid) opportunities for Dubsmashers and, many times, has been the workhorse ensuring that Dubsmash's top content creators are not getting lost in the fold. To support this work, in January 2020, the company launched the Dubsmash Artist Development program as a tool to aid its top content creators and give them resources that will help boost their cultural capital and, as such, elevate their careers. Indeed, as the story of Jalaiah Harmon indicates, an act such as receiving credit may seem simple, but it is anything but that.

JALAIAH HARMON AND THE POWER OF DANCE CREDIT

Jalaiah Harmon (depicted in Figure 3.1) may have begun the 2019–2020 school year like any other fourteen-year-old, but she didn't end it that way. She became known as not only the Original Renegade, but as a prolific dancer who was anything but a one-hit wonder. And much like other Renegades discussed in this book, Harmon's experience as a dancer has been shaped by digital media. Her training in hip hop, ballet, lyric, jazz, tumbling, and tap are all on display throughout her growing oeuvre seen on Dubsmash, Instagram, and TikTok. Harmon's story is perhaps the best example of how receiving credit can be transformative for Dubsmashers. During the media storm following the *New York Times* story, Harmon's follower count on Instagram and TikTok increased exponentially, topping 652,000 and 2.9 million followers, respectively. As her follower count grew, so did lucrative media opportunities. Harmon was featured on nearly every national news outlet. She performed the dance on *The Ellen DeGeneres Show*, where she was presented with a jacket that said "The Original Renegade Dancer" on the back. Each pocket had a surprise in it—$1,000 for a total of $5,000. She was named to Variety's annual Power of Young Hollywood List 2020. She created the Scoob Dance to help launch the Hollywood film *Scoob!* (2020), and Renegade became a Fortnite emote in July 2020. The opportunities kept rolling in for Harmon throughout 2020.

In perhaps the pinnacle of Harmon's media tour, she performed the Renegade dance during the NBA All-Star Game, where thousands saw her

Figure 3.1 Jalaiah Harmon. Photo courtesy Jalaiah Harmon; photo by Thiree Pinnock and Ty "Creed" Smith.

at Chicago's United Center and millions saw her from their homes. The NBA had initially invited several members of the Hype House, in particular Charli D'Amelio and Addison Rae Easterling, who had until that time been connected to the dance, often mistaken as its creators. D'Amelio and Easterling were to be part of the weekend's activities and help bridge the gap between TikTok culture (i.e., Gen Z culture) and the mainstream basketball community. Easterling was invited to teach the All-Star Game cheerleaders the dance while Charli D'Amelio and Dixie D'Amelio performed Renegade with basketball player Aaron Gordon during the All-Star Dunk Contest. When Harmon's story broke in tandem with the announcement of D'Amelio and Easterling's role at the All-Star Game, Harmon's "absence was met with anger online."[55] Writing for SB Nation, Zito Madu admits, "In Harmon, many people recognized a historical problem that has been exacerbated by social media, in which the ideas of minorities are profited from by those who were 'inspired' by it. Meanwhile, individuals who created the idea often fade into obscurity."[56] Indeed, Black girls' cultural production writ large penetrate mainstream culture even as systems of White supremacy and misogynoir—misogyny directed toward *Black* women—work to exploit Black women.[57]

On the Friday of the weekend, K-Camp, the artist behind the Renegade song, tweeted a video of him and Harmon dancing to the song, thanking this young Black woman for making his song a mega hit. In many ways, the timing of the All-Star weekend worked in Harmon's favor; if a last-minute invite wasn't extended then the professional sports league that is arguably the most in touch with the Black community would be turning its back on one of its own, and would have become yet another example of White creatives benefiting from the talents of Black artists. The NBA, perhaps more than any other professional sport, has historically included and celebrated hip hop culture.[58] From the beats and music selection that teams play during the game to special halftime performances and the allure of sitting courtside, hip hop culture is thoroughly integrated into the NBA. The NBA is a "space where Blackness has been normalized, and Whiteness treated as Other."[59] And, as such, the artists take notice. Being aligned with a particular NBA team, such as the Lakers or the Knicks, is a key piece of cultural capital and can help an artist cement their ties to a city and, by extension, a fan base. Not to mention that the NBA All-Star Weekend is a spectacle and the crown jewel of the season. Having the creator of the country's most popular dance was a no-brainer and a key late addition to the docket.

Although Harmon had other high-profile appearances, her NBA All-Star game performance on February 16, 2020, is especially pertinent to this study given the relationship between the NBA, hip hop, and Black communities. During Harmon's All-Star game performance, mega celebrities courtside such as Kim Kardashian West posted Harmon's dance on her Instagram story for her 164 million followers to see and then follow Harmon. Michelle Obama tweeted a video of the performance, saying "Jalaiah, you crushed it—love seeing your talent shine!"[60] Although it is too early to see what Harmon's future holds, the NBA's act of inviting her helped her gain a level of recognition that will enable her to profit from the dance. The NBA did something so basic—they simply acknowledged her. By all means, this was a win-win-win weekend for everyone involved. The NBA got to further cement its place in Black culture by doing the right thing. Harmon's stock rose. And the TikTokers still got to do their thing.

And do their thing they did. Although Harmon's All-Star weekend experience included many high-profile performances, perhaps the most pertinent is preserved in a grainy video of her dancing with TikTok influencers in an expansive hotel ballroom lobby. The video, posted on February 16, quickly became immortalized on social media. In it, Harmon is front and center doing the original Renegade dance. Behind her are D'Amelio and Easterling, performing as her backup dancers complete with huge smiles. While comments on Instagram and TikTok videos may have tried to manufacture girl drama between Harmon and D'Amelio, in the end, the kids showed us that they are all right. There was no feud. The video's top comment, "i'm so glad you're getting the long needed recognition you DESERVED," is liked 78,500 times while other top comments with tens of thousands of likes all preach the same message—"im genuinely so happy youre getting the recognition you should have gotten from the start," "YESS FINALLY PEOPLE ARE SEEING YOU!," "A sister finally get recognition."[61]

Shortly after, Harmon was finally able to financially capitalize on Renegade. In March 2020, she signed with United Talent Agency, which can use its leverage as one of the top talent agencies in the United States to create opportunities for Harmon to appear in film and television, write a book, become a recording artist, or do anything else she sets out to do. The possibilities are endless. And, while so many things in her life have changed, her goal remains the same. In a *Teen Vogue* profile, she admits, "I really just want to be a choreographer. It's good that I influence other people, but I just like to dance."[62] While a career as a choreographer is perhaps a long way off given her age, because of social media dance app culture Harmon is on a trajectory that virtually no choreographer in the history of the world has ever been on up to this point.

CONCLUSION

I return to this chapter's central guiding question—Can a dance app have a shared set of values? The story of Jalaiah Harmon's journey to gaining credit for creating the Renegade dance uncovers how Dubsmash does, in fact, operate with a community culture that privileges the work of content creators. A key aspect of privileging Black artists is recognizing their unique contributions and, to that end, giving them credit for their work. Indeed, the larger national conversation surrounding Renegade reached a tipping point when Dubsmashers and TikTokers disagreed about the need and subsequent power of giving dance credit. While mostly White TikTokers claimed Renegade was just a trend that did not need to be credited, Black Dubsmashers saw this as another example of how Whites have historically appropriated the work of Black artists for their own gain. Even if Charli D'Amelio's work was unintentional—and, to her credit, she has been consistent in her stance to acknowledge Harmon's work since the issue erupted in February 2020—it played into systems of White supremacy that has disadvantaged people of color since the first European colonizers arrived in the so-called Americas and the United States was born.

While Harmon's story potentially could have ended in anonymity like so many other Black digital dancers whose work is not acknowledged, this was not the case. Harmon's stock has only continued to rise. Her story, while unique in its own right, illustrates how social media culture can in fact shift. By foregrounding values entrenched in hip hop culture—namely peace, love, unity, and having fun—Dubsmash was able to rally its digital community to shift the social media culture around crediting dancers. Doing so relied on Renegades of all shapes and sizes, on those with large follower counts and those with little to no clout, to double down on something that was never published or publicly proclaimed—valuing and crediting the work of content creators. As a natural extension of hip hop culture, Renegades instinctively embedded these guiding principles into social media digital dance culture. While it is still too early to see where this movement will go, one thing is certain: Renegades will not be silenced. They will be heard. They will be seen. This is the Renegade Nation. Now is the time to pay attention.

CHAPTER 4

Gone Viral

Creating an Identity as a Hip Hop Artist

In early February 2020, basketball star and global icon Lebron James joined his son Bryce in their living room to do something that has become a common practice in intergenerational bonding: they made a TikTok. But this wasn't just any TikTok. Rather, Lebron and Bryce hit the Mop, a new dance set to TisaKorean's song of the same name. By the end of 2019, the Mop had joined the Woah and the Wave as signature moves that would become part of the viral dance toolkit. The brief, fifteen-second video may seem simple but if you look further, there is more than meets the eye. Bryce is smiling ear to ear, clearly having not only convinced perhaps the most famous athlete in the world to learn the dance, but also engaged his father in a meaningful act of culture-sharing. Undoubtedly, Lebron learning the Mop and making a TikTok is on the same level as putting Bryce's artwork on the fridge. And, as with all the case studies in this book, there is a backstory that reveals the fundamental role that social dance plays in US culture. A week earlier, on January 26, the former Lakers star Kobe Bryant unexpectedly died in a helicopter crash that also killed his thirteen-year-old daughter Gianna and seven other people. Lebron, who was traded to the Lakers in 2018, said that the entire Lakers organization had "the toughest week of some of our lives."[1] The night before Bryant died, James passed him on the NBA's all-time scorers list, moving into third place. Following the game, Kobe tweeted, "Continuing to move the game forward @KingJames. Much Respect for my brother #33644."[2] There was deep respect between the two legends that went beyond the basketball court. As seen in Lebron

Renegades. Trevor Boffone, Oxford University Press. © Oxford University Press 2021.
DOI: 10.1093/oso/9780197577677.003.0005

and Bryce's TikTok, in addition to Kobe and Gianna's storied relationship, part of that connection is the way that both stars engage with their children, learning about their culture, and celebrating them. At first glance, the Mop might look like an easy dance and a quick fad, but there is more to it. It is an intergenerational hip hop dance that brings people together, whether to have fun or to relieve stress after the worst week of your life.

By the time Lebron and Bryce hit the Mop in February 2020, the dance had already cemented its place in Zoomer culture. Lebron didn't make the Mop popular. In November 2019, Houston rapper TisaKorean (Domonic Patten, b. 1994) and his squad—namely Kblast, Huncho Da Rockstar, and producer Mighty Bay—released "The Mop" with the corresponding dance.[3] The trio met in college at Prairie View A&M University after TisaKorean saw their video for "The Arrow" and decided then and there that they needed to meet and become friends. The result has been a generative relationship that has seen each rapper and dancer build their career with the support of the group. A key facet of their work and how they have crafted their identities and budding careers as rappers has relied on viral dance trends that eventually make their way to Dubsmash and TikTok, where they end up being picked up by major celebrities, as was the case with Lebron.[4] The Mop is no different. The song begins with a call to action:

Ayy,
I get it crunk, I get it wide, I get the party lit outside,
I get it crunk, I get it wide, I get the party lit outside,
I get it crunk, I get it wide, I get the party lit outside.[5]

At this point, TisaKorean invites people to the dance floor. The party is about to go cray and get wild, which, as TisaKorean claims, is exactly what his squad does—"we really do get the party wild."[6] Once on the dance floor, the best way to get the party lit is to hit the song's titular dance move:

Left hand first, put your right hand on top,
Mop, Mop, Mop, Mop,
Left hand first, now put your right hand on top,
Mop, Mop, Mop, Mop.[7]

As the lyrics evidence, part of the dance's success harkens back to the instructive nature of the song. In this moment, TisaKorean and Kblast quite literally explain how to begin the dance. Hold out your left hand in a fist then place your right fist on top of it and move them as if you are rowing a boat. Want to make it sizzle? Lean into it. Pick up your right leg and go deep. The variations are endless despite the primary action being so simple that virtually anyone can do it.

Although the song is credited to TisaKorean, it is truly a collaborative effort. As TisaKorean has stated, Huncho Da Rockstar and Kblast were already doing the dance move long before the song was even an idea. After the trio became friends, TisaKorean explains, "when we linked, probably like the third time, I think they both were like, 'Man, I aint going to lie, T-SA, we want to do a song.' And I'm like, 'What y'all want to do man, like for real?' He like, 'We going to do something like 'mop, mop, mop.' And I'm just open, I'm like, 'Well shit let's swag it.'"[8] And swag is exactly what they did because, as the artists in this book demonstrate, having swag is critical to building a Renegade identity.

In this chapter, I explore how Dubsmash, TikTok, and other social media apps become fundamental digital spaces for hip hop musicians to cultivate a unique identity and to cement their work as an integral part of Zoomer culture. These apps serve as critical spaces to try out new music and test original dance moves and extended choreographies. That being so, in the digital age, social media is where young hip hop artists *must* perform identity in order to build their careers. They don't merely post content for likes. Rather, content is specifically curated to position the artist as a trendsetter. Zoomers subsequently flock to these profiles to stay up to date on who and what is hot. "In-the-know" Zoomers must not only be aware of the content that the Renegades in this book produce, they also must be able to execute the related dances in order to gain clout and credibility within their own circles. Moreover, as this chapter details, social media is seen as a necessary way to build communities and a dedicated fan base. After all, there are no successful rappers without followings. Musicians need people who will stream their music, who will go to their live shows, and, of course, who will make videos dancing to their music. Accordingly, digital spaces can make or break a rapper's career.

One of the main spaces for these artists is Dubsmash, which, as I detailed in previous chapters, is accessible and grassroots in many ways, much like the hip hop movement itself. While New York City and Los Angeles remain important cities for this cultural work, cities like Atlanta, Detroit, Dallas, and Houston are just as relevant. Bolstered by social media's ability to democratize access, Dubsmash users from all parts of the country—and world—can use the platform to network, build a brand, or simply dance. Youth of color no longer need to be in one of the United States' traditional entertainment capitals to be a part of the entertainment industry. And this isn't just about dancers. Rappers and singers such as the ones in this chapter—TisaKorean, Brooklyn Queen, and Kayla Nicole Jones—and others such as Famous Ocean, Chris Gone Crazy, Debo, the Wicker Twinz, and Jay Go Crazy use Dubsmash to disseminate their music and build a dedicated following. That none of these artists lives in Los Angeles or New York City should not be lost on the casual observer. Social media has quite literally leveled the playing field.

Much of TisaKorean and his group's swag emerges from their various viral dance moves that have become hallmarks of Black Zoomer culture. Everyone was doing the Mop when it came out.[9] Soon after, the dance leaped from the realm of TisaKorean's specific song to become an important move in the larger Dubsmash community repertoire. As Huncho Da Rockstar claims, "You can mop anything. How you feeling? Just mop it up."[10] Without a doubt, as the story of TisaKorean, Kblast, Huncho Da Rockstar, and Mighty Bay reveals, a fundamental component of making a career as a hip hop artist in the age of social media revolves around viralness and the ability to not only create a ten-to-fifteen-second sound bite but, perhaps more important, the ability to choreograph a corresponding dance that can grow into a larger viral trend. The Mop demonstrates how creating a viral song and dance can be the difference between having regional success as a rapper versus having the likes of Lebron James make TikToks to your music.

With stories such as TisaKorean and the Mop in mind, in the pages that follow, I interrogate the nuanced ways that Renegades engage with social media dance culture to forge identities as hip hop artists. By closely reading the digital presence of Renegades such as TisaKorean, Brooklyn Queen, and Kayla Nicole Jones, I explore how musicians position themselves as both music and dance content creators on Dubsmash to gain followings. In the case of TisaKorean, his trajectory as the rapper who introduced the world to the now-iconic the Mop speaks to the power of going viral in the digital age. Likewise, hip hop artist Brooklyn Queen has been able to leverage her popularity on Dubsmash and TikTok to cement her rap and R&B career. The third case study, Kayla Nicole Jones, demonstrates the limitations of going viral. Although her music has gone viral on Dubsmash and TikTok, she is still not known for her music. Rather, she is best known for her memes that have emerged from her comedy videos on YouTube. Although she is tremendously successful, Kayla Nicole Jones exists in a gray area that allows us to tease out the possibilities and constraints of social media dance culture.

Notably, each of TisaKorean's, Brooklyn Queen's, and Kayla Nicole Jones's work in this chapter engages in the genre of the dance instruction song, which links these artists to a popular oral tradition that has firmly African roots. Dance scholars Sally Banes and John F. Szwed claim that the dance instruction song "is about the mass distribution of dance and bodily knowledge and thus served crucial aesthetic, social, and political functions."[11] Part of a longer history of oral tradition in afro-diasporic communities, dance instructionals help produce Black community. Because they are often easy and repetitive movements set against great songs, they have also been highly marketable, which we can see in the popular spread of dance instructionals like the Twist, the Loco-Motion, the Mashed Potato, the Hustle, the Vogue, the Electric Slide, and the Tootsie Roll, or something ultra-contemporary such as the Mop.[12] Renegade artists extend what we might call an Africanist aesthetic, and its corporate commodification, into the digital age. Naming dance moves makes them "teachable" and ripe for repetition, cementing them into generational culture. Having a name, therefore, is power, and artists such as TisaKorean, Brooklyn Queen, and Kayla Nicole Jones are the ones with that power in their hands. Their instructional social dances and social media performances at large have turned signifiers of Zoomer culture and identity, this revealing how Renegades are making impacts and impressions.

SOCIAL MEDIA AS IDENTITY PERFORMANCE

As *Renegades* illustrates, Gen Z culture is thoroughly entrenched in the digital. As Zoomers have grown up during a time in which digital spaces have been the norm, it is quite literally impossible to separate online life from face-to-face socialization for these so-called digital natives. To this end, Danah Boyd claims that young people today "face a public life with the possibility of unimaginably wide publicity."[13] Whereas teens from previous generations may have had to pay their dues to become an artist and, if they were lucky, get famous for their art, in the digital age, an artist's stock can dramatically increase overnight.[14] While all the artists in this book do, in fact, "have the goods," they have all relied on viralness, which is a stroke of luck as much as anything else. Charli D'Amelio didn't expect to go viral on her ninety-minute drive to dance camp. And I didn't intend to immediately go viral on Instagram after making my first post dancing with my students. It just happened. And as it happened, I was forced to navigate public life and cultivate my digital image and brand. This may have been new to me, but for Renegades, it's simply another step in their journey. They don't have to come up with a brand on the fly as I did because they are legitimate artists and social media is another platform that they use to make art and engage with their communities.

Building a brand on social media is, first and foremost, a question of presenting a certain type of image to the public. Although at times this may appear to be a free-wheeling process, it is in fact quite calculated. Speaking of a time before the digital age, sociologist Erving Goffman uses the term "impression management" to speak to the ways that performance, interpretation, and adjustment are part of a self-presentation process in which people attempt to influence how their image is perceived.[15] Naturally, the body becomes a crucial site to perform identity. That is, people use their bodies to project information about themselves, which ultimately shapes how others perceive them.[16] Social media networks encourage such management self-presentation because, in part, nearly every app is built around user profiles.[17] User profiles, therefore, are where the journey to craft a digital identity as a hip hop artist begins. By creating content that aligns with these profiles, hip hop artists use social media dance apps, in particular to, as digital media scholar Jenny Sundén contends, perform themselves into being.[18]

As Howard Gardner and Katie Davis suggest, "digital media open up new avenues for youth to express themselves creatively."[19] That is, artistic practices such as video production, music composition, and photography editing made readily available on cell phones are more accessible for youth today than they were in the pre-digital era. They are cheaper to purchase (if a purchase is required), easier to use, and provide a wider array of possibilities than previous generations enjoyed.[20] Essentially, while apps support diverse communities and a variety of artistic practices to materialize, they, perhaps most significant, increase access and democratize the music industry. What is more, as I explain throughout this book, social media culture has made it easier for artists to find an audience and community to support their artistic practice and help them pivot leisure social media use into legitimate careers as recording artists.

Artists have long seen the internet and social media as key sites for capitalizing on youth's desire to get their music fix.[21] Just as young people did in the age of MySpace, contemporary young music aficionados find their music and engage with the culture that surrounds musicians on Instagram, Dubsmash, and TikTok.[22] This is a symbiotic relationship: artists want a central location wherein they can grow their fan base, and fans want to connect with their favorite musicians. Youth are active participants in music (sub) cultures and can be the difference between a recording artist lingering in anonymity or going viral and capitalizing on their art. Digital, social media spaces give fans a type and level of access that wasn't previously available. All music fans need is a phone and an internet connection; there is no need for expensive concert tickets or backstage passes. In essence, social media democratizes access to musicians. Fans can simply follow an artist on a variety of social media sites and immediately be able to interact with them. On Instagram, for instance, fans can engage with artists by means of comments, story posts, sharing content, and, the crown jewel of fan engagement, "talking" to the musicians during an Instagram Live session. Dance apps, like other video-sharing apps, have increased artists' audience base and expanded the possibilities that musicians have for forging careers.[23] And, perhaps most relevant to *Renegades*, digital media has "affected virtually every facet of the creative process, encompassing who can be a creator, what can be created, and how creations come into being and find an audience."[24]

As digital capabilities have broadened, so too have the opportunities for aspiring hip hop artists to use social media as a necessary building block in the path toward a successful career. In early internet culture, certain social media platforms were like an added bonus in an artist's toolkit. Today, Zoomer artists are virtually irrelevant if they are not on Instagram or TikTok. To that end, places like Dubsmash with smaller user bases serve as critical sites for artists to test their brand identity before taking themselves to the masses on larger apps such as Instagram, YouTube, and TikTok, where virality is the name of the game. Yet, as media studies scholar Brooke Erin Duffy posits, young social media artists can be both enterprising and digitally networked, but still unpaid for their labor.[25] Since so often this work is met without compensation, Duffy uses the term "aspirational labor" to speak to the "(mostly) uncompensated, independent work that is propelled by the much-venerated ideal of *getting paid to do what you love*."[26] While it perhaps feeds into neoliberal capitalism and the so-called American Dream, the idea is that if an artist works hard enough then it will eventually pay off once their work catches on and, if they are lucky, goes viral. In that case, the "investment of time, energy, and capital will later lead to a fulfilling career."[27]

As well-known Dubsmashers grow in popularity and can capitalize from their agency, they gain confidence—or they become skilled at performing confidence—that they can then use as an integral part of their digital identity performances. In *Foundation: B-boys, B-girls and Hip-Hop Culture in New York*, Joseph G. Schloss advocates for a deeper understanding of the "relationship between creativity and self-confidence" that is associated with hip hop dance and, to a larger extent, hip hop aesthetics.[28] That is, hip hop artists rely on self-assurance to develop their art and to find success in it. Schloss notes, "one must project an absolute certainty that, if one does something valuable, no matter how subtle, it will be appreciated."[29] Despite their youth, Dubsmashers are already engaging with brand management and projecting self-assuredness. It bears repeating that artists' social media is anything but random. Rather, the Renegades in this book strategically engage with social media as a core component of fashioning an identity as a hip hop artist and cultivating a community of followers who will continue to support the work even when Gen Z moves on to the next digital platform.

Such is the work of the next two case studies in this chapter—Brooklyn Queen and Kayla Nicole Jones. Both artists present the various performance strategies that Black Zoomers in the hip hop industry actualize to render aspirational labor into a bona fide career as an artist and influencer. Like TisaKorean, social media dance apps are not an optional part of the artist's repertoire but are fundamental tools that each serve a specific purpose on the journey to building a lucrative career in the music industry.

BROOKLYN QUEEN TAUGHT ME

On March 4, 2020, I walked into a dance studio in Midtown Houston to meet Brooklyn Queen (depicted in Figure 4.1), who was in town to perform

Figure 4.1 Brooklyn Queen. Photo by Dove Clark.

at the Houston Rockets NBA game the following day. During our brief DM exchanges on Instagram setting up our meeting to collab, she told me she had rehearsal. That's all I knew. When I walked through the door, I quickly realized that what I thought was going to be a quick collab with Brooklyn Queen was so much more. Awaiting Brooklyn were a dozen Black tweens who comprised 2xclusive Performing Arts. As soon as Brooklyn walked in the door, the girls collectively lost their minds, giving her hugs, high-fives, and the like before jumping into a perfectly choreographed dance sequence to a mega-mix of Brooklyn's songs. At the end of their routine, the girls gathered in a circle and chanted:

> Who believes? She believes!
> Who believes? I believe!
> I believe in myself!

I stood to the side, blown away by what was happening. While Brooklyn was only a few years older than these girls, she might as well have been Beyoncé to them. She made the music and the culture, and these girls fully embraced it, furthering the reach of Brooklyn's identity through their dance.

Brooklyn's rehearsal, it turns out, was actually a rehearsal for her *and* the young women of 2xclusive Performing Arts, who would be performing alongside Brooklyn at the Rockets game. Brooklyn's content and personality spreads positivity and empowerment to young girls, two things that were on display. Hip hop scholar Cheryl L. Keyes suggests that, historically, Black female rappers from MC Lyte and Queen Latifah to Roxanne Shante' and Monie Love "have created spaces from which to deliver powerful messages from Black female and Black feminist perspectives."[30] According to Brooklyn, "I encourage my supporters to always follow their dreams and stay away from negativity. Also, be kind. A smile can go a long way."[31] This was the type of energy that was present at 2xclusive. Although brief, Brooklyn's interactions and collaborations with and at 2xclusive reveal the power that Renegades have to influence generational culture. Although a teenager herself, Brooklyn has already cemented herself as an integral cultural influencer who is rapping the lyrics and choreographing the dance moves that young Zoomers across the United States are all adding to their own repertoires.

Born in 2005, Detroit rapper and social media personality Brooklyn Queen's career has been entirely shaped by social media and digital technologies. Despite her age, she has already had a prolific career that expands across many social media platforms. When she was five years old, she wrote her first song for her kindergarten talent show. The experience gave her the music bug and she has yet to look back. She continued dabbling in music, being trained by her mother Nailnotorious Kim, an influential nail artist who is also a rapper. Brooklyn began recording songs when she was eight years old, but her career took off in 2017 when the music video for her song, "Keke Taught Me," went viral on YouTube, gaining 30 million views in its first month. The music video, which also features comedian Eastside Ivo, now has over 54 million views and remains her most well-known song. Like so many viral hits in the social media dance age, "Keke Taught Me" is didactic. That is, the lyrics explain how to do the dance, not unlike TisaKorean's "The Mop" or Kayla Nicole Jones's "Move Like a Snake." Other notable songs by Brooklyn Queen include "Beat the Baby," "Pretty Girls Stuff," "Emoji," "Feeling So Wavy," and "Rich Girl Problems." While her digital presence has helped solidify her place with young members of Generation Z, her work also pays homage to hip hop history, featuring collaborations with legends such as Salt-n-Pepa and Rob Base.

Brooklyn Queen's name is part of this homage. Artists' names and social media account usernames (e.g., Instagram handles) are one of the most important parts of crafting their identity. As Joseph G. Schloss acknowledges regarding hip hop dancers, in particular, it is rare for them to use their given names. Rather, it is more common to "choose a name that suggests the qualities they wish to project in their dance, and they may go through several names before they find the one that really fits them."[32] The world of Dubsmash is no different. For Brooklyn Queen, the choice to adopt the word "Queen" positions her as Gen Z royalty, following a lineage of female rappers who have adopted "Queen" into their names and personalities. For example, hip hop scholar Cheryl L. Keyes points to the work of Queen Kenya, Queen Latifah, Sister Souljah, Nefertiti, Queen Mother Rage, Isis, and Yo-Yo to demonstrate the "Queen Mother" category of female rappers "who view themselves as African-centered icons."[33] On her use of "Queen," Queen Latifah admits, "It felt good saying it, and I felt like a queen. And you know, I am a queen. And every Black woman is a queen."[34] The word "Queen," then, is as strategic as any other facet of a female rapper's identity. The title also connotes leadership, ways of knowing, and connection to the legacy of female rappers in hip hop.

With a name intact, the artist can then focus on the music. And with the song comes the dance. While Brooklyn has far more traction on TikTok, simply due to the platform being larger, Dubsmash remains a key tool in her digital identity performance as a musician, a dancer, and choreographer. Brooklyn routinely releases new dance challenges that begin on Dubsmash before they circulate on other social media platforms. For instance, in April 2020, Brooklyn introduced a dance challenge to Phil Collins's 1981 song "In the Air Tonight." The challenge, #brooklynxair, matches classic viral dance moves to Collins's iconic drum section of the song. This challenge is particularly noteworthy since most Zoomer Dubsmash challenges make use of contemporary music. So, using a rock song from the early 1980s stands out. One Instagram user even commented on Brooklyn's Instagram post of the video, "Why is this my grandma ringtone tho." #brooklynxair exemplifies how Brooklyn influences her followers to hit virtually any dance challenge she creates.[35]

When I met Brooklyn at 2xclusive Performing Arts, she told me about her new single, "Dance Baby," which was set to drop later that week. As with her most viral hits, this salsa-infused song is not only catchy but also instructive. The lyrics explain:

> Now left, then right,
> Now left, then right,
> Now front, then back,
> Now front, then back,
> Now work the middle, work the middle,
> Work your hips, just a little,
> And work the middle, work the middle,
> Work them hips just a little.

She asked me if I wanted to make some videos with her for the drop, along with her frequent collaborator, Detroit-based La La So Lit, also a social media influencer. As is customary in these collaborations, La La So Lit and I would also post the videos on our social media accounts. Dubsmashers frequently rely on such in-person collaboration, and collaborative distribution of their content, to help grow their follower counts. With Brooklyn, though, one thing stood out. Rather than distribute the same video across all platforms, she wanted to modify the dance to speak to the differences of each platform. So, as Brooklyn showed me the dance to be posted to TikTok she also asked me how she should modify it for Dubsmash. As is typically the case, the TikTok version of her dance is easier to execute, as it is meant to speak to a broad community of dancers and non-dancers. The Dubsmash version, however, was to be like nearly any dance that migrates from Dubsmash to TikTok in that it goes harder (i.e., it's more complicated).

Ultimately, the "Dance Baby" choreography didn't change much as the song's dance doesn't provide much opportunity to elaborate or go harder. That said, Brooklyn was keenly aware of the two social media platforms and how she imagined that audiences would perceive her and the work on each. Adjusting the dance was a matter of how Brooklyn wanted to position herself for her audience(s) as well as an exercise in how Brooklyn recognizes how *others see her* which, as an artist, is imperative. That Brooklyn understands this at fourteen years old, as her career is still on the rise, reveals how nuanced the work of Renegade recording artists are. Each move—each post, song, caption, etc.—is a calculated part of their identity performance.

As Dubsmashers have a culture of crediting choreographers, the result is a collection of repetitions that all point back to Brooklyn. That is, as more Dubsmashers hit the challenge, Brooklyn's name proliferates. Since usernames are hyperlinks on Instagram, it only takes one click to visit her profile. By clicking her username, the viewer has shown interest, which makes them more likely to want to see more of Brooklyn's content and, ultimately, follow her. As I quickly realized when I went viral myself, having clout on Instagram ensures that nearly everything a popular account posts will go viral to a certain extent. While a post might not go viral enough to be picked up by popular meme accounts or the likes of *Good Morning America* and *The Tonight Show*, even minor instances of virality help to extend the reach of a social media influencer.

Every post that Brooklyn Queen makes on Instagram, for instance, makes up a component of the Renegade blueprint toward cultivating Zoomer aesthetics and generational culture. As Brooklyn Queen exhibits, performance can be used as a strategy to bring the audience in and help them identify with a collective culture.[36] Performance has long been considered a form of resistance and politics.[37] For instance, in *The Archive and the Repertoire*, performance studies scholar Diana Taylor proposes, "embodied performance . . . makes visible an entire spectrum of attitudes and values."[38] Moreover, in *Choreographing Empathy: Kinesthesia in Performance*, dance scholar Susan Foster acknowledges that choreography theorizes identity and embodiment, at both the personal and the communal levels.[39] As such, the cultural work of Renegades like Brooklyn Queen also pushes against and, at times, averts stereotypes of youth identity. Considering that, as musical theater and dance scholar Phoebe Rumsey claims, "the body is a prime site to examine historical agency and ownership of cultural mores," we can begin to understand how hip hop artists use embodied performance on social media apps as a strategy to write themselves into the narrative as culture creators and to position themselves as agents of social change.[40] They are not merely bystanders who wait for culture to shift; they are actively using social dance, social media, and virality as a form of ownership and generational leadership. The fact that youth are leading the widespread cultural changes that comprise the subject of this book should not be lost. That is, to disregard Brooklyn Queen's art-making because she is a young teen would be a mistake.

I've always been afraid of snakes. The mere sight of a picture of a snake will send shivers down my body. But in fall 2019, I couldn't stop moving like one. There I was in my classroom, on Instagram Live, on Dubsmash, you name it, moving like a snake. The song and corresponding dance move "Move Like a Snake" is the brainchild of Kayla Nicole Jones. Born in 2001 in Montgomery, Alabama, Jones is one of the most well-known Zoomers in the world. According to her website, Jones is "gifted, eye-catching and unforgettable."[41] While people might not know her name, her work routinely penetrates the mainstream, demonstrating Jones's knack for virality. Of all the artists in this book, Jones's work is the most wide-reaching even if most of her contributions remain without her name attached. Using a mixture of digital platforms, each serving a specific use, Jones has positioned herself as both a hit recording artist and a comedic goldmine. As her website bio attests, "Jones doesn't aspire to follow anyone else's path. She's making a lane of her own."[42] Jones strategically uses social media to engage in what African American Studies scholar Regina Bradley calls "black girl awkwardness," which allows "black women to visualize themselves, establish communities and share/document their experiences online."[43] Her Black girl awkwardness is precisely what sets her apart from other artists in her generation. Despite a myriad of successes, she is best known through viral GIFs and memes that have emerged from her YouTube content on Nicole TV, where she has 5 million subscribers. Nicole TV features a regular assortment of comedic beauty tutorials, sketches, and vlogs. Her Instagram (@kaylanicolejones), where she has 6.5 million followers, has the most variety of content than other Renegades in this book. This reflects her career being further along, no doubt because her work as a YouTuber dates to at least 2015 with the video "How to be on FLEEK." Regardless of the platform, Jones shows a consistent knack for going viral. Yet, despite her successes, there are few resources about Jones online, which mirrors the larger disregard for Generation Z culture and, specifically, the cultural contributions of Black teenage girls.[44]

Her most famous contribution to pop culture has been the "Looking Up and Down" meme, which is a three-second video that features Jones sitting on the sofa looking up and down. The clip turned into a meme through a plethora of viral tweets and Instagram posts that added witty captions to Jones's video.[45] Yet, the further such memes circulate beyond the content's original posting and context, the more detached from the creator's identity they become. That is, because Jones is quite literally performing a character that doesn't resemble her day-to-day appearance or her persona as a rapper, the work is siloed off from her other art-making. The range that Jones demonstrates through her art raises questions of when the artist takes on certain personas and how Renegades vary identity performances according to the platform. In her research on how Black girls use YouTube as a site to theorize and perform twerking, Kyra D. Gaunt lingers on the moment before an artist hits record: "As you watch yourself recording a video from a webcam before you upload to YouTube, every new subscriber or vlogger must confront—begin to come face-to-face—with one question: *Who am I and for what audience am I presenting and managing myself/ identity?*"[46] I find Gaunt's question particularly relevant to understanding the work of Kayla Nicole Jones. While other artists in this book strategically use social media as an accurate extension of their lives, Jones presents a different persona on each platform. That is, she is different on YouTube than in real life. She is different on Dubsmash than she is on Twitter. Each platform, therefore, serves a different purpose and helps paint a full picture of the artist.

Even though she is primarily known for her comedic sketches on YouTube, Jones is also a prolific rapper who uses her full arsenal of social media platforms to disseminate her music. As is often the case with Renegades, and Zoomer recording artists in general, the key to a song's success relies on social dance. Performing and visual arts scholar Barbara Cohen-Stratyner declares that "the best way to bring attention to a song was to attach a dance to it."[47] Although Cohen-Stratyner is speaking of musical theater in the 1920s (quite literally a world away), the work of Renegade rappers is no different. In nearly every example in this book, a song's success and longevity has relied on a popular dance associated with the song. And, in turn, an important part of being "in the know" is knowing and being able to execute the dances that correspond to certain songs, post yourself dancing to the song on social media, and, subsequently, engage in the viralness of the song and dance.

Jones's 2019 song "Move Like a Snake" is no different. Like the music to so many viral dance challenges, "Move Like a Snake" is instructional:

Move like a snake, like a snake,
M-move like a snake, like a snake,
Put your hand on your face, move like a snake, move like a snake,
    move like a snake,
Put your hand on your waist, move like a snake, move like a snake,
    m-move like a,
Move like a sssssssnake.[48]

The song's official music video, which has over 14 million views on YouTube, features Jones working as a teacher at the fictional Zone 4 High School. While picking up some papers that she frantically drops, she stops the Wicker Twinz and asks them why they aren't in class.[49] They quickly flip the question on Jones, asking her why *she* isn't in class. "I'm grown and I'm a teacher," Jones tells them while making her new "teacher's pets" pick up the remaining papers. She then sits down with the principal, who has called the "snake charmer" into his office because he doesn't think she's been doing her job. When she pushes back, voicing the work she has done, he responds, "Grades? Grades? All I see is Dubsmash, Dubsmash, Dubsmash."[50] The two then get into an argument about the role of social media in Jones's classroom. According to her, dancing with her students is an essential part of her job and, as a result, doesn't violate any of the school's policies. After she gets fired for making Dubsmash videos with her students, she storms out of his office and the beat drops. Still at school, it is time for Jones to teach us a lesson about moving like a snake. As Jones sings "Move Like a Snake," she makes use of her classroom's chalkboard to teach the students the lyrics as she shows them the dance moves: move your hips back and forth from left to right while putting your hand on your forehead as if trying to block the sun. The students eagerly follow Jones's every move, demonstrating how valuable they find the lesson. It is worth noting that the "students" in Jones's class are also popular Dubsmashers. The music video, therefore, mirrors the ways that viralness transpires on social media: Jones sets the trend and other popular Dubsmashers engage with the trend before it extends into the masses. Indeed, soon after the video's release, teenagers across the world were making videos in which they moved like snakes. They posted them on social media using the appropriate hashtags and, before you know it, the next viral trend was firmly rooted in Zoomer generational culture.

It should come as no surprise that moving like a snake became an iconic dance move within the Dubsmash community. Compared to most trending dances on Dubsmash, moving like a snake is remarkably simple. Of course, there are countless variations and Dubsmashers enjoy adding their own unique spins to popular dances, especially dances that are simple. Riffing off popular dances is quite common on Dubsmash and is something that my students and I frequently do. We often discuss a given dance and talk about what we like about it, what we don't like about it, and how we can alter it to fit our aesthetic. Dancers will also change dance moves to make them easier to execute. In other instances, when a dance features a difficult move, dancers will swap it out with an easier move. For example, I can't do helicopter hands, so I instead do other dance moves when choreography calls for them. In other instances, I will attempt helicopter hands but will exaggerate my movements and try to be funny to distract from my inability to do the dance as choreographed. As I continued to make Dubs, move like a snake became one of my signature dance moves. I would sneak it into as many Dubs as I could, and I couldn't get on Instagram Live in fall 2019 without my followers asking me to move like a snake for them. The move was everywhere and, as Dubsmashers made more and more videos, the song continued to go viral and become part of mainstream US popular culture.

In the social media dance world, songs and dances achieve canonization when they are performed across time. That is, the viral repetition that builds on an original video helps the dance challenge enter what theater scholar Jonathan Miller calls the "afterlife."[51] Although Miller is specifically referring to how Shakespeare's plays are canonized, I find his analysis particularly helpful in unpacking the ways that trends go viral and *stay* viral, becoming, as a result, canonical pieces of Gen Z culture. Each subsequent video performance builds a body of work that comprises a challenge's afterlife. The larger this body of work becomes, the more likely it is that a challenge's afterlife will lead to canonization and the cultural capital and public life that is tied to becoming part of the pop culture canon. Such virality helps sustain relationships between artists and their followers, ultimately bridging communities. Viral song-and-dance repertoires bind generational community together, as happened with Gen X and the Macarena, and with Millennials and the Wobble and the Cha Cha Slide. These dance trends are ingrained in our collective memories as generational culture, and are easily accessed even if listener-dancers haven't heard their related songs in years. The afterlife of the song and dance continually brings people together. And, with a prolific afterlife and a sustained collection of repetitions (that is Dubs and TikToks), cultural capital continues to accrue and, as a result, the dance challenge enters into a public life that extends beyond the artist themself. This is precisely how Kayla Nicole Jones uses cross-platform virality to cement herself as an influencer of generational culture. What begins as a Dub then becomes a YouTube tutorial before spreading like wildfire across social media. As Jones's work attests, this is where her success lies.

CONCLUSION

Although I began this chapter by demonstrating TisaKorean and his squad's knack for virality, many of the Gen Z trendsetters are, in fact, women. But, as has historically been the case for women in hip hop, credit is more often than not given to male artists. That is, Black girls must work twice as hard to see results on social media. This isn't the case of Charli D'Amelio posting a simple dancing video on TikTok and going viral during the ninety-minute drive to dance camp.[52] Unlike her, artists such as Brooklyn Queen and Kayla Nicole Jones didn't go viral overnight and have to scramble to find a way to continue their viral fame. Rather, their viralness is a direct product of their dedication to their art-making and of strategically using social media as a form of identity performance and impression management. Although specifically referring to twerking videos on YouTube, Kyra D. Gaunt observes that each view on social media—each impression—of a Black girl doing a specific dance "is not just casual audio-visual consumption for entertainment. It is also a cipher for creating the discourse of racial and gender ideology, as well as for the actual exchange of commerce as social capital in the attention economy surrounding rap and popular music videos."[53] That is, every time a Dubsmasher engages with "Dance Baby" by Brooklyn Queen or "Move Like a Snake" by Kayla Nicole Jones, for example, it adds to a growing body of work that positions artists like Brooklyn Queen and Jones as culture creators and trend setters.

As virality works, a generational culture that draws from Black girlhood proliferates. These young women are positioned as knowers, which, as this book reveals, is antithetical to the ways that systems such as White supremacy seek to discount the work of Black teen influencers. Although these artists may face systemic roadblocks that are largely out of their control, their art-making and strategic use of social media uncovers a shared politic and rebelliousness that demonstrates how these young people will not be silenced or relegated to second tier status. In the world of social media, they have a level of agency that might have been impossible to achieve in the pre-digital era. That is, as their follower counts have organically grown, so has their clout and, subsequently, their reach. Whether it is the dance students at 2xclusive Performing Arts or the "students" in Jones's class at Zone 4 High School desperately learning how to move like a snake, Zoomers look to these Black women to set the culture.

CHAPTER 5

Moving as One

Unison Dancing, Muscular Bonding, and Hip Hop Pedagogy

Ashley was a late addition to my second period Spanish II class. We were already a few weeks into the 2019–2020 school year by the time her schedule changed, and she was now taking a class with me for a second year in a row. While I know teachers aren't supposed to admit that they have favorite students, Ashley had become one of mine the year prior. We bonded over our love of dance and Ashley quickly became my most vocal supporter and teacher as I began to learn how to dance. So, as you can imagine, I was excited to see her walk through my door that day. But Ashley looked anything but excited. In fact, she looked quite miserable to be in my class. She came in, handed me her schedule, and sat at the table next to my desk (i.e., as far away as possible from other students). I began the lesson and once students were off and running with the classwork, I went and sat by Ashley. I asked her why she didn't want to sit by her classmates. "I don't like anybody in this class," she told me. I then started naming students that I knew she knew. She then proceeded to tell me, in quick fire style, what she thought about each student in the class: "She's too much. He's aggy. She's ok. He tries too hard. I don't like her voice. He's too quiet. She's too loud." Ashley seemed miserable to be in my second period because, well, she didn't like anyone in the room except for me. This soon changed.

Within a few months, Ashley made a story post on Instagram that was a picture of some other girls in the class, Ashley, and me. We were

Renegades. Trevor Boffone, Oxford University Press. © Oxford University Press 2021.
DOI: 10.1093/oso/9780197577677.003.0006

wearing matching shirts that Sauce Avenue sent us. The caption read "This is family." Now, you might be wondering how Ashley went from loathing my classroom community to calling it family—I became her "cousin"—but, if you are still reading this book, then you have probably guessed that this transformation happened through Dubsmash. Herein lies the power of Dubsmash as a tool for community building in the classroom (see Figure 5.1). When I began teaching at Bellaire High School, I recognized that my students and I had a similar interest in dance and, to a larger extent, an intergenerational understanding of hip hop.[1] While this commonality enabled us to begin building relationships in a way I previously hadn't seen in my classroom, something was missing, something that could unite us. As this book demonstrates, dance can create a sense of community and a sense of belonging, two things that high school students are desperate to have, even if they don't always give voice to those desires. As we had done the previous school year, in second period, I strategically used social media dance apps as a way to build stronger relationships with my students and, by extension, a more robust sense of classroom community. Ashley became one of the leaders in this movement. She didn't change overnight; rather, Ashley gradually saw the value of positioning herself as a knower and a culture creator. She helped choose songs we would dance to, she would come up with the choreography, and teach us the dance moves. As she did these

Figure 5.1 Bellaire High School students and author show off their Dubsmash hoodies. Photo by Luke Parker.

things, her grades improved, her sense of self-esteem rose, she became a leader, and she developed kinship bonds with other Black girls in her class.

Although Ashley's story is best seen through the events of the fall 2019 semester, her journey—and mine—began during the previous school year. From the first day of school at Bellaire in 2018, my students and I quickly bonded over our love of music and dance. Almost immediately, I showed a genuine interest in my students' culture and, with that authenticity, my students became more willing to share with me. In between classwork, they would tell me about the music they were listening to and I would tell them about the music I grew up listening to. And with music comes dance moves. Now, I've always loved to dance and I've always been eager to learn new styles of dance, but I wasn't ready for what they were about to teach me—the Woah. The Woah is the definitive Generation Z dance move. They throw it up and they hit it like they are getting paid to do it. The Woah was everywhere so my students taught me how to hit it. Admittedly, our time dancing together was limited. It happened irregularly and with almost no sense of obligation or urgency.

Enter Dubsmash. When Dubsmash relaunched as a dance challenge app in 2018, we were provided with the missing link. One day in October, I was sitting at my desk one day waiting for the bell to ring when a group of Black girls propped up a phone against the window sill, pressed a purple button on the screen, and, without so much as a conversation, began doing a highly choreographed dance in perfect unison. I was both perplexed and spellbound. It looked like something out of a 1990s teen movie and I needed to know everything about it: what was the app, how did everyone already know the dances, and where did the choreography come from? At this point, my students already knew that I loved to dance—even if I couldn't even remotely execute their dance moves—so they invited me into the circle.

As our dancing became more formalized during breaks during the school day, the sense of obligation entered the picture. Obligation, according to Juan Flores, is a key facet of building and sustaining community.[2] Typically, in a high school classroom, obligation is framed around compliance; students are obligated to behave in a certain way and to do their work under certain rules and constraints.[3] By foregrounding Dubsmash as a fundamental part of my pedagogy, obligation to each other instead became a way for my students and me to trouble the traditional hierarchies and relationships seen in urban public education. By embracing the values that define the larger digital Dubsmash community, my students and I entered into an unofficial contract of obligation that saw us fully committed to teaching each other dance challenges through a non-hierarchical model built on patience, love, and support. Put simply, we were obligated to our Dubsmash community in a way that the public educational system doesn't always support. This obligation felt more authentic than other obligations students have because it felt necessary and real. As a result, this obligation changed the classroom dynamic and allowed us to take this work beyond simply posting short dance videos on Dubsmash and Instagram. What I found was that by engaging in Dubsmash and learning about their cultures in a genuine way, my students attained a higher level of buy-in when they arrived for my class. Shortly after my students and I went viral, I began to question *everything*.[4] I wanted to know what made dancing work. Sure, it was fun, but from the beginning I knew that there was something to it beyond simply having fun and relieving stress at work.

In the pages that follow, I explore the transformative power that social media dance holds to forge an inclusive, hip hop pedagogy. To do this, I use my own classroom and experiences with my students as a case study in community-focused pedagogy. Through an analysis of the Renegades in my classroom, I argue that unison dancing helps Renegades create stronger relationships and a more formidable sense of community. Building on research on Broadway chorus lines and military formations/drills, this chapter analyzes how unison movement and muscular bonding create an affective response that helps build stronger relationships between students and teachers. As such, this chapter is a testament as to how Dubsmash can be used as a tool of hip hop education and culturally responsive teaching. To further demonstrate how Renegades materialize in the high school classroom, this chapter also features interviews with other dancing teachers. Indeed, Dubsmash pushes against the barriers typically seen between teachers and students in public education, effectively becoming a tool of anti-racist community building.

HIP HOP EDUCATION

If you attend virtually any professional development workshop for high school teachers, you will inevitably hear one word—*engagement*. Teachers are always looking for new ways to improve student engagement and, as a result, help improve the educational experience. It seems that teachers are constantly trying to get students who appear disinterested to care about their education. To this end, one of the current buzzwords in teacher training has become "culturally relevant pedagogy." As educational researcher Gloria Ladson-Billings describes, culturally relevant pedagogy requires teachers to consider the cultures and identities of the students in their classrooms before any instructional or environmental decisions can be enacted.[5] Dance scholar Nyama McCarthy-Brown recognizes the need for culturally relevant teaching in dance education, as well, noting that, "What is at stake for these students is a connection to their identity and culture."[6] That is, teachers must not only learn about their student's cultures, but they must privilege them and, as an extension, work to embed them in the educational experience.

To address the need for culturally relevant pedagogy, the hip hop education movement was formed. Better known by the hashtag #HipHopEd, hip hop education infuses hip hop methods such as rap battles, cyphers, and shared leadership into the classroom to create culturally responsive educational experiences. While the #HipHopEd movement is indebted to the work of scholars and educators such as Edmund Adjapong, Amil Cook, Timothy Jones, Ian Levy, Bettina L. Love, Emery Petchauer, Jason R. Rawls, John Robinson, and Courtney Rose, my work has most been informed by Christopher Emdin, whose *For White Folks Who Teacher in the Hood . . . and the Rest of Y'all Too: Reality Pedagogy and Urban Education* remains the most valuable scholarship in regards to my teaching.[7] Emdin explains how teachers can address the need for culturally responsive teaching by means of what he calls "reality pedagogy":

> Reality pedagogy is an approach to teaching and learning that has a primary goal of meeting each student on his or her own cultural and emotional turf. It focuses on making the local experiences of the student visible and creating contexts where there is a role reversal of sorts that positions the student as the expert in his or her own teaching and learning, and the teacher as the learner. It posits that while the teacher is the person charged with delivering the content, the student is the person who shapes how best to teach that content. Together, the teacher and students co-construct the classroom space.[8]

Reality pedagogy requires a willingness to both learn how to teach youth of color and to learn about the students themselves. By not acknowledging the differences between student cultures and the traditional cultures that dictate how students are supposed to act in classrooms, the divide between students and teachers can only increase. That is, by not allowing the cultures of our students to hold space in the classroom, inequities in education will only persist, leading to a perpetual cycle in which systemics of racism, sexism, homophobia, and the like are replicated rather than eradicated.[9]

Responding to how education is not always a safe space for students of color, Emdin explores ways to increase student engagement through anti-racist teaching and culturally responsive pedagogy. A key facet of this is knowing your students and understanding what their interests are and *how* they create individual and collective sense of identity. As Emdin demonstrates, urban teens strategically use dress, music, and their creativity and artistry in general to separate themselves from the larger mainstream culture. Yet, the creation of a youth subculture is not typically met with praise. Rather, "in much public discourse, the ways in which they express themselves creatively are denigrated."[10] With regard to digital media, Kirsten Drotner notes how the innovative ways that young people push culture forward is typically met with normative responses.[11] In the case of urban youth cultures in schools, adults sometimes regard these creative innovations as inferior in cultural quality. For instance, many adults and other outsiders dismiss much hip hop music and dance as being vulgar. As Emdin explains, however, "the skill and innovation it takes to create this type of art are entirely secondary to the surface-level thing that people hear."[12] As I always tell teachers with whom I work, an essential aspect of building high-quality relationships with students relies on respecting and elevating their cultures. That is, when my students introduced me to the Woah, I didn't criticize the dance or tell them that it was inferior to dance styles that I was more familiar with. In the same vein, when they told me about the contemporary rap music they enjoy such as NBA Youngboy, Blueface, and City Girls, I didn't create value judgments about their rap music as different from the rap music I grew up with such as Tupac, Queen Latifah, and Dr. Dre. Belittling or dismissing students' cultures is *not* best practice. To prioritize a reality pedagogy, there *has* to be listening and respect.

This is all to say that to fully understand how Dubsmash works in the classroom, one must first understand Dubsmash as another expression of hip hop culture that can aid in building relationships and help students perform their cultures at school. Although I had been practicing culturally responsive teaching long before I had a name for it, it wasn't until I read Emdin's work and began to engage with the #HipHopEd community through scholarship and weekly Twitter conversations that I truly understood the potential that students hold to radically shift the classroom environment. With these tools in my teaching toolbox, I opened my classroom up and the Renegades took over. Dubsmash was the missing link that I had been looking for as an educator. That I wasn't the one to introduce it to my students is even more noteworthy. I didn't invent this or create it. My students were engaging with Dubsmash already; I simply opened the doors for them to engage with it in the classroom. My students not only brought their culture into the classroom, which they had already been doing in a variety of informal ways, but they demonstrated its value to their formal education. That is, the way my students and I work using Dubsmash is perhaps even more important than the subject matter of my courses. This is a pedagogy that goes beyond classwork and test scores. Rather, reality pedagogy creates a space where students' identities matter in a way that works against traditional models of public education.

MUSCULAR BONDING ONE DUBSMASH AT A TIME

Dancing in collective holds transformative power to build community and (re)enforce a positive self of individual and group identity. In *The Games Black Girls Play: Learning the Ropes from Double-Dutch to Hip-Hop*, Kyra D. Gaunt exposes "how black musical style and behavior are learned through oral-kinetic practices that only teach an embodied discourse of black musical expression, but also inherently teach discourse about appropriate and transgressive gender and racial roles (for both girls and boys) in African American communities."[13] I extend this to demonstrate how Black girl expression in the classroom fosters an environment in which young women become leaders in a space that has historically worked to disenfranchise them—public education. That is, social media dance facilitates an embodied practice that positions the artistic and cultural contributions of Black girls as an act of resistance. In "Twerk Sumn!: Theorizing Black Girl Epistemology in the Body," African American Studies scholar Aria S. Halliday proposes that Black girls strategically use twerking videos as a way to render their cultures significant and visible, thus placing the practice of twerking within a lineage of African diasporic dances.[14] Indeed, as the work of the Dubsmash community and my student dancers reveals, this work is about more than simply twerking or hitting the Woah. Rather, as Halliday reveals in her study of twerking videos, "Whether professional music videos or amateur videos online, many of the popular twerking videos show multiple Black girls dancing together, encouraging each other, complimenting each other's movement, laughing, and celebrating successful new moves."[15] Digital dance spaces, then, serve as spaces for building self-esteem and community, which are core tenets of Black women's spaces.[16]

Dubsmash, as a space that encourages unison dancing, exemplifies what Gaunt refers to as "musical blackness," or the ways that Black girls engage in "practices, communications, and traditions that lead to cultural identification."[17] That is, executing a Dubsmash video relies on a series of choreographed movements, which in turn lead to cultural identification.

Naturally, young people come to depend on such embodied consciousness as intrinsically tied to socialization and to fitting in with group culture. For social media dance apps, embodied consciousness takes the form of a series of dance moves that dancers *must* learn to become one with the group. I often refer to these viral dance moves as puzzle pieces. While it may take a particular dancer a while to build out their toolkit, once each choreographic move is mastered, making a Dub becomes a process of putting the puzzle pieces together. Having these puzzle pieces in your repertoire is essential to having cultural capital and being able to feel a sense of group belonging. Even if someone is not a master dancer, knowing these dance moves allows individuals an entry point into the community. And, as this chapter reveals, there is power in making puzzles together. That is, there is power in doing Dubsmash and engaging in unison dancing. There is power in group movement that is enhanced by learning as a group and gaining literacy in Dubsmash. And, since Black girls have historically been marginalized by the public education system, that the work in my classroom is led by Black girls is even more noteworthy, as the story of Ashley that began this chapter illustrates.[18] Dancing, then, becomes a space for Black Zoomers to navigate stereotypes about "our social and musical bodies, our somebodiness, as well as the internalized assumptions we carry and impose upon ourselves and other black bodies."[19] Black girls present how Dubsmash is another game that Black girls play and a strategic act of rebellion that positions them as leaders in the classroom.

Whereas dance challenges on apps such as TikTok and Triller encourage individuality in their dance movements, Dubsmash dance challenges rely on uniformity. Even a brief perusal of both apps will show this discrepancy—TikTokers, for the most part, simply learn the dance moves, whereas Dubsmashers who dance in pairs or groups will record their dance videos as many times as necessary until they have achieved unison or at least near perfect unison. The latter has been the case with my students and me while using Dubsmash. The app encourages users to become perfectionists and polish their dance moves as much as possible. Moreover, Dubsmash, as an app that encourages unison movement, builds feelings of community in its users when recording a duo or group video. Throughout the process of attaining cohesion through unison dancing, my students and I have slowly chipped away at the traditional barriers placed between teachers and students by a public educational system that privileges hierarchies.

Shortly after my Instagram account went viral, people began to ask me about how my students and I worked together and, specifically, why it was working so successfully. While there are several answers to these questions, one I continually returned to was the idea of what dancing in unison does to the individuals involved. I knew something was happening, but I couldn't quite put a finger on it. And then I attended dance scholar Adrienne Oehlers's presentation on unison dancing in the musical *A Chorus Line* at the Association for Theatre in Higher Education conference in August 2019 and everything clicked. In "In Sync/On Stage: 'One Singular Sensation,'" Oehlers proposes that the unison dancing and collective movement in *A Chorus Line*'s famed curtain call creates an affective response in audiences that routinely leads to thunderous applause.[20] I extend Oehlers's work to consider what the feeling of becoming "one singular sensation" does for the performers themselves. The euphoric feeling that audiences feel following "One Singular Sensation" were exactly the same as what my students and I had been experiencing with our Dubsmash videos.

Dance and Dubsmash become collective movement rituals that my students and I use to create group cohesion in our videos and beyond. In *Keeping Together in Time: Dance and Drill in Human History*, historian William Hardy McNeill uses his experience in the military to examine this phenomenon. As he details, moving in unison with his fellow soldiers created a "strange sense of enlargement; a sort of swelling out, becoming bigger than life, thanks to participation in collective ritual."[21] It should come as no surprise that it is difficult to put words to what this feeling does to an individual; words can be limiting and, as was the case with me, I struggled with putting to words what my students and I felt while dancing together (not to mention going viral together). In a sense it felt larger than life, like something that couldn't be contained to a brief description or theory. Creating a Dubsmash together is an act that triggers an emotional response that, to quote McNeill, constitutes "an indefinitely expansible basis for social cohesion among any and every group that keeps together in time, moving big muscles together and chanting, singing, or shouting rhythmically."[22] The experience of unison dancing was visceral and enabled us to develop kinship bonds between teacher and students and, furthermore, it gave my Renegade students the opportunity to develop kinship bonds marked by Black girlhood. There was something magical happening in our classroom and on social media that we simply couldn't describe. And this magic is precisely what charged us forward.

In his journey to understanding his experiences of collective ritual in the military, McNeill introduces the theory of "muscular bonding" to explain how collective movement rituals lead to a positive feeling among participants. According to McNeill, this euphoric response is a leading reason that military troops are efficient, loyal, and equal.[23] Not to mention that veterans often continue to practice unison drills even when the movement has no practical use in their lives. It's something that they just can't shake off. Although military formations would seem a world away from the world of social media dancing, the focus on moving as one and the affective response it creates is not so different. I posit that McNeill's theory of muscular bonding extends into the classroom, as well, as evidenced by the work of my students. Muscular bonding, as a result, functions as a form of enculturation for student Renegades. This is not unlike what A. R. Radcliffe-Brown notes in saying that group dance is marked by a surrender of the individual in favor of a collective identity:[24] "As the dancer loses himself in the dance, as he becomes absorbed in the unified community, he reaches a state of elation in which he feels himself filled with energy or force immediately beyond his ordinary state, and so finds himself able to perform prodigies of exertion."[25]

By succumbing to group cohesion, the individual dancer increases their sense of self-worth. That is, unison dancing is intrinsically linked to forming a positive self-value. And, as feelings of positive self-esteem grow, so do feelings of obligation to group identity. Dance leads to situations in which harmony in the community is at a maximum and, as a result, can be felt by each individual member.[26] This joint feeling and fusion of individual and collective identity becomes one of the primary functions of social media dance. This work is even more noteworthy when Black girls do it, especially in an educational setting. When Black girls move as one, they are learning racial and gender identity through acts of embodied consciousness.[27] As Gaunt proposes, "the embodiment of social interactions that produce musical events is a primary site for discovering how black musical aesthetics are learned and communicated as self and social experience."[28] While Gaunt describes Black girl-girl relations, I find her work also can describe intergenerational, interracial exchange. These processes often happen simultaneously.

As I mentioned earlier, Dubsmash encourages cohesive movement; when making a Dubsmash it is imperative to be moving as one. Consequently, making a Dubsmash is to become equal with fellow dancers and to engage in a form of culture sharing. Students being on equal footing with their teachers is an uncommon occurrence, even in the arts. While it is quite common for arts teachers and professors to be artistic collaborators with their students, this often takes the form of teachers leading students—be it as a director, conductor, or mentor. Even if teachers perform alongside their students, the teacher has most likely been a leader throughout the process of developing the piece. Much like other #HipHopEd pedagogies, my Dubsmash methodology disrupts this narrative by situating the students as leaders from the beginning. In my classroom, students not only teach the dances, but they often choose the material we work with and lead the process from idea to final product. We rehearse together, correcting each other's techniques as need be as we work to create a tight ensemble in which we are moving as one. This leads to a form of muscular bonding that is often unseen in the public high school classroom. And with that comes a set of benefits that demonstrate how a Renegade politic can penetrate the educational experience. Crafting an inclusive classroom and dance community depends on unity and equity. That is, without harmony realized through dance, the type of group cohesion that muscular bonding allows will be lost. The work of Dubsmash in the classroom, therefore, isn't a gimmick that happens every now and then. Rather, it is something that is thoroughly ingrained in my pedagogy, which allows my teaching to reach a higher level as it engages the cultures and identities of my students in a way that pushes against the traditional public education system.

This process of collaboratively creating a Dubsmash video creates a corporeal transference between teachers and students. Put simply, doing complicated dances in unison such as Jalaiah Harmon's Renegade to K-Camp's "Lottery" and D1 Nayah's choreography to Blueface's "Holy Moly Donut Shop" fosters a level of synchronicity that releases endorphins. Moreover, these endorphins and the sense of community extend beyond the students featured in the video itself. Not only does Dubsmash cohesion create a euphoric feeling among dancers, but it passively releases endorphins to other students who become our spectators, building an affective experience of "feeling together." All in all, my students become self-aware of the work we are doing to forge community.

Muscular bonding and unison dancing enabled the Renegades in my classroom to form a type of digital kinship that was fostered by social media dance.[29] In "When Social Media Yields More than 'Likes': Black Girls' Digital Kinship Formations," Ashleigh Wade defines digital kinship as "a relational practice through which familial ties—with both origin family and chosen family—are established and/or maintained through digital technologies."[30] Similar to the Black teenage girls in Wade's class as seen in her article, my students formed "complex digital kinship structures that reveal how digitality enters into discourses on Black relationship and communication practices."[31] As Black girls' identities have historically been policed and, thus, rendered invisible in school spaces, digital spaces such as Dubsmash and Instagram are uniquely positioned to allow new forms of kinship to materialize in which Black girlhood is the norm.[32] In these spaces, Black girls fashion support networks and acknowledge the agency that they hold to control space. That is, digital spaces become spaces in which Black girls run the show. This book is a testament to that. Although Renegades come in all gender identities, Renegade girls are the leaders in the digital dance world. They are the ones exercising agency in a movement in which collaboration is fundamental.

HOW WE WORK TOGETHER

One of the questions other teachers most frequently ask me is how my students and I work together. They often assume that I am still maintaining my position as the teacher. They assume I pick the songs and choreograph the dances. They assume that I teach the students the dances. Yes, I have done all these things, but on rare occasions. My students are the ones who run the show. I am simply an active participant (see Figure 5.2). After all, I firmly believe that they are the ones bringing their gifts to the table and sharing them with me. My students' work reveals a Renegade politic that can lead to a transformative public education experience. This isn't to say that dance is a classroom management tool; rather, it's a relationship building tool. And it extends far beyond Dubsmash to create a positive feedback loop into the larger classroom community. On account of this, I propose that the way my students and I work together reveals the power of hip hop education, unison dancing, muscular bonding, and social media dance to break down traditional institutional structures within the classroom, both the community and the teacher/student hierarchy. Considering

Figure 5.2 Bellaire High School students and author do the Mop. Photo by Luke Parker.

that the premise of culturally responsive teaching is to bring the culture and background of students to the forefront of the learning environment, this work can help students feel safe and more eager to apply their cultures to their learning.

Once my Instagram account—@dr_boffone—was off and running in late February 2019, Takia and Talia—the identical twins that were featured in my first videos—and I quickly realized our desire to continue making dance videos. We were bolstered by the wave of positive feedback we received from students and teachers from all across the world who were inspired by our collaborative work. We didn't fully understand what was happening, but we knew that we were in the middle of an inexplicable lightning-in-a-bottle moment and wanted to ride this momentum wherever it was going to take us. I asked the girls to pick out a dance challenge for us to do and we would work on it during lunch the next day. They arrived the next day, eager to teach me a new Dub. I was excited and in completely new territory. As I've mentioned before, these weren't my dance moves; they didn't entirely make sense to me and I would wake up sore the next day in the strangest places. Hitting the Woah came with its own set of challenges.

I told Takia and Talia that they had to teach me the dance and that they needed to be patient with me, but not to worry because I was a quick learner. All in all, I knew I could do it and they believed in me. They slowly walked me through the moves, making sure I understood what I needed to do and how I was going to transition quickly between the moves. As I learned the dub, I became keenly aware of how these two young Black teens were teaching this Millennial White man how to dance. I noted the language they used to instruct and how they effortlessly code-switched between proper dance terminology and urban slang. In between, we laughed quite a bit whenever I would mess up or do something absolutely ridiculous (e.g., one time I punched myself in the face). And, maybe most important, I was aware of—not to mention impressed by—their patience with me. If you've never done a dance challenge, it can be excruciatingly annoying when you continually mess up the same moves. Once you've mastered them, you will inevitably forget another transition in the dance. It isn't just learning the individual puzzle pieces but is a matter of remembering the sequences, learning the transitions, staying in the rhythmic pocket, keeping formation, and having your face engaged. That is, Dubsmash is more than an inconsequential social media app that teens use to record silly dancing videos. Rather, Dubsmash is a form of social dance that is as legitimate as any other dancing tradition. It requires much skill to execute and master it. It can be a rocky road and, in unsupportive company, it can be toxic. The twins never made me feel bad and in fact always encouraged me and told me I could do it. Without any teacher or leadership training, they were both effortlessly teaching me how to dance and leading me through the process of making a Dubsmash. Our roles shifted and my students gained the agency to teach *me*. The shift in power shifted the relationship. The roles were reversed; I was the student, they were the teachers. I had to be vulnerable. They had to be patient. We had to work to build community in a new and exciting way that would prove transformative to our experiences at Bellaire.

That entire week, they would choose dance challenges for us to do, we would meet during lunch to make Dubs, and I would continue to witness their leadership skills. I would brag about them to anyone who would listen, always giving credit to the twins for passing on their knowledge and culture to me.[33] But, as fun as it was to dance with only Takia and Talia, I knew I needed to expand my repertoire and dance with other students. After all, I had already been dancing with other students for much of the school year—but I hadn't gone viral with them. Going viral with the twins positioned them as the most visible personalities on @dr_boffone (not to mention they each amassed tens of thousands of followers themselves), but I knew that this was an opportunity I had to share and experience with other students. I would always dance with the twins, but I had 150 students I needed to serve, in addition to mention a school of 3,500 who would soon be interested in working with me in just about any capacity.

After a few weeks, I invited some of my students who I knew liked to dance to make Dubs with me, usually on Fridays after they had finished all their work for the week. They were excited to be joining in on the fun. Other students or people we didn't know on Instagram would say they were doing it for clout and followers, but I never once questioned these girls' motives. Yes, they did in fact get clout and followers, but that was never the intent. We were never, have never, and will never do this to go viral or get invited on *The Ellen DeGeneres Show*. As I told them from the beginning, we are doing this for a more important reason—to build a stronger relationship between teacher and student. This was always my goal. Everything else was a bonus. And my students get this. When we are together, it is all about music, dance, and giving them a sense of ownership in the classroom. It's about Black girl games and musical identities being at the forefront of their high school experience.

As I noticed with Takia and Talia, I saw how these girls easily took on leadership roles as they taught me how to dance and how to do dance challenges. They each brought to the table their unique talents and voices to do so. For the most part, they chose the Dubs, taught me the dances, helped me with captions, and offered any support they could to me.

Sometimes, I would hear a song on the way to school and ask them to help me choreograph a dance and they would always enthusiastically agree even if they secretly thought the song was "old" and "cringey" ("Gettin' Jiggy with It" comes to mind). They recognized that part of us doing this was respecting the artistic choices that everyone brought into the dance "studio" (the classroom or hallway).

Despite the ways in which Dubsmash saturated my experience at school, it was still ancillary to the classroom experience for most of my students (see Figure 5.3). It wasn't something that all of my students did or have to do. I didn't make a behavior chart and add gold star stickers when students danced with me. I didn't ditch teaching Spanish and dance with my students all day, every day. There was still content to cover and Spanish to learn. It wasn't even a formal part of my teaching. Rather, Dubsmash became a bonus for kids who were interested in dancing with me, watching me dancing with other students, helping me with captions, or suggesting new songs to dance to or other Instagram dancers to connect with. We would find extra time during the day to dance—before school, during lunch, after school, during class when there was some free time. While the Instagram videos would showcase a specific group of students, they engaged the majority of my room in some capacity. There was a role for anyone who was interested in being part of our community. Everyone benefited from the euphoric feeling that unison dancing had created.

Figure 5.3 Bellaire High School students and author. Photo by Luke Parker.

To that end, my experience with my students speaks to the power that Renegades hold to influence classroom culture. By foregrounding a space for Black teens—and mostly girls—to bring their unique identities and cultures into the classroom, it changed school for not only this particular group of Renegades, but for every student in my classes and, subsequently, my school. As I saw the positive effects that Renegades were instilling in my classroom, I too noticed that other teachers at my school became increasingly interested in the work. They wanted to know how we did it and what made the work click. While this work is far more complicated than a how-to manual, one thing I constantly tell other teachers is that the first step is trusting the students and giving them space to bring their cultures into the classroom. From there, it is simply a matter of respecting the nuances of those cultures and finding ways to organically include them into the curriculum. As my work uncovers, embracing social media dance cultures in the classroom can make a difference, but teachers don't have to dance on social media to do this work. Sure, this book and this chapter specifically speak to the power of dance, but, as I always tell people, this work is truly about centering students in education. It might take the form of dance in my classroom, but it could be puzzles, rapping, fashion, sports, or photography for another teacher. There is no single blueprint. You just have to trust the Renegades.

THE DANCING TEACHERS SPEAK

By any measure, unison movement depends on listening, learning, and watching together, which builds (and depends upon) a supportive environment that enhances the classroom community and increases student success. It bears repeating, Renegade aesthetics goes far beyond what people see during a fifteen-second video. That is, it creates an affective response in more than just the students in the video. While the euphoric feeling that unison dancing enables impacts dancing students in one way, it also has a reverberating effect. Since I have introduced Dubsmash into my pedagogy, I have seen my students in general exhibit a stronger work ethic and an increased eagerness to participate in classroom activities. Even students who don't actively participate in our classroom Dubsmash activities show signs of enjoying and benefiting from this classroom culture. Admittedly, measuring work ethic and eagerness are nearly impossible tasks even if they can be obvious to the classroom teacher. These experiences are not unique to my classroom. Since @dr_boffone was created, I have had teachers from across the country reach out to me. Many times they ask me specific questions about how to re-create what I am doing. Other times they message me with excitement to tell me that they now dance with their students, as well. The usual narrative is that their students see my videos and then ask their teacher to dance with them. Then the teacher reaches out to me to tell me about how successful it was and how it's been a game-changer in their classroom. Indeed, giving space for students to be Renegades in the classroom can be transformative. While I could write a chapter based on those conversations, I would like to highlight two educators here: Debbie A. Simmonds-Barber and Meghann Hogan.

Simmonds-Barber, an intensive reading teacher at Whiddon Rogers Educational Center in Ft. Lauderdale, has been making music and dancing for over twenty years, at times dancing and creating choreography with students who have helped in her music videos. After watching @dr_boffone videos, Simmonds-Barber, who is Black, began to loosen up more in the classroom and merge education, music, and dance together. According to Simmonds-Barber, @dr_boffone "helped me take it to a whole new level":[34]

It all started with one of my former student faves, Cassy. She kept sending me DMs of you and the twins dancing. I was honestly annoyed. Then a week later, another student, AJ, sent a video to me. The more I looked at how technical those Dubsmash moves were, I grew even more annoyed that I wasn't doing that with my kids. So, yeah, I developed a jealousy because I knew that my students would absolutely appreciate making Dubsmashes with their teacher. I just didn't want to put in the work. I'm so glad that I did though, because there's power in fostering relationships with today's youths. It's the key to our students' motivation, well-being, and success.[35]

Notably, Simmonds-Barber acknowledges that she initially didn't want to do the work, but as she attests, collaborations between students and teachers are both gratifying and something that is needed right now and going forward.

Meghann Hogan, a White math teacher at Central High School in Louisville, Kentucky, explained to me that dancing has helped her build relationships with her students while also being a way to shed positive light on public education. Much like myself, Hogan began this work as a result of listening to her students and centering their identities in the classroom. Hogan details:

The way it all got started was when a student of mine asked me if I knew how to do The Mop. I had no idea what she was talking about, so she taught me and we recorded it. She posted it on her Instagram and students came to school the next day and said they saw me dancing with LaRoya. The students were the ones that said I should do more dances, and they came up with my handle (Meghann Thee Teacher, like Megan Thee Stallion).[36]

Students come to Hogan every day with new dances, they dance together, and then she posts them to her account. She centers her students and has created an inclusive community in which any student at her school is welcome to dance with her.

Initial messages among Simmonds-Barber, Hogan, and me focused on dancing as classroom community building, but these digital relationships soon led to valuable spaces for us to talk about pedagogy (what works and what doesn't), to bounce around ideas to incorporate into our classrooms, and to seek advice about how stay to above water in a profession that often throws us into the deep end. That these conversations were happening with like-minded educators from across the country through social media made it even more powerful. Dancing with our students brought us together and dancing with our students would bring us forward.

CONCLUSION

Giving authentic space for students of color to bring their cultures and identities into the classroom is the first step toward forging a more inclusive classroom space, one that can allow the success stories like mine to materialize. While my classroom became a home for Renegades, there are teachers across the United States engaging with #HipHopEd in ways that have always made me feel inferior. I may have a wider reach than other educators simply because of my follower count, but this shouldn't be mistaken for superior teaching. For instance, HipHopEd STEM sponsors Science Genius Battles, a program that uses hip hop to engage youth of color in science, and HipHopEd Therapy creates counseling spaces at schools and community centers that are aligned with urban youth culture. While each of these projects is unique, they all share one commonality—they are all forms of culturally responsive teaching that privilege student identities first and foremost. That is, parts of the educational experience such as standards and test scores are secondary. If a teacher doesn't know their students and, consequently, doesn't have an authentic relationship with them, then how can a genuine learning experience even begin to occur?

In my classroom, culturally responsive teaching takes the form of performance. Using performance pedagogies in the common curriculum shouldn't be a rare occurrence, yet often I am told that my teaching is outside-the-box. As my teaching demonstrates, by foregrounding performance as a fundamental aspect of my classroom community, my students have taken a higher level of ownership than I had seen before. My students show up excited and ready for class. As I discussed in this chapter, this pedagogy works because the teacher-student role has been flipped, where students become the teachers and dictate content and culture, and because my students and I dance in unison. Such muscular bonding creates a euphoric feeling that reverberates throughout the classroom, making it a safe and inclusive space where students can be themselves and not have to adhere to a rigid idea of what a high school student should look like and how they should act.

Dubsmash—in addition to other dance apps—has allowed this work to take place and has changed my relationship to my teaching, but also how I view my PhD. While I may not be living the dream that I once had of working in academia as a tenure-track professor, I am living another dream that I didn't even know I had. Every day I am using my doctoral training in theater studies, ethnic studies, and community engagement in ways that I never could have imagined. There is power in theater and performance. There is power in working side by side with students. And there is power in community.

CHAPTER 6

When Karen Slides into Your DMs

Race, Language, and Dubsmash

As the spring 2019 semester rolled along, I truly felt like I was living in a movie. What had once been a pretty standard high school teaching job changed overnight once my students and I went viral. Suddenly, I couldn't walk down the halls of my school without students taking pictures of me, asking me to dance, or whispering about me. I would joke that I felt like Beyoncé, which the media loved, naming me "The Beyoncé of Bellaire."[1] I hadn't realized before how much I valued having some modicum of anonymity at school. I would never go back to that life. This was the new normal. I was no longer a teacher, but a teacher with notoriety, which changed the way students—both mine and ones I didn't know—viewed me. I was unexpectedly living in the fictional worlds of *Sister Act 2: Back in the Habit*, *School of Rock*, or *AP Bio*. What was happening felt larger than life. My Instagram follower count skyrocketed and with this newfound clout came the media. During the last month of school, the local ABC affiliate in Houston called me and asked to profile my students and me. Within hours after the segment airing, I was on the phone with *Good Morning America* to appear on the show the following day. Although talking to Robin Roberts, Michael Strahan, and George Stephanopoulos live before 5 million people felt like the peak of this journey, it was only the beginning. My students and I would get used to regular media appearances, packages filled with swag, and the like. I'd field phone calls from casting directors during lunch—*The Amazing Race*, the Disney Channel, Netflix, you name it. I'd make a morning radio show appearance instead of grabbing a latte

Renegades. Trevor Boffone, Oxford University Press. © Oxford University Press 2021.
DOI: 10.1093/oso/9780197577677.003.0007

at Starbucks on my way to school. Everything had changed. It was so unexpected.

But something interesting happened along the way. I began to receive feedback from many people celebrating my work, but the standout negative feedback was about one thing—the language in the videos, which largely feature contemporary rap music using African American Vernacular English (AAVE). These critical messages almost always came from White women who reacted negatively when faced with language and cultural identifiers that were not part of their predominately White cultures and communities. Notably, the messages lingered on rap music. While not all rap music includes expletive lyrics, it is nevertheless common, including in the music that trends on Dubsmash. To be clear, most of my videos don't include swearing, but occasionally they do. A part of my methodology is that the students choose the songs and teach me the dances. There are parameters, of course, but my mission is to fully embrace what my students bring to the table and situate them as the experts in the room. My goal is *not* to police their music choices and, by extension, their cultures and identities.

But some people disagree with my approach and, to be honest, they don't have to agree. My goal is to serve the students in my classroom and, with that in mind, I privilege their opinions more than those of individuals that have virtually no impact on my classroom. So far, those who show their disagreement by sending me a direct message have almost entirely been White people who argue that the language is inappropriate for a teacher and his students to dance to. What is more, these messages rarely, if ever, ask me about my methodology. Rather, they tell me it is wrong in a very matter-of-fact way. Even so, I have received even more messages from Black people praising me and my students, recognizing the powerful bonds we have created through music and dance. So, what gives?

This chapter engages with critical race theory, sound studies, and hip hop pedagogy to explore how listening is indeed a racialized act. My argument is that a racial divide between White and Black viewers exists on social media platforms such as Instagram, something that Renegades push against through their music selection and dance styles on Dubsmash. Specifically, I analyze the ways in which my White followers attempt to police language and, by extension, the cultures of my students. I contrast this with the messages I have received from Black followers who praise the very things my White followers criticize. On account of this, I examine the relationships between language, race, and power and how these intersections affect my digital classroom community on Instagram as well as my face-to-face classroom as Bellaire HS. I explore what dominant (read: White) US society determines is appropriate and inappropriate and, specifically, what that means for Black students. Ultimately, this chapter reveals the potential role that White allies (read: teachers) can play in public education. I linger on the following questions: Where does this racial divide come from? Why do Black and White audiences hear different things?[2] And, perhaps most significant, how can teachers and other adults become allies to Zoomers of color? Ultimately, while White audiences perhaps demand civility from Dubsmashers, these artists reject marginalization through their sustained social media dance performances.

SEE THEM AS THEY ARE, HEAR THEM AS THEY ARE

An integral aspect of becoming an ally to Zoomers is to hear them as they hear themselves, and to see them as they see themselves. Oftentimes, many of the issues that Black students face in public education come down to cultural differences and the discrepancy between how teachers and administrators see the students versus how the students sees themselves. Unsurprisingly, this inconsistency is rooted in systems of race and privilege that dictate power dynamics in the United States. There is a hidden curriculum, an unwritten set of rules that dictate what the schooling experience is supposed to look and sound like.[3] To be successful is to always follow the hidden curriculum. Students are expected to adhere to these rules and norms even if they conflict with the students' beliefs and cultures. Coincidentally, many of these norms reinforce and privilege Whiteness. For instance, even charter schools that primarily serve communities of color oftentimes attempt to replicate elite White prep schools. Rather than focus on individuality, these schools work to create a monolithic culture. Christopher Emdin claims, "students are taught to dress, talk, act, and behave in ways that are in opposition" to their identities.[4] "Making it out of the hood" is to be "White." As such, the role of education becomes as much about teaching students to conform to Whiteness as it does about teaching content.[5] By and large, one of the major issues facing urban education is the discrepancy between how the teacher sees the student versus how the student sees themself. This is largely influenced by systems of race and privilege that influence nearly everything in the United States. Many of my students feel invisible. And the first step in rendering them invisible is seeing them for who they are rather than who *we want* them to be (see Figure 6.1).[6] This materializes in different ways, but perhaps the most visible example revolves around what is considered to be "appropriate" behavior in the classroom and in digital spaces.

Figure 6.1 Bellaire High School student and author dance to "Move Like a Snake" by Kayla Nicole Jones. Photo by Luke Parker.

I offer the case of Seth, a Black student who was constantly getting in trouble for minor reasons (for instance, showing up late or talking during class) and who never seemed to understand why what he did was deemed inappropriate. While Seth's story isn't exclusively about listening, it does reveal the discrepancy between how Black youth are oftentimes misunderstood by the White adults in their lives. Whether these misunderstandings materialize in the classroom, at work, or online, they fit into a system that disproportionately targets youth of color and, in particular, Black boys and girls. One day I noticed that Seth wasn't in class because he was suspended. It is quite common at Bellaire HS Students for students to be suspended or receive in-school suspension (ISS). Whenever I see that a student is in ISS or is suspended, I ask around to see what the student did. Once I have the information, I run it through my head and analyze it. I'm not trying to get "the tea," as the kids say, but I'm trying to better understand our campus culture and what sort of things are tolerated and what things are not—not to mention *which* students are being targeted. And, perhaps most significant, I am trying to better position myself as an ally and educator to my students. If I don't know the inner workings of the system were are in, then how can I expect to help my students navigate it?

"Does anyone know why Seth is suspended?" I asked my class. They usually had the information or could at least point me in the right direction. And, at this point, my students trusted me with this insider info.

"He did 'Bust Down Thotiana' in front of Ms. Black," one student said without hesitation.

"What's that?"

"You know it! You did it in a video last week!"

"I did?"

"And you snapped. No cap."

The student then demonstrated how to properly bust down Thotiana. Truth be told, I had seen this move a lot in the preceding weeks and I had mastered it, as well. It had become a common viral dance move that went far beyond its source material—Blueface's song "Thotiana." To bust down, you take one hand and grab the top of your pants and pull them up. You take your other hand and raise it into the air. You then lean and rock back and forth. While Blueface's song may indeed be sexual and, accordingly, the dance can take on a sexual connotation, the dance move alone is not vulgar, even though it was perceived to be by the White teacher who wrote the student up.

How was this any different from the mostly White kids I went to high school with dancing to Juvenile's "Back That Azz Up?" "Back That Azz Up" might as well have been the soundtrack to the private Christian school I attended in New Orleans throughout middle school and high school. Although Juvenile's song is about sex, popular rap songs such as "Back That Azz Up" and "Thotiana" extend far beyond the lyrics to include related social dances. Yes, lyrics are a part of the equation and to disregard language from Seth's scenario would be suspect. I give this example to draw attention to the ways that Black students are treated differently from White students. White kids in the suburbs dancing to Juvenile was perfectly acceptable, but a Black boy busting down with no music was grounds for punishment. And, it bears repeating, my Whiteness enables me to do this same dance move on social media and reap the benefits—followers, comments, praise—while my Black students get in trouble within the White supremacist school system. This isn't fair, but this is the reality my students face.

Did this student, a Black male, get written up by a White teacher and consequently suspended by a White assistant principal for doing a nonvulgar dance move in class? He did and I had no clue what to do about it. When he returned the next day, I asked him about it and he laughed and smiled. I didn't know what to say to him, but this was a student who listened to me and I felt like I needed to offer some sort of advice. I told him that he needs to respect the classroom culture of this teacher and save his dance moves for other parts of the day. I'm not even sure I believed what I said, but it felt like the best survival tactic to make it to the end of the year. But deep down, I knew something was wrong. I told some other teachers at my school and from other places who share my values and they all agreed that the student being suspended for this particular action went too far. The student was simply doing a popular dance move at school, but his identity was rendered inappropriate and vulgar by a teacher who had taken no time to actually get to know him. A few months later when I chaperoned the senior prom, I saw dozens of students doing the same exact dance move while administrations and teachers happily looked on. Perhaps a school dance requires a different set of cultural norms, but what sort of message are we sending to our students, especially Black students, about how they dance in one space versus another?

HOW IS LANGUAGE RACIALIZED?

As I detailed in the previous chapter, the use of social media dance in my high school classroom is almost entirely dictated by my students. Although I am an active participant in this work and at times suggest the songs or dance moves, most of the time the process of making a video from start to finish is led by students. The typical classroom roles are flipped: my students become the experts and I become the student. Accordingly, this system privileges student voices and situates them as both experts and curators. I simply open up space for them to bring a Renegade aesthetic and sensibility into the room, which then penetrates the classroom space and, by extension, digital spaces once our art-making is complete and ready to share with the masses. A fundamental part of the art of social dance is music and, with the song, comes the lyric.

As a Title I school, Bellaire HS features a student body with incredible racial and ethnic diversity. We have students from nearly every racial and socioeconomic background and White students are the minority. Given that I teach lower-level, general education classes (i.e., I don't teach AP or higher-level classes), the school's demographics are skewed in my classes, which include a higher percentage of Black and Latinx students. This is not because my students are inferior or less smart than those in AP and higher-level classes; rather, it speaks to the limited access to high-quality education and social services that my students have on their way to high school. That is, my school represents the inequities that exist in the community at large. Indeed, like many large urban high schools, Bellaire HS is largely a segregated school. If I taught AP or Dual Credit college classes, then I might be writing a book about students who are more interested in Adele, Billie Eilish, and BTS than in Blueface, Cardi B, Nicki Minaj, and Travis Scott. This is not to say that my mostly students of color *only* listened to rap music, but rap music was the common denominator among my Black and Brown students. And, when Dubsmash relaunched in October 2018, rap music was far and away the most popular genre on the app. It dominated the trending music page and was the soundtrack to nearly every viral Dubsmash dance challenge. In this way. Dubsmash is synonymous with rap music.

When my students and I danced on Dubsmash and they posted the videos on their Instagram accounts, I didn't think much about the music. But when I started my own account, I was immediately forced to listen to the music in a different way. What once was something I overlooked suddenly became attached to my name and to my teaching. I couldn't continue to take a passive role in the process anymore. So, I set some ground rules with my students. They were still in charge of picking out songs and dances, but the songs could not include any lyrics about guns or sex. The songs also couldn't have excessive cursing. Rather than give them a limit on curse words, I let them bring me songs to approve. Soon, students learned what type of music would work for us. Anytime I told them no, it was always framed around the optics of me—a White man—dancing with Black teen girls. My students and I needed to always be aware of the racial and gender dynamics of the work we were doing. If the song wouldn't work for us, I always encouraged them to dance to it on their own or with friends.

But still, I didn't outright reject songs with curse words in them. It was never a matter of me telling them the song wasn't good or that it didn't have value. My standpoint from the beginning was that my classroom should reflect the real world since my classroom already is the real world. And, therefore, our work on Dubsmash should mirror the lives of my students. Their cultures and identities should be respected and celebrated. They shouldn't have to hide who they are just because the public education system historically privileges Whiteness, and so shouldn't have to hide with me. I'm not saying that students curse or use excessive slang in my classroom, but that my pedagogy gives students opportunities to be themselves and bring their unique identities and cultures into the classroom in a variety of ways. Sometimes that includes "bad" language but, rather than police the way they speak, I instead try to teach them about skills like code-switching and how language can be a tool of resistance.

While my classroom may be a safe(r) space where my students can play with identity, everything changes once they leave the four walls of my classroom. As our social media dance videos began circulating the internet, becoming memes and viral clips along the way, our work was susceptible to the criticism of people who didn't really know us. Our ten-second micro performances allowed spectators to include their own biases and prejudices in the viewing experience. Often this took the form of focusing on the language, specifically any song that included a curse word in it. Although my school administration, fellow teachers, and students' parents never once criticized this work or brought attention to the language in the videos, I began to receive messages from White followers who took issue with the language.

As these messages filled my inbox, I began to linger on the ways that the White/Black binary penetrates the world of social media dance. In the United States, White supremacy and listening are intertwined.[7] In *The Sonic Color Line: Race and the Cultural Politics of Listening*, sound studies scholar Jennifer Lynn Stoever uses the term "sonic color line" to explain "the process of racializing sound—how and why certain bodies are expected to produce, desire, and live amongst particular sounds—and its product, the hierarchical division sounded between 'whiteness' and 'blackness.'"[8] As White ways of listening become mainstream so, too, do the ways that the dominant culture imposes a particular style of listening that confirms the racial biases and prejudices that mark the sonic color line. That is, even though race is most often understood as something visual, it can also be heard and, as a result, racist systems are replicated in sonic landscapes. Indeed, Stoever asserts, "listening operates as an organ of racial disenfranchisement, categorization, and resistance in the shadow of vision's alleged cultural dominance."[9] Often the ways that White people (mis)hear and imagine Blackness feed into systems of oppression that go far beyond, say, simply watching a short video on Instagram. What might seem inconsequential on social media is part of a larger system that can be a matter of life and death for people of color in the United States.[10]

Listening, then, is a political act that shapes how spectators engage with social media dance apps as well as how teachers approach the language of their students. Indeed, the politics of racialized listening are experienced in both digital and face-to-face spaces as Zoomers are scrutinized by those who don't understand the nuances of their identities. Oftentimes, the language of high school students is coded as a behavior issue. Christopher Emdin claims that urban youth of color often behave in ways that are deemed outside the traditional norm in schools.[11] Consequently, they are seen as academically and intellectually behind their peers who come from traditionally privileged racial and socioeconomic backgrounds. Teachers carry inherent biases and prejudices that can radically affect how students experience the classroom. In turn, as Emdin notes, "when these students speak or interact in the classroom in ways that teachers are uncomfortable with, they are categorized as troubled students, or diagnosed with disorders like ADD (attention deficit disorder) and ODD (oppositional defiant disorder)."[12] This leads to a vicious cycle in which students of color—in particular, Black students—are harshly disciplined in ways that lead to them engaging less in academic work. Black girls often face unique challenges at school. In *Pushout: The Criminalization of Black Girls in Schools*, Monique Morris explores how schools often criminalize Black girls, which, consequently, affects their mobility. Morris notes, "Black girls are sixteen percent of the female student population, but nearly one-third of all girls referred to law enforcement and more than one-third of all female school-based arrests."[13] Morris's work reveals how education isn't always an equitable place as historically marginalized identities remain disenfranchised when they walk into the classroom. We must question how listening plays into these racialized and gendered dynamics. As I advocate for in this chapter—and Emdin does in his work—(White) teachers must understand and analyze how we engage with students outside of our own identity markers. By acknowledging and reconciling cultural barriers and differences we have with our students, we are taking an instrumental step to dramatically alter the way that we engage with students in larger urban schools. And, as an extension, teachers can facilitate a form of culture sharing that amplifies student voices and identities both in the classroom and beyond.

WHEN KAREN SLIDES INTO YOUR DMS, OR "A TALE OF FOUR MESSAGES"

After posting a video on January 17, 2020, of my students and me dancing to ZaeHD & CEO's "COOKIE SHOP," I received four messages within an hour that ranged from White people criticizing and questioning the language in my videos to Black people praising the work of my students and me. To be clear, this was not the only instance in which I received similar messages, but it marked the tipping point that prompted me to address it in a formal way through writing. The first message was from a White, female high school Spanish teacher who had sent me similar messages before: "Hey FYI your latest video, the first word out of the artist mouth is fuck while in the dance y'all thrust your hips . . . do you not listen to the songs before doing these?" Within minutes, a Black Army Veteran commented on the post: "Somewhere on the planet is a teacher that is hating on the fact that this is better than any other method of growing with your students." To be honest, when I received this message immediately following Karen's,

I cackled.[14] The timing could not have been more perfect. I then received a message from a Black teenage girl:

> "Ok idc if u read this or not but u low key fye. Like no matter what nobody say u is soooooo fyeee. Like tbh u can dance better than me. And it's gonna be haters but all u gotta do is he the woah on them. Like just to let u know I wish u were my teacher. . . . . But yea ur fye and me and my frans love u."

And finally, I received a message from a Black woman telling me: "You are something like amazing! I pray my children have teachers in HS like you."

As these messages reveal, White and Black audiences are quite literally "hearing" two different things—one deemed inappropriate and the other seen in a significantly more positive light. As Stoever proposes, "Without ever consciously expressing the sentiment, white Americans often feel entitled to respect for their sensibilities, sensitivities, and tastes, and to their implicit, sometimes violent, control over the soundscape of an ostensibly 'free,' 'open,' and 'public' space."[15] Indeed, as I began to dive deeper into the messages I had received from the White teacher in tandem with looking at her content on TikTok and Instagram it became apparent that we don't share the same values or viewpoints as educators. This is not to say that my style is superior to hers, but that we approach working with students of color in different ways. What I see as respecting their culture, she sees as inappropriate for an educational setting. What I see as acceptable, she sees as distasteful. It bears repeating that I don't believe that my students' identities and the experiences (Figure 6.2) they bring into the classroom-turned-dance studio need to be policed—especially given that much of what students listen to, read, and interact with *is policed* in a system like school.

To be transparent, I don't know this Karen teacher. I don't know where she teaches or what type of students are in her classroom. I don't know what her training is or what her life experiences are. But I do know by means of her messages to me that she projects her values and beliefs onto my work and, specifically, what music and dance styles are acceptable for a teacher and students to engage with. I ask, how can someone know what is appropriate for a classroom if they don't actually know the personalities and life experiences that make up that classroom? How should we define appropriate? Is it offensive to all or just a few? Who is being protected or silenced in educational spaces? Each classroom is unique and, for this reason, the educational experience must be adapted accordingly. What I do with my students might not work for other teachers nor should it have to. It works for me and that's what matters in my classroom.

Figure 6.2 Bellaire High School students and author dance during a TV shoot for *Localish*. Photo by Luke Parker.

At the root of messages that seek to censure language is a culture of promoting so-called civility. In an essay on tone policing, applied sociologist Zuleyka Zevallos recognizes, "The language of 'civility' has been used throughout history to justify the colonialization of Indigenous people, the slavery of Black people, and racial stratification all over the world."[16] In the public education system, notions of civility bring this colonization into the classroom and seek to transform educational spaces into places where there is only one "appropriate" way of self-expression, one that is inevitably coded as "White." If students don't adhere to the dominant culture then they run the risk of being marginalized for the way they speak, dress, and behave. That is, school transitions from being a safe space into a space of potential harm that mirrors many of the power dynamics that mark the "real world." While this harm can take many different shapes, in today's urban public schools it can lead to encounters with the police. As Morris explains, "the surveillance to which Black girls are subjected and the punitive responses to either their (sometimes poor, sometimes typical) decision making or their reactions to perceived injustice have made contact with law enforcement a frequent occurrence."[17] In other words, Black girls—and Black students in general—are held to a different set of standards than are students of other racial identities. Because of the roadblocks they face— namely, potential harm at school and general misunderstanding about their identities and cultures—it is imperative that Black girls have safe spaces that they can define and dictate.[18] This is precisely why my students select the music we dance to. It is an opportunity for them to take on agency in a way that is uncommon in public education.

Interestingly enough, on my Instagram account, my Black students do not experience such criticisms directly. Rather, my students become passive bystanders while a White adult messages another White adult *about them*. While criticisms are inevitably directed at me given my position as both the teacher and the owner of the Instagram account, my students are in the videos with me, often strategically placed *in front of* me. Therefore, when people message me saying that the language in our videos is inappropriate, they are saying, by extension, that my students' language is inappropriate and that their cultures are unacceptable—in both the realms of education and social media. They are questioning the civility of me, but also of my students.

My students are being told what words to use and when they can use them without any understanding of my students' identities. In "Policing Language Is Just Another Way to Silence Women," journalist Jess McHugh notes, "When women and people of color are told what words to use, and how to use them, it's more than mere political correctness gone awry. It's a form of silencing that sustains a moral, class, and racial hierarchy."[19] Linguist Robin Lakoff adds, "If you're black, you are judged; you're policed. Every syllable you utter, every way you dress, everything you do with your hair is found fault with, is 'too white or not white enough.'"[20] People of color face additional roadblocks regarding equality and inclusion. Blackness is surveilled in ways that White people will never understand. Sometimes this takes obvious forms, as with police brutality, and other times it is in the seemingly minor forms of direct messages on Instagram. Both large and small acts of surveillance are part of the system of White supremacy that continues to disadvantage the lived experiences of teens of color.

While many well-intentioned White people may in fact recognize these systems of oppressions, the work of actively dismantling racism is another story. In other words, being anti-racist is quite different from talking about racism or even calling out racist actions.[21] In "Stop Policing My Language," writer Tori Williams Douglass explains how, rather than work to dismantle racist structures, many White people in the United States attempt to censure Black language:

> To police our language is to pull the rug, once again, out from under us. Whiteness refuses to without even acknowledging the bruises we carry from yesterday first. Because whiteness dictates reality—pain, suffering, love, legitimacy—to black

America, they are able to cause harm and claim it was not in fact harm. . . . What is more vulgar? When I say the word "fuck," or when babies in Yemen starve to death? . . . All of this is I suspect, the result of whiteness historically assuming that it has the power to dictate the terms of our humanity to us.[22]

McHugh, Lakoff, and Williams Douglass's assertions speak to the ways in which White audiences hear and process language in Dubsmash videos and then attempt to dictate what standards and expectations my classroom—and my students—should have. They do this without ever engaging with my students and learning about them, effectively projecting their own experiences, viewpoints, and standards of Whiteness onto a group of Black teens who they quite literally know nothing about.

Notably, this silencing features an interesting racial dynamic considering that I am White and most of the students in my videos are Black. As I detailed in the previous chapter, the work on my @dr_boffone Instagram page reflects my students. They are the artistic directors. They typically select the music. They choreograph and teach me the dances. They manipulate the lighting in the classroom so the video looks just right. Throughout the experience, they are in the driver's seat and I genuinely take on a passive role. I may be the one that people associate with my Instagram and Dubsmash accounts, but the work is truly reflective of my students and the creative potential they hold. Therefore, to criticize me is to criticize them. Anyone saying what I should or should not be dancing to is inevitably saying that same message to my students. Policing language doesn't meet any of my goals as an educator nor does it serve my student population.

To be transparent, I am not advocating for my students or any other young people to swear, even if many believe it is a powerful act.[23] Part of my work as an educator is to respect the diverse cultures that my students bring into my classroom. Sometimes this includes music with swear words. My job isn't to police language, but instead to teach about more relevant things such as code-switching and how to navigate various challenges outside of the classroom. Code-switching, although often disregarded, is a complicated linguistic system that relies on the speaker shifting between various dialects or languages in a single conversation or social interaction, sometimes even alternating within the same sentence. Code-switching requires deep knowledge of multiple linguistic registers and, as a result, is an advanced form of communication. Emdin recognizes:

Some of the most successful people in the world have an uncanny ability to fit in across multiple social settings. They read the codes or rules of engagement in a particular social field, identify which ones have value, adopt them, enact them, and through this process, form powerful connections to new people.[24]

As Black feminist theorist Audre Lorde argues, "the master's tools will never dismantle the master's house. They may allow us to temporarily beat him at his own game, but they will never enable us to bring about genuine change."[25] Following Lorde, my role as an educator, both in the classroom and on digital spaces, is to teach my students how to work within systems of oppression while also developing their own set of tools that come from their own lived experiences, identities, and cultural background. That being so, my classroom is not another academic space to replicate structural racism, sexism, homophobia, and the like, but rather I position my classroom as a space to validate my students and help them develop tools that will help them find success once they leave my class. Teaching my students about code-switching is an essential part of this process.

Urban slang is often seen as "lowbrow antiacademic culture,"[26] even though it is difficult to use with ease. Like any other language or dialect, it requires knowledge of an intricate linguistic code and rules that one must intimately know before they can speak it with fluency. African American Studies scholar Marcyliena Morgan claims, "In Hip Hop culture, language is not simply a means of communication. Rather, language use is viewed as a series of choices that represent beliefs and have consequences."[27] Morgan draws upon landmark theoretical studies such as Foucault's *The Discourse on Language*, Bakhtin's *Dialogic Imagination*, and Labov's *Language in the Inner City* to unpack the power that language holds in the realm of hip hop and, by extension, the Black community at large. Morgan adds, "Hip Hop uses language rules to mediate and construct a present which considers the social and historicized moment as both a transitory and stable place."[28] In the same vein, Emdin notes that the intellectual capacity of urban youth to code-switch in such a way "cannot be appreciated by educators who are conditioned to perceive anything outside their own ways of knowing and being as not having value."[29] Thus, the cultural choices and identity performances of Black Zoomers on social media run the risk of being misunderstood or held to standards that disregard their artistic and cultural contributions.

Moreover, much like the cultural work seen throughout *Renegades*, mainstream determinations of what language is appropriate and not is often gendered. In *Swearing Is Good for You: The Amazing Science of Bad Language*, Emma Byrne posits that women aren't afforded the same luxuries as men are when it comes to using profanity or slang.[30] Indeed, swearing can have a negative impact for women. Byrne signals a 2002 study by sociologist Robert O'Neill that reveals a significant gendered divide in how people perceive swearing. The study asked 277 people to rate how offensive uses of swearing were based on a transcript of a conversation. Male swearers were consistently seen as more dynamic, whereas female swearers were seen as weak. Indeed, O'Neill's results reaffirm a double standard that should come as no surprise. Byrne adds, "It doesn't matter if you ask men or women; we've all been schooled to believe that male swearing is the norm, while a woman swearing is some kind of fuck-up. It just isn't 'ladylike' to swear."[31]

The double standard takes on added layers when one considers an intersectional approach to examining how the mainstream perceives swearing. Accordingly, mainstream (i.e., White) audiences view swearing differently when it is done by a White teen compared to a Black teen. In the world of social media dance, Zoomers aren't necessarily voicing profanity so much as dancing to songs that include these words. And, in my experience, choosing a song on Dubsmash is often about finding a song with a good beat that will lend itself to digital dance moves. TikTok is filled with videos of White teens using sound clips with Black voices singing or saying swear words. In fact, a running gag on TikTok relies on the profanity and shock value of lyrics. For instance, a trend that has proliferated on TikTok since 2018 involves a White teen playing a clip featuring profanity for their parents with the hopes of capturing a funny reaction. As soon as the parent hears the profanity, they inevitably act shocked or they play along with the joke. In any case, these White teens are not reprimanded for engaging with vulgar content that is mostly created by Black artists. Instead, they use this content to rack up views, likes, comments, and followers. Therefore, language becomes yet another battlefield in the racial politics of TikTok that lets users of different non-Black racial identities capitalize on certain sounds and trends while others don't get these same privileges. That is, White TikTokers co-opt Blackness while actual Black teens continue to be policed, as has been the case with my students.

Despite the attempts at surveilling Black Zoomer identities and cultures, Renegades lean into the subversive. They lean into the rebelliousness that defines much of the Renegade experience. In an essay for *Elle*, Byrne proposes that rather than police their language, women lean into profanity as an act of rebellion: "And I think that to fight it, women need to insist on our right to strong words, strong ideas, and strong feelings."[32] This is precisely what Renegades do—it is up to the adults that surround them to recognize their power, as opposed to attempting to control or silence it. Accordingly, Emdin notes, "The work for white folks who teach in urban schools, then, is to unpack their privileges and excavate the institutional, societal, and personal histories they bring with them when they come to the hood."[33] The more teachers and other people who interact with teens consider the culture of students and Zoomers in general, the more relevant, impactful, and accessible the educational experience can be. That is, learning about all parts of a student's identity—including their language—is a fundamental way to find connections that can lead to mutual, shared interests. Emdin questions, "What new lenses or frameworks can we use to bring white folks who teach in the hood to consider that urban education is more complex than saving students and being a hero?"[34] The result can become a transformational high school experience that privileges the cultures that have typically been marginalized at school. That this work can transpire on a digital stage is all the more noteworthy, as Black students can (re)claim space in a way that has often been denied to them. In the social media dance world, Renegades don't need the approval of a teacher or a White critic.

CONCLUSION

One of my teaching philosophies is that my classroom should reflect the real world because my classroom *already* is part of the real world. As such, I argue that my students' cultures should play a fundamental role in how the class atmosphere is constructed. My students shouldn't be expected to check their identities at the door when the bell rings. Now this doesn't mean that my students and I casually use profanity throughout the day, but it does mean that profanity isn't necessarily a bad thing that we should dance around. My students listen to music with cursing in it. They watch movies with cursing in them. And they themselves curse (because, well, they are people, too). So, as a natural extension of my classroom, my Instagram account does include some content with cursing in it. It is minimal, but it is there. Privileging Renegades' sense of identity is imperative as I create digital and IRL space for them to express themselves and influence generational culture. Classrooms and social media apps are not spaces for me to surveil them and mold them into what I think they should be. Rather, they provide opportunities for me to guide them on a journey of self-actualization and building a positive sense of self.

I recognize that the values that I bring into my classroom do not always align with what is popular in education. What I do know is that my work as a teacher, as a form of reality pedagogy, is rooted in knowing the students I teach. As Emdin notes, reality pedagogy can take many different forms and, consequently, mean different things for each student. He adds, "Some will leave the classroom feeling like their culture is worthy of being considered academic or intelligent. For others, this may mean that the classroom provides some affirmation of their beliefs about themselves and their intelligence."[35] Now is the time to listen to our students. We must hear them and work to understand who they are beyond what we see. Only then can we transform education in addition to the other spaces we occupy. My Instagram is first and foremost for my student and school population and, as such, content on my account should reflect this reality.

And in line with the landmark 1957 Supreme Court decision in *Roth v. United States* testifies, my teaching meets my community standards.[36] My administration approves of the work. My students' parents approve of the work. And my students approve of this world in which their sonic cultures are not policed, but are celebrated and treated on equal footing as anything else in my class. The sounds of my students matter. They will not be silenced.

Outro

The Revolution Will Be Dubsmashed

On May 25, 2020, life in the United States came to a screeching halt. George Floyd was arrested for allegedly using a counterfeit bill. While in custody, officer Derek Chauvin kneeled on Floyd's neck for 8 minutes and 46 seconds while Floyd repeated that he couldn't breathe and called out for his deceased mother. During the final two minutes, Floyd laid motionless on the concrete with no pulse. All the while, fellow officers Tou Thao, J. Alexander Kueng, and Thomas Lane aided Chauvin and prevented onlookers from intervening. Bystanders filmed from their cell phones, pleading for Chauvin to remove his knee as Floyd died right before the country's eyes. Footage of the murder quickly circulated social media and before we could even grasp what we had witnessed, the course of our nation's history had changed forever. It's not hyperbolic to state that the entire country witnessed George Floyd die that day. Like Trayvon Martin, Philando Castille, Alton Sterling, Eric Garner, Sandra Bland, and Tamir Rice before him, George Floyd became a hashtag. But this hashtag was different. Following the murders of Breonna Taylor and Ahmaud Arbery in the spring of 2020, the majority of the United States—including White people who had been resistant to the Black Lives Matter (BLM) movement—had had enough with the systemic racism that had worked to devalue Black bodies since this country was founded. Although the BLM movement began in July 2013, after the acquittal of George Zimmerman following the death of Black teenager Trayvon Martin, the movement found renewed interest,

Renegades. Trevor Boffone, Oxford University Press. © Oxford University Press 2021.
DOI: 10.1093/oso/9780197577677.003.0008

and what was once deemed as radical politics became the norm in the United States.

As I sat at home watching the news about the murder of George Floyd around the clock, I doom scrolled on my phone, flipping back and forth between Facebook, Twitter, and Instagram to learn about the protest marches that were happening in nearly every city, large and small, in the United States. Even during the deadly COVID-19 pandemic that had kept the majority of the population social distanced in their homes, masses of people took to the streets clad in masks, goggles, hoodies, and the like to collectively speak out against racial injustice. As a diversity of people protested and organized, the Renegades also mobilized. Black teens, in particular girls, were central to the renewed Black Lives Matter movement. They were making "moves" on the streets in much of the same way they had been doing on social media, as documented in this book. And, as always, these Renegades put their social media accounts to use to advocate for racial justice. With a great platform comes great responsibility, and these Zoomers didn't back down.

While scrolling on Instagram, I first noticed my student Rian, the same girl who first attempted to teach me the Renegade dance, as I detail in this book's preface. On June 2, Rian posted a picture on Instagram of her standing among a sea of people in front of Houston's city hall at the culmination of a march that saw over 60,000 people traverse the country's fourth largest city. The march was one of the largest in Houston's history and Rian was just one of my students in attendance. In Rian's picture, she is standing alongside her little brother. She is raising her fist high into the air with a wide smile on her face. The caption reads: "All lives won't matter until black lives matter!"[1] Born in 2003, Rian forms part of a collective of Renegade Zoomers who voiced their support of Black Lives Matter in the wake of the murders of Taylor, Arbery, and Floyd. This is the world that this generation of Black Zoomers have always known; they have always had to deal with the collective trauma of people who look like them being murdered and becoming hashtags that continually reiterate the systemic disregard for Black lives in the United States.

Rian's Instagram post was part of a large body of social media activity by the Renegades in this book and their fellow cohort of Dubsmashers. While my students were actively involved in the movement, they weren't alone. Writing for the *New York Times*, Mihir Zaveri noted how George Floyd's death had energized teenagers across the country and, in particular, high school students in Greenville, Michigan; Laurel, Maryland; Berkeley, California; and Katy, Texas, who organized marches in their communities.[2] In the conservative Houston suburb of Katy, Black teen Foyin Dosunmu was compelled to organize after experiencing racism while coming of age in the affluent suburb, and recognizing that someone had to take charge to make a difference. She thought, why couldn't she be that person: "I need people to hear my voice. I need Katy to hear what I'm thinking."[3] Indeed, a critical step in achieving racial justice is to not simply amplify the voices of Black women, but to listen and respond to them.

On June 3, Jalaiah Harmon posted a selfie on Instagram claiming her power as a Black woman. The caption reads: "We are BLACK WOMEN! . . . . We have a VOICE . . . . . . We don't tear down other BLACK WOMEN! . . . . . . we have felt the pain of NOT BEING HEARD and we have decided we will deliberate about building others! . . . All too often, we women find it easier to criticize each other, instead of building each other up. With all the negativity going around let's do something positive!! Upload one picture of yourself. . . . ONLY you. Then tag as many sisters to do the same. Let's build ourselves up, instead of tearing ourselves down."[4] In the post, Harmon tagged six of her friends, all Black girls, and the challenge grew. While Harmon didn't initiate this Instagram challenge, her participation was noteworthy. She used her platform and role as a legitimate social media influencer to, well, influence. There was not a promotional deal. There was no monetary gain. The work was done simply to amplify the voices of Black women at a time when the country desperately needed to listen to Black women.

As Renegades were attending BLM marches and using their social media platforms to elevate Black voices, a new dance challenge was in the works as well. At the end of the day, these Zoomers are dancers and dance is the vehicle through which their expression is best manifested. On June 5, the Dubsmash Instagram account posted a collection of Dubs set to "Black Lives Matter" by Dae Dae featuring London on Da Track. The primary dance, choreographed by well-known Dubsmasher Niyah (@Niyahgotcurls), had all the hallmarks of a viral dance challenge, combining standard dance moves such as the Woah, the Wave, and the Clap with moves invoking the Black Lives Matter movement and protests, such as freezing with one's hands up and the Black Power fist. At end of the dance, Niyah holds out her hands, inviting the viewer in before the words "#Blacklivesmatter" hover over her open hands. While other dancers offered their own spin to the dance, Niyah's version gained the most popularity, likely due to her popularity on Instagram and Dubsmash. Even so, nearly every version of the Dub featured the hands up and the Black Power fist gestures, marking these moves as essential parts of viral dance repertoires during this time.

Later, on August 21, Brooklyn Queen dropped new music that she had been working on during the summer. Her song, "Trying to Breathe," invokes the death of Breonna Taylor and the systemic racism that Black people experience in the United States. Brooklyn raps:

> 400 years we've been fighting for this
> living just to fight
> we just fighting to live
> it's like we fighting for our rights and our rights to exist.

Throughout the song, Brooklyn sings about the various hardships that Black people face today, from microaggressions to hate crimes. Since the first slave ships from Africa arrived in what is now the United States in 1619, the system has been rigged against Black people and, accordingly, as Brooklyn raps,

> Trayvon could have been you
> Breonna could have been me.

Brooklyn doesn't want to become the next hashtag even if that is largely out of her control. She's "just trying to breathe" despite how much the system is rigged against her and her community. In addition to the song's pointed social commentary, the music video features Brooklyn clad in black from head to toe and sporting a beret. Invoking the iconic dress of the Black Panther Party, Brooklyn places herself within a lineage of Black recording artists who have used their platforms as spaces for social commentary.[5] In the music video, Brooklyn leads her community on a march for Black lives, similar to the real protest marches that happened in nearly every part of the country in 2020. At the end of their march—and the music video—the group raises their collective fist, telling us that, although they are "just trying to breathe," their voices will not be silenced any longer. With Brooklyn Queen leading the way, they have all the tools they need to advocate for social change and an end to systemic racism.

One thing was apparent in the summer of 2020—the Renegades didn't let this movement pass them by. Even though they may be young, this is the world they have grown up in and they are ready to transform it. Having a viral social media platform was unthinkable when I graduated high school in 2004, yet this is the reality of Renegades and other members of Generation Z who are coming of age in a digital world. As their summer 2020 actions demonstrated, they are keenly aware of their collective power. This book is a testament to this cultural work. They are not only the next generation of activists, artists, influencers, and leaders; they are the present. They privilege their individual and collective identities through digital performance methods that foster community and social media interconnectedness in the twenty-first century. Renegades take up space on social media platforms to construct identity, create supportive digital communities, and exercise agency. And, as this collective work reveals, this revolutionary work will be Dubsmashed.

ACKNOWLEDGMENTS

I had the idea for this book for nearly a year but knowing how much time and energy goes into writing a book, I always said that I'd only write it if I had interest from a publisher. And then one day I woke up to an email from my editor Norman Hirschy, who saw that I was writing a book on using Dubsmash in the classroom and wanted to know if I had found a publisher. While he was asking about a different book, I pivoted and pitched Hirschy the idea that would become *Renegades*. Throughout this process, Hirschy has been a fervent supporter of this project. The entire staff at Oxford University Press has exceeded all expectations and has been a joy to work with. At every step of this project, I have felt in good hands. The anonymous peer reviewers were fantastic and offered crucial insight that only improved my work. I am forever grateful for their expertise and belief in this project. Thank you for your attention to my work, especially reviewing at the height of the Black Lives Matter protests and the ever-growing COVID-19 pandemic in the summer of 2020.

This book would not exist without the Dubsmash community. To them, I owe an enormous amount of gratitude. That I have been fully accepted and integrated into the Dubsmash community has been one of my life's most unexpected and cherished gifts. I owe a special thanks to Barrie Segal, who has believed in my work from my very first Dub and continues to support me to this day. Segal has been instrumental in helping me build my social media platform and refine my understanding of the intricacies of the social media dance community. Segal is a force and I am lucky to call her my friend. While there are far too many Dubsmashers to name here, I would like to thank the ones who fill the pages of this book: Jalaiah Harmon, Brooklyn Queen, D1 Nayah, TisaKorean, Kayla Nicole Jones, and the many others who drive this movement forward. Moreover, I am grateful for Kim Nailnotorious and Naveed Hassan for their help in securing several of the pictures that appear in this book.

While my work in this book reflects my face-to-face and digital classrooms, I am forever indebted to the faculty and administration at Bellaire High School who has supported the work of my students and me every step of the way. I owe special thanks to Ebony Cooksey, Sarah Humphrey, Mica Segal de la Garza, Freddy Davalos, Tania Andrews, Jane Baker, Maria Gloria Borsa, Debra Campbell, Kori Catlin, Stephanie Clayton, Heidi Florian, Lil Harris, Jenni Ho, Margy Laufe, Jennifer Mathieu, Michael McDonough, Miriam Mulet, Jimmy Newland, Amanda O'Leary, Michael Rossow, Jamie Schaff, Hillary Schulze, James Scott, Jacqueline Tellez, Allison Underhill, and Terri Williams, who have made this work possible. I am fully aware that my style of teaching wouldn't fly at every school and I am fortunate to work at a place that trusts me to reach my students the best way I know how to.

Of course, I am indebted to my students at Bellaire High School, who not only introduced me to the world of Dubsmash and TikTok, but welcomed me into the fold. From my first week at Bellaire in 2018, my students have generously shared their music, dance, and culture with me, which has made this book possible. I know it sounds clichéd, but my students truly inspire me in so many ways. I thank them for the creativity, joy, and positivity that they bring to my classroom. I am forever grateful for them.

This journey has also introduced me to other dancing teachers from across the United States. I extend my deepest thanks to Debbie A. Simmonds-Barber, Daisha Taylor, Meghann Hogan, Luis Eladio Torres, Audri Williams, Callie Evans, PJ Howard, and Jakeb Knight for being my online professional learning community. I hope to visit each of your classes one day and see firsthand the joy you bring to the world.

Since 2015, I have grown in my writing practice through the University of Houston's Write on Site. I began formally writing this book at the onset of the COVID-19 pandemic and was inspired to tell this story during daily Skype writing sessions with Willa Friedman, Lea C. Hellmueller, Rachel Afi Quinn, Eesha Pandit, Rikki Reiss Bettinger, Caryn Tamber-Rosenau, Kavita Singh, Gabriela Baeza Ventura, Jess Waggoner, and Sandra Zalman. They kept me accountable and motivated to finish this book. To be honest, I don't know how I wrote this book during the pandemic, but I am certain that my Skype Write on Site group is primarily to thank.

While this project happened at an unusually rapid pace, I was still fortunate to be able to present portions of this research in different educational and scholarly settings. Special thanks to Troy Scheid for inviting me to give a keynote at the 2019 Houston Arts Partners Conference, which forced me to write down what was happening. I owe thanks to fellow panelists and audience members at the Mid-American Theatre Conference and Telephone Hour: A Quarantine Colloquium, whose observations and suggestions greatly informed the shape of this book. And, finally, I extend my warmest thanks to Gina Sandí-Díaz and Micha Espinosa, who invited me to present this research at Fresno State University and Arizona State University, respectively. In a similar vein, I owe thanks to my editors Margaret Downing at *Houston Press* and Tom Berger at Edutopia, who helped push my thinking that helped shape chapters 5 and 6 of this book.

Since 2014, my scholarly home has been the Association for Theatre in Higher Education and this network of brilliant artists/scholars proved crucial to my work. I especially owe my deepest gratitude to the Music Theatre/Dance Focus Group, who supported this research and, in particularly Lindsey Barr, Jordan Ealey, Brian Eugenio Herrera, Meg Kirchhoff, Caitlin Marshall, Dustyn Martincich, Ariel Nereson, Phoebe Rumsey, Stacy Wolf, and Elizabeth Wollman. Moreover, I would like to thank Barrie Gelles, Laura MacDonald, and Bryan M. Vandevender for their enthusiasm for my teaching and research. Informal conference talks, phone calls, and Zoom sessions with them kept me focused and helped me to see the value in my writing. Gelles once told me, "what you are doing with your students *is* musical theater," which completely revolutionized my approach to being an artist/scholar writing about my own creative practice.

Along the way, I also benefited from digital conversations and support from Ashleigh Greene Wade, Aria S. Halliday, Kyesha Jennings, Jasmine Johnson, and Safiya Umoja Noble. I am forever grateful to this cohort of scholars who are revolutionizing the fields of media studies and African American Studies (to name a few). You inspire me to become a better version of myself.

I extend special thanks to Carla Della Gatta, Jessica Hinds-Bond, Marci R. McMahon, and Adrienne Oehlers, who read chapters drafts and gave incredibly useful feedback. Claire M. Massey, the Cagney to my Lacey, kept a fire lit under me all the way from Germany. Josh Inocéncio helped me significantly to work through my understanding of Gen Z culture. Abigail Vega, Kevin Becerra, Emilio Rodriguez, and Franky D. Gonzalez have been fervent champions of my work. I also owe thanks to my dear friend and writing and teaching buddy Sarah Jerasa, who has encouraged me from day one when I began working at Bellaire HS. Sarah read nearly every chapter in this book and provided critical feedback and shaped much of the scope of this book. On a similar note, I am forever indebted to my hermana Cristina Herrera. When I told her about possibly writing this book, she told me I had to do it and she would help push me along. When I say she read the proposal, every single chapter (sometimes multiple times), the response to reader reports, you name it, she did and more. I am so lucky to have a colleague like Cristina. Nerd power!

"Mother says I was a dancer before I could walk/She says I began to sing long before I could talk/And I've often wondered, how did it all start?" Well, it all started with an incredibly supportive family. My parents fostered my creativity and encouraged me to be myself, even if I was different. My mom is my biggest fan and supporter. She taught elementary school for twenty years, helping me to see firsthand the power that lies in education. I only hope to be half as good of a teacher as she was. Although going viral has had far more highs than lows, it saddens me that my father never got to see any of this. But, even so, his light paved the way and gave me the tools to make this a reality. I know he would be proud of me. I feel as though I danced out of the womb and my earliest memories are singing and dancing along to "I Just Want to Dance with Somebody" and "Get outta My Dreams, Get into My Car." My siblings, of course, offered support whether it was as my hype man (Terry) or my scene partner (Frances). Over thirty years later and their roles have not changed. The only difference is that they have more experience and simply could not be replaced with anyone better.

Moreover, I extend my deepest thanks and neck rubs to Teddy HoneyBear Boffone, who served as my research assistant, keeping me company during long days at the computer and reassuring me that I could write this book (his meows are very telling). I also thank Pickles Boffone, my research assistant who came on board late in the project but nevertheless helped me finish it on time. And, last but certainly not least, I wish to thank my partner Kayla for fully supporting me and believing in this project from the very beginning.

NOTES

PREFACE
1. Title I is a label given to public schools that educate large populations of socioeconomically disadvantaged populations. Title I schools receive supplemental funds from the government to better meet student educational goals.
2. For more on the ways that Whiteness operates, see Ruth Frankenburg, *White Women, Race Matters: The Social Construction of Whiteness* (Minneapolis: University of Minnesota Press, 1993); John Gabriel, *Whitewash: Racialized Politics and the Media* (London: Routledge, 1998); Cynthia Levine-Rasky, *Working through Whiteness: Intersectional Perspectives* (Albany: SUNY Press, 2002); Ashley W. Doane and Eduardo Bonilla-Silva, *White Out: The Continuing Significance of Racism* (New York: Routledge, 2003); Michael Eric Dyson, *The Michael Eric Dyson Reader* (New York: Basic Civitas, 2004); Shannon Winnubst, *Queering Freedom* (Bloomington: University of Indiana Press, 2006); David S. Owen, "Towards a Critical Theory of Whiteness," *Philosophy and Social Criticism* 33, no. 2 (2007): 203–22; Steve Garner, *Whiteness: An Introduction* (London: Routledge, 2007); and France Winddance Twine and Charles Gallagher, "Introduction: The Future of Whiteness: A Map of the Third Wave," *Ethnic and Racial Studies* 31, no. 1 (2008): 4–24.
3. There is also a rich body of hip hop scholarship written by White scholars who explicitly address their Whiteness. As I do here, these scholars typically take an ethnographic approach that relies on embeddedness in the community in question. For these perspectives, see Murray Forman, *The 'Hood Comes First: Race, Space and Place in Rap and Hip-Hop* (Middletown, CT: Wesleyan University Press, 2002); Mark Katz, *Groove Music: The Art and Culture of the Hip-Hop DJ* (New York: Oxford University Press, 2010) and *Build: The Power of Hip Hop Diplomacy in a Divided World* (New York: Oxford University Press, 2019); and Joseph G. Schloss, *Making Beats: The Art of Sample-Based Hip-Hop* (Middletown, CT: Wesleyan University Press, 2004) and *Foundation: B-boys, B-girls and Hip Hop Culture in New York* (New York: Oxford University Press, 2009).
4. Imani Perry, *Prophets of the Hood: Politics and Poetics in Hip Hop.*(Durham, NC: Duke University Press, 2004), 27.
5. bell hooks, *The Will to Change: Men, Masculinity, and Love* (New York: Washington Square Press, 2004), 17.
6. For more on systemic racism and White supremacy in digital spaces, see Safiya Umoja Noble, *Algorithms of Oppression: How Search Engines Reinforce Racism*

(New York: New York University Press, 2018); and Ruha Benjamin, *Race after Technology: Abolitionist Tools for the New Jim Code* (Boston: Polity Books, 2019).

7. For more on "world"-traveling, see Maria Lugones, *Pilgrimages/ Pereginajes: Theorizing Coalition against Multiple Oppressions* (New York: Rowman & Littlefield, 2003), 77–100.

8. Marilyn Frye, *The Politics of Reality: Essays in Feminist Theory* (Trumansburg, NY: Crossing Press, 1983), 75.

9. See, for example, Inderpal Grewal and Caren Kaplan, *Scattered Hegemonies: Postmodernity and Transnational Feminist Practices* (Minneapolis: University of Minnesota Press, 1994).

10. Trinh T. Minh-ha, "Not You/Like You: Post-Colonial Women and the Interlocking Questions of Identity and Difference," *Inscriptions* 3–4 (1988), https:// culturalstudies.ucsc.edu/inscriptions/volume-34/trinh-t-minh-ha/.

11. Rachel Afi Quinn, "This Bridge Called the Internet: Black Lesbian Feminist Activism in Santo Domingo," in *Transatlantic Feminisms: Women and Gender Studies in Africa and the Diaspora*, eds. Cheryl R. Rodriguez, Dzodzi Tsikata, and Akosua Adomako Ampofo (Lexington Books, 2015), 26.

INTRODUCTION

1. Taylor Lorenz, "The Original Renegade," *New York Times*, February 13, 2020, https://www.nytimes.com/2020/02/13/style/the-original-renegade.html.

2. The song's release was untimely; rapper and close friend of K-Camp Nipsey Hussle died unexpectedly the day before the song was set to be released, prompting the team to push back the song's release date.

3. Music Ally, "How K Camp's 'Lottery' (aka 'Renegade') Went Viral—and What Happened Next," March 9, 2020, https://musically.com/2020/03/09/k-camp-lottery-renegade-viral/.

4. For a list of the most-followed TikTok accounts, see https://en.m.wikipedia.org/ wiki/List_of_most-followed_TikTok_accounts.

5. With clout comes so-called clout chasers, who want to collaborate with well-known influencers so that they can gain followers. At Bellaire High School, "clout chaser" is frequently used as an insult, given to anyone who doesn't appear genuine in their interest to dance with me and Dubsmasher students.

6. Dance scholar Harmony Bench notes that repetition in dance practices relies on user interaction and, as an extension, makes a dance common. See Harmony Bench, *Perpetual Motion: Dance, Digital Cultures, and the Common* (Minneapolis: University of Minnesota Press, 2020), 21.

7. Music Ally.

8. Ibid.

9. K-Camp, for instance, has over 7.6 million monthly listeners on Spotify, and "Lottery (Renegade)" has been streamed over 60 million times on Spotify alone. Popular YouTube videos of the song have 15 million, 21 million, and 30 million viewers.

10. Anthea Kraut, *Choreography Copyright: Race, Gender, and Intellectual Property Rights in American Dance* (New York: Oxford University Press, 2015), 4. For more on the racial politics of US dance, see Brenda Dixon Gottschild, *Digging the Africanist Presence in American Performance: Dance and Other Contexts* (Westport, CT: Greenwood Press, 1996); Susan Manning, *Modern Dance, Negro Dance: Race in Motion* (Minneapolis: University of Minnesota Press, 2004); Jacqueline Shea Murphy, *"The People Have Never Stopped Dancing": Native American Modern Dance*

Histories (Minneapolis: University of Minnesota Press, 2007); Priya Srinivasan, *Sweating Saris: Indian Dance as Transnational Labor* (Philadelphia: Temple University Press, 2011); and Yutian Wong, *Choreographing Asian America* (Middletown, CT: Wesleyan University Press, 2010).

11. Rebecca Jennings published an article for Vox on February 4, 2020, that included Harmon's story. However, Lorenz's *New York Times* piece "The Original Renegade," dated February 13, was what led to Harmon's meteoric rise to fame, no doubt in large part because of the cultural capital that comes with a feature story in the *New York Times*. As such, I view Lorenz's article as the one that "broke the story."

12. Lorenz, "The Original Renegade."

13. Michael P. Jeffries, *Thug Life: Race, Gender, and the Meaning of Hip-Hop* (Chicago: University of Chicago Press, 2010), 2.

14. Bench, *Perpetual Motion*, 3.

15. Gwendolyn D. Pough, *Check It While I Wreck It: Black Womanhood, Hip-Hop Culture, and the Public Sphere* (Boston: Northeastern University Press, 2004), 3.

16. Marcyliena Morgan, "'Nuthin' but a G Thang': Grammar and Language Ideology in Hip Hop Identity," in *Sociocultural and Historical Contexts of African American English*, ed. Sonja L. Lanehart (Amsterdam: John Benjamins), 187.

17. Katrina Hazzard-Gordon, "Dance in Hip-Hop Culture," in *It's the Joint! The Hip Hop Studies Reader*, eds. Murray Forman and Mark Anthony Neal (New York: Routledge, 2004), 513.

18. Jasmine Johnson, "The #OptimisticChallenge: Decisive Black Joy," in *Black Futures*, eds. Kimberly Drew and Jenna Wortham (New York: One World, 2020), 152–55.

19. Emmett George Price III, *Hip Hop Culture* (Santa Barbara, CA: ABC-CLIO, 2006), 17.

20. Raymond Williams, *Culture* (London: Fontana Press, 1981), 200.

21. Imani Perry, *Prophets in the Hood: Politics and Poetics in Hip Hop* (Durham, NC: Duke University Press, 2004), 10. Perry's point notwithstanding, hip hop's multiethnic and multiracial roots and impact are not to be elided here. See Mark Katz, *Build! The Power of Hip Hop Diplomacy in a Divided World* (New York: Oxford University Press, 2019); Ian Maxwell, *Phat Beats, Dope Rhymes: Hip Hop Down Under Comin' Upper* (Middletown, CT: Wesleyan University Press, 2003); Tony Mitchell, *Global Noise: Rap and Hip Hop Outside the USA* (Middletown, CT: Wesleyan University Press, 2002); and Patricia Herrera, *Nuyorican Feminist Performance: From the Café to Hip Hop Theater* (Ann Arbor: University of Michigan Press, 2020).

22. Dubsmash, "Dubsmash Teaser Q3," dubsmash.com, July 2020.

23. Ibid.

24. See, for instance, Katrina Hazzard-Donald, *The Rise of Social Dance Formations in African-American Culture* (Philadelphia: Temple University Press, 1992); Tricia Rose, *Black Noise: Rap Music and Black Culture in Contemporary America* (Middletown, CT: Wesleyan University Press, 1994); Robin D. G. Kelley, *Race Rebels: Culture, Politics, and the Black Working Class* (New York: Free Press, 1996); Gwendolyn D. Pough, *Check It While I Wreck It: Black Womanhood, Hip-Hop Culture, and the Public Sphere* (Boston: Northeastern University Press, 2004); Kyra Gaunt, *The Games Black Girls Play: Learning the Ropes from Double-Dutch to Hip-Hop* (New York: New York University Press, 2006); Jayna Brown, *Babylon Girls: Black Women Performers and the Shaping of the*

Modern (Durham, NC: Duke University Press, 2008); and Aimee Meredith Cox, *Shapeshifters: Black Girls and the Choreography of Citizenship* (Durham, NC: Duke University Press, 2015).

25. Hazzard-Donald, *The Rise of Social Dance Formations*, 513. See also Kyesha Jennings, "City Girls, Hot Girls and the Re-Imagining of Black Women in Hip Hop and Digital Spaces," *Global Hip Hop Studies* 1, no. 1 (2020): 48.

26. Kyra Gaunt, *The Games Black Girls Play: Learning the Ropes from Double-Dutch to Hip-Hop* (New York: New York University Press, 2006).

27. For more on how Black women use dance as a critical site of play, joy, and labor, see Jasmine Elizabeth Johnson, "A Politics of Tenderness: Camille A. Brown and Dancers' BLACK GIRL: Linguistic Play," *Black Scholar* 49, no. 4 (2019): 20–34.

28. Stephanie Leigh Batiste, "Introduction: Black Performance II: Knowing and Being," *Black Scholar* 49, no. 4 (2019): 1.

29. See, for example, Claudia Megele, *Safeguarding Children and Young People Online: A Guide for Busy Practitioners* (Chicago: University of Chicago Press, 2016); Yalda T. Uhls and Patricia M. Greenfield, "The Rise of Fame: An Historical Content Analysis," *Cyberpsychology: Journal of Psychological Research on Cyberspace* 5, no. 1 (2011); and Jake Halpern, *Fame Junkies: The Hidden Truths behind America's Favorite Addiction* (Boston: Houghton Mifflin, 2007). Moreover, in *The App Generation: How Today's Youth Navigate Identity, Intimacy, and Imagination in a Digital World*, Howard Gardner and Katie Davis propose that unpopular teens and teens with low self-esteem are more likely to be obsessed with social media fame.

30. Kelley, *Race Rebels*, 11.

31. Aimee Rickman, *Adolescence, Girlhood, and Media Migration: US Teens' Use of Social Media to Negotiate Struggles* (Lanham, MD: Lexington Books, 2018).

32. Howard Gardner and Katie Davis, *The App Generation: How Today's Youth Navigate Identity, Intimacy, and Imagination in a Digital World* (New Haven, CT: Yale University Press, 2013), 8.

33. The Rosa Cinematic Universe is the creation of Adam Martinez, a twenty-year-old from San Antonio, Texas. Rosa went viral in January 2020 in a series of TikToks in which we learn about Rosa's love for Arizona Iced Tea, Hot Cheetos, and, of course, chisme (or, hot goss aka gossip). For more on Rosa, see Javier Moreno and Pablo Valdivia, "Meet Adam Martinez, The Guy behind Everyone's Viral Fave Rosa," *Buzzfeed*, February 14, 2020, https://www.buzzfeed.com/pablovaldivia/rosa-tiktok-adam-rodriguez.

34. Florence Martin, Chuang Wang, Teresa Petty, Weichao Wang, and Patti Willkins, "Middle School Students' Social Media Use," *Journal of Educational Technology & Society* 21, no. 1 (2018): 215.

35. Kirsten Drotner, "Leisure Is Hard Work: Digital Practices and Future Competences," in *Youth, Identity, and Digital Media*, ed. David Buckingham (Cambridge: MIT Press, 2008), 169.

36. Ibid., 170.

37. Alicia Corts, "(Un)limited: Virtual Performance Spaces and Digital Identity," *Theatre Symposium* 24 (2016): 113.

38. Danah Boyd, "Why Youth Heart Social Network Sites: The Role of Networked Publics in Teenage Social Life," in *Youth, Identity, and Digital Media*, ed. David Buckingham (Cambridge: MIT Press, 2008), 120.

39. Gardner and Davis, *The App Generation*, 32.

40. S. Craig Watkins, "Black Youth and the Ironies of Capitalism," in *It's the Joint! The Hip Hop Studies Reader*, eds. Murray Forman and Mark Anthony Neal (New York: Routledge, 2004), 557.

41. Ibid., 558.

42. See, for example, Erin Ranft, "Blogs as Alternative Spaces for African American Literature and Student Voices," *CLA Journal* 59, no. 3 (2016): 232–41; Stephanie Vie, "'What's Going On?' Challenges and Opportunities for Social Media Use in the Writing Classroom," *Journal of Faculty Development* 29, no. 2 (2015): 33–44; and Gardner and Davis, *The App Generation*.

43. Ashleigh Wade, "New Genres of Being Human: World Making through Viral Blackness," *Black Scholar* 47, no. 3 (2017): 33–35.

44. André Brock Jr., *Distributed Blackness: African American Cybercultures* (New York: New York University Press, 2020).

45. For more on how Black youth respond to mainstream hip hop artists such as Drake and Rihanna on Instagram, see Della V. Mosley, Roberto L. Abreu, Ashley Ruderman, and Candice Crowell, "Hashtags and Hip Hop: Exploring the Online Performances of Hip Hop Identified Youth Using Instagram," *Feminist Media Studies* 17, no. 2 (2019): 135–52. While this work is in conversation with my own, *Renegades* focuses on Black youth as the creators of mainstream culture rather than simply a community that engages with the culture.

46. Jennings, "City Girls," 81. African American Studies and Media Studies scholars such as Kyra D. Gaunt, Ruth Nicole Brown, Andre Brock Jr., Ruha Benjamin, Sarah Florini, Aria S. Halliday, Kyesha Jennings, Jasmine Johnson, Safiya Noble, and Ashleigh Greene Wade have made key interventions into our understandings of the various ways that the Black community uses social media.

47. Ashleigh Wade, "When Social Media Yields More Than 'Likes': Black Girls' Digital Kinship Formations," *Women, Gender, and Families of Color* 7, no. 1 (2019): 80–97.

48. Jennings, "City Girls," 49.

49. Boyd, "Why Youth," 119.

50. Jennings, "City Girls," 48–49.

51. Price, *Hip Hop Culture*, 11.

52. For more on b-boying, see Joseph G. Schloss, *Foundation: B-boys, B-girls and Hip-Hop Culture in New York* (New York: Oxford University Press, 2009).

53. Sally Banes, "Breaking," in *It's the Joint! The Hip Hop Studies Reader*, eds. Murray Forman and Mark Anthony Neal (New York: Routledge, 2004), 14.

54. Schloss, *Foundation*, 4.

55. Gwendolyn D. Pough, *Check It While I Wreck It: Black Womanhood, Hip-Hop Culture, and the Public Sphere* (Boston: Northeastern University Press, 2004), 17.

56. Ibid.

57. Banes, "Breaking," 14.

58. Tricia Rosa, quoted in Angela Ards, "Organizing the Hip-Hop Generation," in *It's the Joint! The Hip Hop Studies Reader*, eds. Murray Forman and Mark Anthony Neal (New York: Routledge, 2004), 314.

59. Pough, *Check It While I Wreck It*, 30.

60. José Esteban Muñoz, *Disidentifications: Queers of Color and the Performance of Politics* (Minneapolis: University of Minnesota Press, 1999), 4. My theoretical framework for understanding these Renegades is indebted to the work of Latinx cultural theorists who have shaped me as a scholar and helped me build the meaningful connections with my students who brought me to writing

this book: Gloria Anzaldúa, Cherríe Moraga, Chela Sandoval, Juan Flores, and Muñoz. While not all the subjects in this book are Latinx, their identity practices and performances fit within a conversation on difference that is largely informed by Latinx theory.

61. DeFrantz, "The Black Beat Made Visible: Hip Hop Dance and Body Power," in *Of the Presence of the Body: Essays on Dance and Performance Theory*, ed. Andre Lepecki (Middletown, CT: Wesleyan University Press, 2004), 71.

62. Judith Butler, *Bodies That Matter: On the Discursive Limits of Sex* (New York: Routledge, 1993), 219.

63. Muñoz, *Disidentifications*, 31.

64. Ibid., 5.

65. Chela Sandoval, *Methodology of the Oppressed* (Minneapolis: University of Minnesota Press, 2000), 225–26.

66. Chela Sandoval, "U.S. Third World Feminism: The Theory and Method of the Oppositional Consciousness in the Postmodern World," *Genders* 10 (1991): 15.

67. Gloria Anzaldúa, *Borderlands/La Frontera: The New Mestiza* (San Francisco: Aunt Lute, 1987), 25.

68. Ibid., 101.

69. Gloria Anzaldúa, "La Prieta," in *This Bridge Called My Back: Writings by Radical Women of Color*, eds. Cherríe Moraga and Gloria Anzaldúa (New York: Kitchen Table), 208.

CHAPTER 1

1. See Howard Gardner and Katie Davis, *The App Generation: How Today's Youth Navigate Identity, Intimacy, and Imagination in a Digital World* (New Haven, CT: Yale University Press, 2013).

2. For more on Dubsmash, see Josh Constine, "How Dubsmash Revived Itself as #2 to TikTok," *TechCrunch*, 31 January 2020, accessed 29 April 2020, https://techcrunch.com/2020/01/31/dubsmash-songs/?guccounter=1; and Suchit Dash, Jonas Druppel, and Tim Specht, "Dubsmash Was Dying. Now Users Watch 1 Billion Videos a month," *Fast Company*, 13 March 2020, accessed 29 April 2020, https://www.fastcompany.com/90476906/dubsmash-was-dying-now-users-watch-1-billion-videos-a-month.

3. Jay Mitra, *Entrepreneurship, Innovation and Regional Development: An Introduction* (New York: Routledge, 2019).

4. Dash, Drüppel, and Specht, "Dubsmash."

5. Ashley King, "Dubsmash Is Back, and Focused Entirely on Dance Challenges," Digital Music News, 21 February 2019, accessed 12 May 2020, https://www.digitalmusicnews.com/2019/02/21/dubsmash-is-back-and-focused-entirely-on-dance-challenges/.

6. King, "Dubsmash."

7. King, "Dubsmash."

8. King, "Dubsmash."

9. Constine, "How Dubsmash."

10. Constine, "How Dubsmash."

11. Constine, "How Dubsmash."

12. Constine, "How Dubsmash."

13. Constine, "How Dubsmash."

14. Dubsmash, "Dubsmash Teaser Q3," dubsmash.com, July 2020.

15. Constine, "How Dubsmash."

16. Danielle Abril, "Meet Dubsmash, the Video Service Stealing Some of TikTok's Thunder," *Fortune*, 14 July 2020, https://fortune.com/2020/07/14/what-is-dubsmash-tiktok-security-concerns-bans/.

17. Todd Boyd, "Check Yo Self before You Wreck Yo Self: The Death of Politics in Rap Music and Popular Culture," in *It's the Joint! The Hip Hop Studies Reader*, eds. Murray Forman and Mark Anthony Neal (New York: Routledge, 2004), 325.

18. S. Craig Watkins, "Black Youth and the Ironies of Capitalism," in *It's the Joint! The Hip Hop Studies Reader*, eds. Murray Forman and Mark Anthony Neal (New York: Routledge, 2004), 559.

19. Thomas F. DeFrantz, "The Black Beat Made Visible: Hip Hop Dance and Body Power," in *Of the Presence of the Body: Essays on Dance and Performance Theory*, ed. Andre Lepecki (Middletown, CT: Wesleyan University Press, 2004), 71.

20. Cherie Hu, "Dubsmash Is Far from Dead—But Can It Survive Its Second Life," *Forbes*, 19 February 2020, accessed 12 May 2020, https://www.forbes.com/sites/cheriehu/2019/02/19/dubsmash-is-far-from-dead-but-can-it-really-survive-its-second-life/#255afb6c4961.

21. Dash, Druppel, and Specht, "Dubsmash."

22. Bryan Clark, "The Clueless Parent's Guide to Understanding TikTok," The Next Web, 31 January 2019, accessed 12 May 2020, https://thenextweb.com/socialmedia/2019/01/31/the-clueless-parents-guide-to-understanding-tiktok/.

23. Notably, ByteDance has a separate version of TikTok for users in China called Douyin.

24. Natalie Jarvey, "TikTok Boom! How the Exploding Social Media App Is Going Hollwyood," *The Hollywood Reporter*, 6 May 2020, accessed 12 May 2020, https://www.hollywoodreporter.com/features/tiktok-boom-how-exploding-social-media-app-is-going-hollywood-1293505.

25. Jarvey, "TikTok Boom!"

26. Jarvey, "TikTok Boom!"

27. See Sam Biddle, Paulo Victor Ribeiro, and Tatiana Dias, "Invisible Censorship," *The Intercept*, 16 March 2020, accessed 29 April 2020, https://theintercept.com/2020/03/16/tiktok-app-moderators-users-discrimination/.

28. Sahil Patel, "Hearst Now Has both Seventeen and Cosmo on Up-and-Coming App Musical.ly," Digiday, 7 March 2018, accessed 29 April 2020, https://digiday.com/media/seventeen-hearst-brings-cosmopolitan-musical-ly/.

29. Sensor Tower, "The Top Mobile Apps, Games, and Publishers of Q1 2018: Sensor Tower's Data Digest, Sensor Tower 1 May 2018, accessed 29 April 2020, https://sensortower.com/blog/top-apps-games-publishers-q1-2018.

30. Jarvey, "TikTok Boom!"

31. Sean Wang, "A Close Look into Tik Tok," Medium, 15 May 2018, accessed 29 April 2020, https://medium.com/@seanzhiyangwangsk/a-look-into-tik-toks-success-6c12ebae572c.

32. Collab houses have been a Los Angeles mainstay since influencer culture became the norm, especially since 2014 with 02L Mansion (Our Second Life), 1600 Vine Street (Vine), and Clout House (YouTubers). Other notable TikToker collab houses include The Sway House, The Clubhouse, The Drip Crib, The Valley House, The Kids Next Door House, The Vibe House, The Alpha House, and Young Finesse Kids. For more on the Hype House, see Taylor Lorenz, "Hype House and the Los Angeles TikTok Mansion Gold Rush," *New York Times*, 3 January 2020, accessed 29 April 2020, https://www.nytimes.com/2020/01/03/style/hype-house-los-angeles-tik-tok.html. In June 2020, the Hype House moved

to the former YouTuber Clout House in the Hollywood Hills. For more on this move, see Carolyn Twersky, "The Hype House Just Moved out of Their Gorgeous LA Mansion," *Seventeen*, 1 June 2020, https://www.seventeen.com/celebrity/a32731655/hype-house-moved-out-of-la-mansion/.

33. Jarvey, "TikTok Boom!"

34. Taylor Lorenz, "Delayed Moves, Poolside Videos and Postmates Spon: The State of Tiktok Collab Houses," *New York Times*, 21 May 2020, https://www.nytimes.com/2020/05/21/style/tiktok-collab-houses-quarantine-coronavirus.html.

35. Tom Ward, "The Hype House Is Changing the Face of TikTok," *Forbes*, 24 February 2020, accessed 29 April 2020, https://www.forbes.com/sites/tomward/2020/02/24/the-hype-house-is-changing-the-face-of-tiktok/#74a32db77c1b.

36. Taylor Lorenz, "Hype House and the Los Angeles TikTok Mansion Gold Rush," *New York Times*, 3 January 2020, accessed 29 April 2020, https://www.nytimes.com/2020/01/03/style/hype-house-los-angeles-tik-tok.html.

37. Taylor Lorenz, "Hype House."

38. @uncle.tomm, TikTok post, 21 December 2019, accessed 29 April 2020, https://www.tiktok.com/@uncle.tomm/video/6772994139010256133?u_code=6dc3cefl1fi8a&preview_pb=0&language=en&timestamp=1577741818&utm_campaign=client_share&app=musically&utm_medium=ios&user_id=144377784793104384&tt_from=copy&utm_source=copy&source=h5_m.

39. Sam Biddle, Paulo Victor Ribeiro, and Tatiana Dias, "Invisible Censorship," *The Intercept*, 16 March 2020, accessed 29 April 2020, https://theintercept.com/2020/03/16/tiktok-app-moderators-users-discrimination/.

40. Sam Biddle, Paulo Victor Ribeiro, and Tatiana Dias, "Invisible Censorship."

41. For more on how tech designers built bias and judgement into tech systems, thus replicating racist systems, see Ruha Benjamin.

42. Safiya Umoja Noble, *Algorithms of Oppression: How Search Engines Reinforce Racism* (New York: New York University Press, 2018), 36.

43. Ruha Benjamin, *Race after Technology*, 3.

44. Ruha Benjamin, *Race after Technology*, 4.

45. The event strategically coincided with Malcolm X's birthday.

46. Alaa Elassar, "TikTokers Stand in Solidarity with Black Creators to Protest Censorship," CNN, 19 May 2020, accessed 23 May 2020, https://www.cnn.com/2020/05/19/us/tiktok-black-lives-matter-trnd/index.html.

47. Tatiana Walk-Morris, "TikTok's Digital Blackface Problem," One Zero, 12 February 2020, accessed 29 April 2020, https://onezero.medium.com/tiktoks-digital-blackface-problem-409571589a8.

48. Brianna Holt, "Teens on TikTok Have No Clue They're Perpetuating Racist Stereotypes," Quartz, 1 November 2019, accessed 12 May 2020, https://qz.com/quartzy/1738478/how-teens-on-tiktok-are-perpetuating-racist-stereotypes/.

49. For more on the history of blackface, see Eric Lott, *Love & Theft: Blackface Minstrelsy and the American Working Class* (New York: Oxford University Pres, 2013).

50. For more on the Freeman/Hume controversy, see Mustafa Gatollari, "Racist Tiktok Video Gets High School Girl's College Offer Rescinded, Expulsion," Distractify, accessed 12 May 2020, https://www.distractify.com/p/stephania-freeman-racist-tiktok-expelled; Jon Greig, "White Girl Who Took Part in Racist TikTok Video with Boyfriend Swiftly Throws Him under Bus amid Backlash," Blavity, 20 April 2020, accessed 12 May 2020, https://blavity.com/white-girl-who-took-part-in-racist-tiktok-video-with-boyfriend-swiftly-throws-him-under-

bus-amid-backlash?category1=news; and Tanya A. Christian, "Georgia High Schoolers Won't Graduate after Posting Racist 'Cooking' Video," *Essence*, 20 April 2020, accessed 12 May 2020, https://www.essence.com/news/carrollton-georgia-high-schoolers-expelled-racist-video/.

51. Greig, "White Girl Who Took Part in Racist TikTok Video."
52. Gatollari, "Racist Tiktok Video Gets High School Girl's College Offer Rescinded, Expulsion."
53. @JamilaGonzale14, "Crazy how they get to be 'just teenagers' but black people never get that," Twitter, 18 April 2020, https://twitter.com/JamilaGonzale14/status/1251651633093783557?s=20.
54. @gmayo28, ""Also, 'stupid teenager stuff' is stuff like underage drinking or climbing onto the roof of your school, not making an incredibly racist video," Twitter, 19 April 2020, https://twitter.com/gmayo28/status/1251742821138272256?s=20.
55. @gmayo28 tweet, 2020.
56. @gmayo28.
57. Fiona Duncan, "A Bunch of People, from Professors to Diplo, Consider the Tiktok Craze," *Interview Magazine*, 23 April 2020, accessed 7 May 2020, https://www.interviewmagazine.com/culture/tik-tok-fame-videos-diplo-content-spring.
58. Fiona Duncan, "A Bunch of People."
59. For more on bell hooks's notion of the imperialist, White supremacist, capitalist patriarchy, see bell hooks, *Feminism Is for Everybody: Passionate Politics* (London: Pluto Press, 2000).
60. The potential TikTok ban did reveal how social media can become ephemeral like other performances. In response to this, TikTokers began downloading their content and trying to migrate their followers to other social media platforms just in case TikTok disappeared in the United States. For more on the instability of digital media performance, see Harmony Bench, *Perpetual Motion: Dance, Digital Cultures, and the Common* (Minneapolis: University of Minnesota Press, 2020).
61. Stephanie Chan, "Installs of India's Top TikTok Alternatives Grew 155% Following Its Ban There," *Sensor Tower*, 23 July 2020, https://sensortower.com/blog/tiktok-alternatives-growth-india.
62. Joe-Marie McKenzie, "Babyface and Teddy Riley Broke Instagram," *Essence*, 21 April 2020, accessed 12 May 2020, https://www.essence.com/celebrity/babyface-teddy-riley-instagram-live-battle/.
63. Jon Caramanica, "How Hip-Hop Royalty Found a New Home on Instagram Live," *New York Times*, 7 May 2020, accessed 12 May 2020, https://www.nytimes.com/2020/05/07/arts/music/hip-hop-instagram-coronavirus.html.
64. Jon Caramanica, "How Hip-Hop Royalty."

CHAPTER 2

1. Dubsmashers use the app PicPlayPost to create video collages. Dancers can make side-by-side duets on Dubsmash, TikTok, and on the dance app Funimate.
2. By April 2020, the short sound bite was used in over 16.2 million TikToks.
3. For more on these Dubsmashers, see their Instagram profiles: @jaygocrazy.16, @jalaiah, @brooklynqueen03, @lalasolit, @barrrie, @bracefacelaii, @thereald1.nayah, @0fficialdvamondx, @baybewil__, @therealeisha, and @dr_boffone.
4. Dara M. Byrne. "Public Discourse, Community Concerns, and Civic Engagement: Exploring Black Social Networking Traditions on BlackPlanet.com," *Journal of Computer-Mediated Communication* 13, no. 1 (2007): 319–40.

5. Ashley Wade, "When Social Media Yields More than 'Likes': Black Girls' Digital Kinship Formations," *Women, Gender, and Families of Color* 7, no. 1 (2019): 80–97.

6. For more on #DemThrones, see Sarah Florini, "Enclaving and Cultural Resonance in Black *Game of Thrones* Fandom," in *Fans of Color, Fandoms of Color*, eds. Abigail De Kosnik and Andre Carrington, *Transformative Works and Cultures* 29 (March 14, 2019). Black Girl Nerds is a webspace dedicated for women of color to celebrate nerdiness and non-normative identities. The website features news stories, interviews, community posts, a podcast, and a shop. For more on how Black girls use twerking videos as a celebration of self-expression, see Aria S. Halliday, "Twerk Sumn!: Theorizing Black Girl Epistemology in the Body," *Cultural Studies* 34, no. 6 (2020): 874–91 .

7. Julie Malnig, ed., *Ballroom, Boogie, Shimmy Sham, Shake: A Social and Popular Dance Reader* (Chicago: University of Illinois Press, 2009), 6, 4.

8. For more on the role of social dance on everyday life, see Kathy Peiss, *Cheap Amusements, Working Women, and Leisure in Turn-of-the-Century New York* (Philadelphia: Temple University Press, 1996); and Linda J. Tomko, *Dancing Class: Gender, Ethnicity, and Social Divides in American Dance, 1890–1920* (Bloomington: Indiana University Press, 1999).

9. Katrina Hazzard-Gordon, *The Rise of Social Dance Formations in African-American Culture* (Philadelphia: Temple University Press, 1990), ix.

10. For more on how young people use digital spaces as key sites of socialization, see Danah Boyd, *It's Complicated: The Social Lives of Networked Teens* (New Haven, CT: Yale University Press, 2014); Nic Crowe and Simon Bradford, "'Hanging Out in Runescape': Identity, Work and Leisure in the Virtual Playground," *Children's Geographies* 4, no. 3 (2006): 331–46; and Patricia G. Lange, *Kids on YouTube: Technical Identities and Digital Literacies* (Walnut Creek, CA: Left Cross Press, 2014).

11. M. Elizabeth Blair, "Commercialization of the Rap Music Youth Subculture," in *It's the Joint! The Hip Hop Studies Reader*, eds. Murray Forman and Mark Anthony Neal (New York: Routledge, 2004), 498.

12. Julie Malnig, ed., *Ballroom, Boogie, Shimmy Sham, Shake: A Social and Popular Dance Reader* (Chicago: University of Illinois Press, 2009), 5.

13. S. Craig Watkins, *Representing: Hip Hop Culture and the Production of Black Cinema* (Chicago: University of Chicago Press, 1998), 65.

14. Nancy Fraser, "Rethinking the Public Sphere: A Contribution to the Critique of Actually Existing Democracy," in *Habermas and the Public Sphere*, ed. Craig J. Calhouson (Cambridge, MA: MIT Press 1992), 123.

15. Murray Forman, "Ain't No Love in the Heart of the City: Hip-Hop, Space, and Place," in *It's the Joint! The Hip Hop Studies Reader*, eds. Murray Forman and Mark Anthony Neal (New York: Routledge, 2004), 155.

16. Bench, *Perpetual Motion*, 3.

17. Cherrie Moraga, *A Xicana Codex of Changing Consciousness: Writings, 2000–2010* (Durham, NC: Duke University Press, 2011), 34–35.

18. Edit L. B. Turner, *Communitas: The Anthropology of Collective Joy* (New York: Palgrave Macmillan, 2012), 3.

19. Tricia Rose, *Black Noise: Rap Music and Black Culture in Contemporary America* (Middletown, CT: Wesleyan University Press, 1994), 11.

20. For more on belonging and unbelonging, see José Esteban Muñoz, *Cruising Utopia: The Then and There of Queer Futurity* (New York: New York University Press, 2009).

21. For more on these creators, see their Instagram accounts: D1 Nayah (@thereald1. nayah), Laii (@bracefacelaii), and Glo Twinz (@glo.twinz).

22. Cherríe Moraga, "Preface," in *This Bridge Called My Back: Writings by Radical Women of Color*, eds. Gloria Anzaldúa and Cherríe Moraga (San Francisco: Kitchen Table Press, 1984), xii–xix.

23. Cherie Hu, "Dubsmash Is Far from Dead—But Can It Really Survive Its Second Life?," *Forbes*, 19 February 2019, accessed 7 May 2020, https://www.forbes. com/sites/cheriehu/2019/02/19/dubsmash-is-far-from-dead-but-can-it-really- survive-its-second-life/#4a6b493c4961.

24. For more on the history of social network sites, see Nicole B. Ellison and Danah M. Boyd, "Sociality through Social Network Sites," in *The Oxford Handbook of Internet Studies*, ed. William H. Dutton (Oxford: Oxford University Press, 2013), 151–172; and Danah M. Boyd, *It's Complicated: The Social Lives of Networked Teens* (New Haven, CT: Yale University Press, 2014), 6–14.

25. Nicole B. Ellison and Danah M. Boyd, "Social Network Sites: Definition, History and Scholarship," *Journal of Computer-Mediated Communication* 13, no. 1 (2007): 210–30.

26. Ellison and Boyd, "Social Network Sites."

27. Kyesha Jennings, "City Girls, Hot Girls and the Re-imagining of Black Women in Hip Hop and Digital Spaces," *Global Hip Hop* 1, no. 1 (2020): 49.

28. Kyesha Jennings, "City Girls," 49.

29. For more on social isolation in the age of social media, see Jacqueline Olds and Richard S. Schwartz, *The Lonely American: Drifting Apart in the Twenty-first Century* (Boston: Beacon Press, 2010); Sherry Turkle, *Alone Together: Why We Expect More from Technology and Less from Each Other* (New York: Basic Books, 2012); Adam Alter, *Irresistible: The Rise of Addictive Technology and the Business of Keeping Us Hooked* (New York: Penguin Books, 2017); Stephen Marche, "Is Facebook Making Us Lonely?," *The Atlantic*, May 2012, accessed 28 April 2020, https://www.theatlantic.com/magazine/archive/2012/05/is-facebook-making- us-lonely/308930/; and David DiSalvo, "Are Social Networks Messing with Your Head?" *Scientific American*, January 2010, accessed 28 April 2020, https://www. scientificamerican.com/article/are-social-networks-messing/.

30. In fact, in *The App Generation: How Today's Youth Navigate Identity, Intimacy, and Imagination in a Digital World*, Howard Gardner and Katie Davis demonstrate that apps can be beneficial in myriad ways.

31. Nancy K. Baym, *Personal Connections in the Digital Age* (Cambridge, MA: Polity Press, 2010).

32. Cherie Hu, "Dubsmash Is Far from Dead—But Can It Really Survive Its Second Life?," *Forbes*, 19 February 2019, accessed 13 May 2020, https://www.forbes. com/sites/cheriehu/2019/02/19/dubsmash-is-far-from-dead-but-can-it-really- survive-its-second-life/#63931e254961.

33. Hu, "Dubsmash, "2019.

34. Rania Aniftos, "How 2018 Became the Year of the Dance Challenge," *Billboard*, 28 August 2018, accessed 7 May 2020, https://www.billboard.com/articles/news/ 8472717/2018-year-of-the-dance-challenge.

35. Jasmine Johnson, "The #OptimisticChallenge: Decisive Black Joy," in *Black Futures*, eds. Kimberly Drew and Jenna Wortham (New York: One World, 2020): 152–55.

36. Johnson, "The #OptimisticChallenge," 152–55.

37. "In My Feelings" rode its dance challenge to stay on top of the Billboard Hot 100 for seven weeks while "Before I Let Go" helped maintain Beyoncé's unmatched momentum following the release of *Homecoming* on Netflix. For more on the "In My Feelings" challenge, see Jasmine Johnson, "b.O.s. 6.4 / *In My Feelings*," *ASAP/Journal*, 13 August 2018, http://asapjournal.com/b-o-s-6-4-in-my-feelings-jasmine-elizabeth-johnson/.

38. Andrew R. Chow, "Lil Nas X Talks 'Old Town Road' and the Billboard Controversy," *Time*, 5 April 2019, accessed 7 May 2020, https://time.com/5561466/lil-nas-x-old-town-road-billboard/.

39. Hu, "Dubsmash," 2019.

40. Josh Constine, "How Dubsmash Revived Itself as #2 to TikTok," *TechCrunch*, 31 January 2020, accessed 29 April 2020, https://techcrunch.com/2020/01/31/dubsmash-songs/?guccounter=1.

41. For instance, Dubsmashers frequently wear T-shirts and hoodies from Thrasher, Sauce Avenue, and Poppin Co. Wearing this clothing is yet another way for users to perform community identity.

42. Judith Hamera, *Dancing Communities: Performance, Difference, and Connection in the Global City* (New York: Palgrave Macmillan, 2007).

43. Hu, "Dubsmash," 2019.

CHAPTER 3

1. For more on the *Friday* film series, Brandon J. Manning, "And You Know This, Man!": Love, Humor, and Masculinity in Friday," *Black Camera* 8, no. 2, (2017: 243–54; and Gail Hilson Woldu, *The Words and Music of Ice Cube* (Westport, CT: Praeger Publishers, 2008).

2. Born in 1997, Blueface's legal name is Johnathan Michael Porter.

3. Blueface's name is a riff off of the Crips, who are known for wearing blue. Coincidentally, the Crips are linked with *Friday*. When they were filming *Friday*, the Crips would watch the shoot every day. According to actor John Witherspoon, they would wear the iconic blue bandanas over their faces and even ask for the actors to take pictures with their kids. For more on *Friday*, see Kelley L. Carter, "After 20 Years, 'Friday' Is (Still) the Most Important Film Ever Made about the Hood," Buzzfeed News, 20 April 2015, accessed 4 May 2020, https://www.buzzfeednews.com/article/kelleylcarter/after-20-years-friday-is-still-the-most-important-film-ever.

4. Blueface's "Holy Moly" is indicative of Zoomer rap for the ways that he blends traditional rap themes with Zoomer culture. For instance, the song references the Disney show *The Suite Life of Zack & Cody* to further its point about gang life: "Twin Glocks names Zack and Cody (holy moly) / Party pooper like Mr. Moseby (Ooh)."

5. Blueface, "Holy Moly," 2019.

6. This was D1 Nayah's profile description as of April 13, 2020, https://vm.tiktok.com/nvB41x.

7. To address the issue of dancer credits, D1 Nayah made a series of TikToks in April 2020 in which she used the green screen video effect to show her doing the original dances on Dubsmash while she pointed to herself and danced with herself. These videos are classic D1 Nayah. They are funny, show off her incomparable dance skills, and are filled with pointed commentary about values.

8. "Bye, Felicia" became a popular meme in 2014 and remains a popular saying. The quote comes from a scene in *Friday* in which Craig dismisses the neighborhood beggar who wants to borrow Smokey's car. Ice Cube's delivery of those two

words demonstrates the comedic power of the film series and its ability to stay relevant nearly three decades after its debut.

9. For more on the origins of hip hop, see David Toop, *The Rap Attack: African Jive to New York Hip-Hop* (London: South End Press, 1985); Dick Hebdige, *Cut 'n' Mix: Culture, Identity, and Caribbean Music* (London: Routledge, 1987); Tricia Rose, *Black Noise: Rap Music and Black Culture in Contemporary America* (Middletown, CT: Wesleyan University Press, 1994); S. H. Fernando Jr., *The New Beats: Exploring Music, Culture, and Attitudes of Hip-Hop* (Edinburgh: Payback Press, 1995); Alex Ogg and David Upshal, *The Hip Hop Years: A History of Rap* (New York: Fromm International, 2001); Murray Forman, *The 'Hood Comes First: Race, Space, and Place in Rap and Hip-Hop* (Middletown, CT: Wesleyan University Press, 2002); Jeff Chang, *Can't Stop Won't Stop: A History of the Hip-Hop Generation* (New York: St. Martin's Press, 2007); and Patricia Herrera, *Nuyorican Feminist Performance: From the Café to Hip Hop Theater* (Ann Arbor: University of Michigan Press, 2020).

10. Emmett George Price III, *Hip Hop Culture* (Santa Barbara, CA: ABC-CLIO, 2006), xi, 1.

11. Marcyliena Morgan, "'Nuthin' but a G Thang': Grammar and Language Ideology in Hip Hop Identity," in *It's the Joint! The Hip Hop Studies Reader*, eds. Murray Forman and Mark Anthony Neal (New York: Routledge, 2004), 187.

12. Joseph G. Schloss, *Foundation: B-boys, B-girls and Hip-Hop Culture in New York* (New York: Oxford University Press, 2009), 45.

13. In 2016, political activist Ronald Savage accused Afrika Bambaataa of molesting him in 1980. Following these allegations of sexual assault, three other men accused Bambaataa of similar acts. While Bambaataa denied any wrongdoing, he resigned from the Universal Zulu Nation, which also disassociated themselves from him. Moreover, all leaders who worked to cover up the allegations were removed from their roles within the organization. Although there are multiple allegations and testimonies that speak to decades of abuse at the hands of Bambaataa, to date he has not been prosecuted for these crimes due to the statute of limitations in New York State, which require that the actions for civil damages must be dealt with within five years of the acts. Accordingly, Bambaataa will likely not be charged with any crimes even if these allegations are widely accepted as the truth.

14. For a comprehensive overview of b-boying, see Schloss, *Foundation*.

15. Gwendolyn D. Pough, "Seeds and Legacies: Tapping the Potential in Hip-Hop," in *It's the Joint! The Hip Hop Studies Reader*, eds. Murray Forman and Mark Anthony Neal (New York: Routledge, 2004), 284.

16. Afrika Bambaataa and James Brown, "Unity (Pt. 1—The Third Coming)," recorded 1984.

17. Richard L. Schur, *Parodies of Ownership: Hip-Hop Aesthetics and Intellectual Property* (Ann Arbor: University of Michigan Press, 2009), 178.

18. Anthea Kraut, *Choreographing Copyright: Race, Gender, and Intellectual Property Rights in American Dance* (New York: Oxford University Press, 2015), 1.

19. Bench, *Perpetual Motion*, 140.

20. Taylor Lorenz, "The Original Renegade," *New York Times*, 13 February 2020, accessed 4 May 2020, https://www.nytimes.com/2020/02/13/style/the-original-renegade.html.

21. John Lorinc, "Your Kids, The Influencers," *Corporate Knights* 14, no. 2 (2015): 50–53.

22. While there is no set rate for paid sponsorship deals on Instagram, there are various Instagram influencer calculators that factor in a particular user's follower count with their engagement rate to give a price range. For example, according to Influencer Marketing Hub, Jalaiah Harmon can command between $1,900 and $3,200 for a single Instagram post given her follower count of 643,911 and engagement rate of 6.44 percent (as of August 2020). These numbers are not set in stone; rather, they offer a place to begin negotiating. Sometimes the client has the money and sometimes they don't. Moreover, they do not factor in other social media platforms such as TikTok, Dubsmash, and Twitter where Harmon can cross-post the content she creates for the promotional deal. That is, she can likely negotiate for a higher rate given her high follower count across these multiple platforms. It is worth noting that the only social media site that actually pays content creators is YouTube. On YouTube, once a user has over 10,000 subscribers, they can begin to make money through ads, which can be extremely lucrative for people with high subscriber counts such as Brooklyn Queen, who has over 1 million subscribers on the platform.

23. Kraut, *Choreographing Copyright*, x.

24. Kraut, *Choreographing Copyright*, xiiv–xiv.

25. M. Elizabeth Blair, "Commercialization of the Rap Music Youth Subculture," in *It's the Joint! The Hip Hop Studies Reader*, eds. Murray Forman and Mark Anthony Neal (New York: Routledge, 2004), 497.

26. Richard Peterson and David G. Berger, "Cycles in Symbol Production: The Case of Popular Music," *American Sociological Review* 40, no. 2 (April 1975): 262.

27. Rebecca Jennings, "On TikTok, Who Owns a Viral Dance?," Vox, 4 February 2020, accessed 4 May 2020, https://www.vox.com/the-goods/2020/2/4/21112444/renegade-tiktok-song-dance.

28. For more on the ways that algorithms work to further disenfranchise already marginalized communities, see Safiya Umoja Noble, *Algorithms of Oppression: How Search Engines Reinforce Racism* (New York: New York University Press, 2018); and Ruha Benjamin, *Race after Technology: Abolitionist Tools for the New Jim Code* (Boston: Polity Books, 2019).

29. Jennings, "On TikTok," 2020.

30. Schur, *Parodies of Ownership*, 35.

31. Schur, *Parodies of Ownership*, 176

32. United States Copyright Office, Copyright Registration of Choreography and Pantomime, Circular 52, https://www.copyright.gov/circs/circ52.pdf.

33. Kraut, *Choreographing Copyright*, xi.

34. Kraut, *Choreographing Copyright*, 167.

35. Austen Goslin, "Fresh Prince's Alfonso Ribeiro Suing Epic Games over Fortnite Carlton Dance Use," *Polygon*, 17 December 2018, accessed 5 May 2020, https://www.polygon.com/fortnite/2018/12/17/18145166/fortnite-carlton-dance-lawsuit-alfonso-ribeiro.

36. For more on copyright in the Fortnite community, see Nick Statt, "Fortnite Keeps Stealing Dances—and No One Knows If It's Legal," *The Verge*, 20 December 2018, accessed 5 May 2020, https://www.theverge.com/2018/12/20/18149869/fortnite-dance-emote-lawsuit-milly-rock-floss-carlton.

37. Jennings, "On TikTok," 2020.

38. Lorenz, "The Original Renegade," 2020.

39. Lorenz, "The Original Renegade," 2020.
40. Lorenz, "The Original Renegade," 2020.
41. *Bring It On*, directed by Peyton Reed (2000; Beacon Pictures; Universal Pictures).
42. For more on Miley Cyrus's use of twerking, see Kyra D. Gaunt, "YouTube, Twerking & You: Context Collapse and the Handheld Co-Presence of Black Girls and Miley Cyrus," *Journal of Popular Music Studies* 27, no. 3 (2015): 244–73; and Aria S. Halliday, "Miley, What's Good?: Nicki Minaj's Anaconda, Instagram Reproductions, and Viral Memetic Violence," *Girlhood Studies* 11, no. 3 (2018): 67–83.
43. Kyra D. Gaunt, *The Games Black Girls Play: Learning the Ropes from Double-Dutch to Hip-Hop* (New York: New York University Press, 2006), 94.
44. Barrie Segal (@barrrie), Instagram post, January 17, 2020, https://www.instagram.com/p/B7bi5I7DIMt/?igshid=ik185vlpwxfl.
45. TikTok Shaderoom (@tiktokroom), Instagram post, January 18, 2020, https://www.instagram.com/p/B7eQbbFnuEK/.
46. Gaunt, *The Games Black Girls Play*, 94.
47. @tiktokroom, Instagram post, January 18, 2020, https://www.instagram.com/p/B7eZgZvHBRM/.
48. Jewel Wicker, "Renegade Creator Jalaiah Harmon on Reclaiming the Viral Dance," *Teen Vogue*, 15 April 2020, accessed 5 May 2020, https://www.teenvogue.com/story/jalaiah-harmon-renegade-creator-viral-dance.
49. Jennings, "On TikTok," 2020.
50. Jennings, "On TikTok," 2020.
51. Darlene Aderoju, "How Megan Thee Stallion Learned Her 'Savage Challenge' TikTok Dance While Social Distancing," *People*, 23 April 2020, accessed 5 May 2020, https://people.com/music/megan-thee-stallion-savage-challenge-tik-tok/.
52. For more on Megan Thee Stallion, her Hotties, and the #SavageChallenge, see Kyesha Jennings.
53. Kyesha Jennings, "City Girls, Hot Girls and the Re-imagining of Black Women in Hip Hop and Digital Spaces," *Global Hip Hop* 1, no. 1 (2020): 58.
54. Lorenz, "The Original Renegade," 2020.
55. Zito Madu, "The NBA invited Jalaiah Harmon to perform 'Renegade' and showed how to address appropriation," SB Nation, 17 February 2020, accessed 5 May 2020, https://www.sbnation.com/nba/2020/2/17/21141239/renegade-dance-nba-all-star-game-jalaiah-harmon-cultural-appropriation.
56. Madu, "The NBA," 2020.
57. Kyra D. Gaunt, *The Games Black Girls Play*, 94.
58. See Todd Boyd, *Young Black Rich and Famous: The Rise of the NBA, the Hip Hop Invasion, and the Transformation of American Culture* (Lincoln, NE: Bison Books, 2008).
59. Todd Boyd, *The New H.N.I.C.: The Death of Civil Rights and the Reign of Hip Hop* (New York: New York University Press, 2002), 23.
60. Obama, Michelle (@michelleobama), "Jalaiah, you crushed it—love seeing your talent shine!", Twitter, 19 Feb. 2020, 8:55 am, https://twitter.com/MichelleObama/status/1230143930664136706?s=20.
61. Jalaiah Harmon (@jalaiahharmon). "Like we hit the lottery 🆙🎶🤞 @addisonre @charlidamelio," TikTok, 16 February 2020, https://vm.tiktok.com/n7EwLX/.
62. Wicker, "Renegade Creator," 2020.

CHAPTER 4

1. Melissa Rohlin, "Watch LeBron James Dance with His Son in TikTok Video," *Sports Illustrated*, 4 February 2020, accessed 22 May 2020, https://www.si.com/nba/lakers/news/lebron-james-dances-with-his-son-in-tiktok-video.

2. Kobe Bryant (@kobebryant), "Continuing to move the game forward @ KingJames. Much respect my brother #33644," Twitter, 24 January 2020, 9:39pm, accessed 22 May 2020, https://twitter.com/kobebryant/status/1221276426164269056?s=20.

3. While TisaKorean's birth year places him on the tail end of the Millennial generation, since his audience base—and corresponding cultural impact—corresponds more with Generation Z, I analyze his work as part of a larger conversation about Zoomer hip hop aesthetics.

4. For instance, Kblast and Huncho Da Rockstar released their song "Get Loose" and a corresponding dance challenge—the Get Loose Challenge—that went viral. Moreover, TisaKorean's music proliferates on Triller, an app that is meant to be used as a vlogging space, but is also another app in the Renegades toolkit. Triller differs from Dubsmash and TikTok by allowing users to film multiple videos and then create edits that feature the videos overlapping with each other. The result feels more like a music video. For more on TisaKorean's music and dances, see Tosten Burk, "Rap Monthly: TisaKorean on His Dance Roots and Outliving the Woah," *Spin*, 10 October 2019, accessed 20 May 2020, https://www.spin.com/2019/10/tisakorean-interview-rap-monthly-dababy-hobo-johnson/.

5. TisaKorean, "The Mop," 2019.

6. TisaKorean, Genius Profile, 2019, https://genius.com/artists/Tisakorean.

7. TisaKorean, "The Mop," 2019

8. TisaKorean, Genius Profile, 2019.

9. Much of this success goes back to music video for "The Mop." The song's music video features the group quite literally mopping while dressed in custodian gear in addition to doing their version of mopping in two locations that have become a hallmark of their work—a playground and a gas station parking lot. In fact, gas station parking lots in the deep country suburbs of Houston have become key sites where TisaKorean and company claim space and perform identity. If you scroll through any of their social media accounts, you will see plenty of highly choreographed viral videos of them dancing at gas stations.

10. Huncho Da Rockstar, Genius Profile, 2019, https://genius.com/artists/Huncho-da-rockstar.

11. Sally Banes and John F. Szwed, "From 'Messin' Around' to 'Funky Western Civilization': The Rise and Fall of Dance Instruction Songs," in *Dancing Many Drums: Excavations in African American Dance*, ed. Thomas F. DeFrantz (University of Wisconsin Press, 2001), 170.

12. For an extensive list of dance instruction songs, see Sally Banes and John F. Szwed.

13. Danah Boyd, "Why Youth Heart Social Network Sites: The Role of Networked Publics in Teenage Social Life," in *Youth, Identity, and Social Media*, ed. David Buckingham (Cambridge, MA: MIT Press, 2008), 137.

14. I do not propose that artists today do not have to pay their dues or that they have an easier road to success. Rather, I believe that the chance to go viral changes everything. Moreover, the ability to build a following via a curated set of posts that are not always dedicated to music helps to create a loyal following that is not only interested in the music, but in the artist.

15. For more on impression management, see Erving Goffman, *The Presentation of Self in Everyday Life* (Edinburgh: University of Edinburgh Press, 1956); and Erving Goffman, *Behavior in Public Places* (New York: Free Press, 1963).
16. For more on identity performances, see Fred Davis, *Fashion, Culture, and Identity* (Chicago: University of Chicago Press, 1992).
17. Howard Gardner and Katie Davis, *The App Generation: How Today's Youth Navigate Identity, Intimacy, and Imagination in a Digital World* (New Haven, CT: Yale University Press, 2013).
18. Jenny Sundén, *Material Virtualities: Approaching Online Textual Embodiment* (New York: Peter Lang, 2003).
19. Sundén, *Material Virtualities*, 121.
20. Sundén, *Material Virtualities*, 121.
21. Danah Boyd, "Why Youth Heart Social Network Sites," 122.
22. For more on music subcultures, see Sarah Thornton, *Club Cultures: Music, Media, and Subcultural Capital* (Middletown, CT: Wesleyan University Press, 1996).
23. Clay Shirky, *Cognitive Surplus: Creativity and Generosity in a Creative Age* (New York: Penguin, 2011).
24. Gardner and Davis, *The App Generation*, 122.
25. Brooke Erin Duffy, *(Not) Getting Paid to Do What You Love: Gender, Social Media, and Aspirational Work* (New Haven, CT: Yale University Press, 2017).
26. Duffy, *(Not) Getting Paid*, 4.
27. Duffy, *(Not) Getting Paid*, 4.
28. Joseph G. Schloss, *Foundation: B-boys, B-girls and Hip-Hop Culture in New York* (New York: Oxford University Press, 2009), 45.
29. Schloss, *Foundation*, 45.
30. Cheryl L. Keyes, "Empowering Self, Making Choices, Creating Spaces: Black Female Identity via Rap Music Performance," in *It's the Joint! The Hip Hop Studies Reader*, eds. Murray Forman and Mark Anthony Neal (New York: Routledge, 2004), 265.
31. YAYOMG!, "Brooklyn Queen Talks Touring, Her Favorite Songs, and Using Her Influence for Good," 18 October 2018, accessed 6 May 2020, https://www.yayomg.com/brooklyn-queen-interview/.
32. Schloss, *Foundation*, 70.
33. Cheryl L. Keyes, "Empowering Self, Making Choices, Creating Spaces: Black Female Identity via Rap Music Performance," in *It's the Joint! The Hip Hop Studies Reader*, eds. Murray Forman and Mark Anthony Neal (New York: Routledge, 2004), 267.
34. Keyes, "Empowering Self," 267.
35. #brooklynxair was one of the challenges that formed #dsxquarantine. For more on #dsxquarantine, see chapter 2.
36. For more on how Black women have strategically used embodiment as a form of identity-making, see Tracy Curtis, *New Media in Black Women's Autobiography: Intrepid Embodiment and Narrative Innovation* (New York: Palgrave Macmillan, 2015). Curtis explores how new media factors into the making of autobiography by Black women in the United States since 1980 such as Audre Lorde, Jill Nelson, and Janet Jackson.
37. For more on embodiment and performance, see Diana Taylor, *The Archive and Repertoire: Performing Cultural Memory in the Americas* (Durham, NC: Duke University Press, 2003); Susan Leigh Foster, *Choreographing Empathy: Kinesthesia in Performance* (London: Routledge, 2010); Mark Franko, *The Work of Dance: Labor, Movement, and Identity in the 1930s* (Middletown, CT: Wesleyan

University Press, 2002); Anthea Kraut, *Choreographing Copyright: Race, Gender, and Intellectual Property Rights in American Dance* (Oxford: Oxford University Press, 2017); and Carrie Noland, *Agency and Embodiment: Performing Gestures/ Producing Culture* (Cambridge, MA: Harvard University Press, 2009).

38. Taylor, *The Archive and Repertoire*, 46.
39. See Susan Foster, *Choreographing Empathy*.
40. Phoebe Rumsey, Embodied Nostalgia: Early Twentieth Century Social Dance and US Musical Theatre" (PhD. diss., CUNY Graduate Center, 2019).
41. Kayla Nicole Jones, personal website, accessed 22 May 2020, iamkaylanicole.com.
42. Kayla Nicole Jones, personal website.
43. Regina Bradley, "Awkwardly Hysterical: Theorizing Black Girl Awkwardness and Humor in Social Media," *Comedy Studies* 6, no. 2 (2018): 149.
44. While Kayla Nicole Jones and Brooklyn Queen are both verified on all their social media platforms, the lack of media coverage of Zoomer artists is a major contributing factor to how difficult it is for an artist who is primarily known as a dancer to get verified on Instagram, for instance. I detailed in chapter 3 how this somewhat changed after Jalaiah Harmon rewrote the narrative, but it remains difficult to be verified without a digital footprint beyond the app.
45. For more on the "Looking Up and Down" meme, see Jayley Soen, "This is what the girl from *that* meme is like in real life," *The Tab*, 26 August 2019, accessed 21 May 2020, https://thetab.com/uk/2019/09/26/kayla-nicole-jones-meme-126839; and "Nicole TV Looking Up and Down," Know Your Meme, 23 September 2019, accessed 21 May 2020, https://knowyourmeme.com/memes/nicole-tv-looking-up-and-down.
46. Kyra D. Gaunt, "YouTube, Twerking & You: Context Collapse and the Handheld Co-Presence of Black Girls and Miley Cyrus," *Journal of Popular Music Studies* 27, no. 3 (2015): 244–73.
47. Barbara Cohen-Statyner, "A Thousand Raggy, Draggy Dances: Social Dance in Broadway Musical Comedy in the 1920s," in *Ballroom, Boogie, Shimmy Sham, Shake: A Social and Popular Dance Reader*, ed. Julie Malnig (Chicago: University of Illinois Press, 2009), 218.
48. Kayla Nicole Jones, "Move Like a Snake," 2019.
49. The Wicker Twinz is an Atlanta-based rap duo comprising twin sisters Yoni and Solai. Born in 2005, the duo's Instagram account has 1.9 million followers and regularly features an assortment of content, including their music and Dubs.
50. Throughout the video, the principal spies on Jones and her students. Once the last bell rings and school is out for the day, the principal dances to the song, admitting that it's catchy and he likes it. But this is something that he can never admit as to acknowledge it would be to relinquish his own power at the school.
51. Jonathan Miller, *Subsequent Productions* (New York: Viking Adult, 1986), 1.
52. I do not mean to undermine D'Amelio's talent. I merely want to draw attention to how race factors into virality. While at times Virality is random, it is also wrapped up in race. D'Amelio going viral is not random, in other words; it is the result of her Whiteness (and how Whiteness plays out differently on TikTok than Dubsmash).
53. Gaunt, "YouTube, Twerking & You," 253.

CHAPTER 5

1. Bellaire High School is a four-year Title I comprehensive public high school in the Houston Independent School District. The school's 2019–2020 enrollment

of 3,456 students is one of the most racial and ethnically diverse in the state of Texas (Latinx 41%, White 24%, Black 20%, Asian 13%, Other 2%). Like many large public schools in urban areas, Bellaire HS's demographics feature a gaping disparity between students enrolled in AP courses compared to academic level courses. As such, my academic Spanish classes feature a higher percentage of Black students than the percentage at the school at large.

2. Juan Flores, *From Bomba to Hip-Hop: Puerto Rican Culture and Latino Identity* (New York: Columbia University Press, 2000), 193.

3. For more on how compliance works in education, see Paolo Freire, *Pedagogy of the Oppressed* (New York: Continuum, 2000); and Christopher Emdin, *For White Folks Who Teach in the Hood . . . and the Rest of Y'all Too: Reality Pedagogy and Urban Education* (Boston: Beacon Press, 2016).

4. For more on my students and my experience going viral and the impact that had on my classroom, see Trevor Boffone, "An Unconventional Approach to Culturally Responsive Pedagogy," Edutopia, 10 March 2020, accessed 22 May 2020, https://www.edutopia.org/article/unconventional-approach-culturally-responsive-pedagogy; Christina Calloway, "Houston Teacher and His Students Continue to Go Viral after Posting Their Classroom Dances," The Shade Room, 10 January 2020, accessed 22 May 2020, https://theshaderoom.com/houston-teacher-and-his-students-continue-to-go-viral-after-posting-their-classroom-dances/; Localish, "This Teacher Dances with His Students to Motivate Them in Class!," ABC, 17 January 2020, accessed 22 May 2020, https://abc.com/shows/all-good/episode-guide/season-01/150-this-teacher-dances-with-his-students-to-motivate-them-in-class; and Susie Tommaney, "HISD Spanish Teacher Dubsmashes the Internet through Dance," *Houston Press*, 3 June 2019, accessed 22 May 2020, https://www.houstonpress.com/arts/bellaire-high-school-teacher-connects-with-students-one-dubsmash-at-a-time-11296065.

5. Gloria Ladson-Billings, "Toward a Theory of Culturally Relevant Pedagogy," *American Educational Research Journal* 32, no. 3 (Autumn 1995): 465–91.

6. Nyama McCarthy-Brown, "The Need for Culturally Relevant Teaching in Dance Education," *Journal of Dance Education* 9, no. 4 (2009): 121.

7. Emdin, *For White Folks Who Teach in the Hood*. Even though the #HipHopEd movement started as a weekly Twitter chat in 2010, there is already a wealth of scholarship that examines its uses in K-12 education. For more, see Christopher Emdin and Edmund Adjapong, eds., *#HipHopEd: The Compilation on Hip-hop Education* (Leiden: Brill/Sense, 2018); Jason Rawls and John Robinson, eds., *Youth Culture Power: A #HipHopEd Guide to Building Teacher-Student Relationships and Increasing Student Engagement* (New York: Peter Lang, 2019); Thurman Bridges, "Towards a Pedagogy of HipHop in Urban Teacher Education," *The Journal of Negro Education* 80, no. 3 (Summer 2011): 325–38; Emery Petchauer, "Starting with Style: Toward a Second Wave of Hip-Hop Education Research and Practice," *Urban Education* 50, no. 1 (2015): 78–105; A. A. Akom, "Critical Hip Hop Pedagogy as a Form of Liberatory Praxis," *Equity & Excellence in Education* 42, no. 1 (2009): 52–66; and Daudi Abe, "Hip-Hop and the Academic Canon," *Education, Citizenship, and Social Justice* 4, no. 3 (2009): 263–72. Moreover, hip hop pedagogy is not unique to the #HipHopEd movement. For representative examples, see Ruth Nicole Brown, *Black Girlhood Celebration: Toward a Hip-Hop Feminist Pedagogy* (New York: Peter Lang, 2009); and Ashleigh Wade, "When Social Media Yields More than 'Likes': Black Girls' Digital Kinship Formations," *Women, Gender, and Families of Color* 7, no. 1 (2019): 80–97.

8. Emdin, *For White Folks*, 27.

9. Emdin, *For White Folks*, 27.
10. Emdin, *For White Folks*, 13.
11. Kirsten Drotner, "Leisure Is Hard Work: Digital Practices and Future Competences," in *Youth, Identity, and Social Media*, ed. David Buckingham (Cambridge, MA: MIT Press, 2008), 187.
12. Emdin, *For White Folks*, 13.
13. Gaunt, *The Games Black Girls Play: Learning the Ropes from Double-Dutch to Hip-Hop* (New York: New York University Press, 2006), 2.
14. Aria S. Halliday, "Twerk Sumn!: Theorizing Black Girl Epistemology in the Body," *Cultural Studies* (2020): 6.
15. Halliday, "Terk Sumn!" 7.
16. For more on the role and importance of digital spaces for Black women, see Moya Bailey and Alexis Pauline Gumbs, "We Are the Ones We've Been Waiting For," *Ms.* 20, no. 1 (2010): 41–42; Sarah Florini, "Tweets, Tweeps, and Signifying': Communication and Cultural Performance on 'Black Twitter,'" *Television & New Media* 15, no. 3 (2014): 223–37; and Kelly Macias, "Tweeting Away Our Blues: An Interpretive Phenomenological Approach to Exploring Black Women's Use of Social Media to Combat Misogynoir" (PhD diss., Nova Southeastern University, 2015).
17. Gaunt, *The Games Black Girls Play*, 38.
18. For more on Black girls and the US educational system, see Monique W. Morris, *Pushout: The Criminalization of Black Girls in Schools* (New York: The New Press, 2016); Ruth Nicole Brown, *Black Girlhood Celebration: Toward a Hip-Hop Feminist Pedagogy* (New York: Peter Lang, 2009); and Leah A. Hill, "Disturbing Disparities: Black Girls and the School-to-Prison Pipeline, *Fordham Law Review Online* 87, art. 11 (2018): 58–63.
19. Gaunt, *The Games Black Girls Play*, 5
20. Adrienne Oehlers, "In Sync/On Stage: 'One Singular Sensation,'" August 9, 2020, Association for Theatre in Higher Education Annual Conference, Orlando, FL. This work is also in conversation with Kellee Van Aken's scholarship on race and gender in Broadway chorus lines.
21. William Hardy McNeill, *Keeping Together in Time: Dance and Drill in Human History* (Cambridge, MA: Harvard University Press, 1995).
22. McNeill, *Keeping Together in Time*, 2.
23. McNeill, *Keeping Together in Time*, 2–3.
24. This also ties into psychologist Mihály Csíkszentmihályi's notion of "flow," or the feeling of being completely immersed in an activity.
25. A. R. Radcliffe-Brown, *The Andaman Islanders* (Cambridge, UK: Cambridge University Press, 2013), 252.
26. Radcliffe-Brown, *The Andaman Islanders*, 252.
27. Gaunt, *The Games Black Girls Play*, 8.
28. Gaunt, *The Games Black Girls Play*, 53.
29. For more on the various forms of kinship, see Margaret K. Nelson, "Fictive Kin, Families We Choose, and Voluntary Kin: What Does the Discourse Tell Us?," *Journal of Family Theory and Review* 5, no. 3 (2013): 259–81.
30. Wade, "When Social Media," 81.
31. Wade, "When Social Media," 81.
32. For more on the ways that Black girls have been marginalized at school, see Morris, *Pushout*; Emdin, *For White Folks*; and Ijeoma Oluo, *So You Want to Talk about Race* (New York: Seal Press, 2018).

33. Part of crediting my students is also correcting false narratives that the media potentially harbors. For instance, when *Good Morning America* called me, they invited me to be on the show, but I insisted that my students and I were a package deal. It was all or nothing. One day later, Talia, Takia, and I were performing live on *Good Morning America*.
34. Debbie A. Simmonds-Barber, in discussion with the author, March 2020.
35. Simmonds-Barber, in discussion with the author, March 2020.
36. Meghann Hogan, in discussion with the author, March 2020.

CHAPTER 6

1. Once the name stuck, I routinely tried to push against it during interviews, but the media continued despite my requests to not co-opt the name of a Black woman to describe the work I was doing.
2. By focusing on Black and White listeners, I do not mean to reinforce the Black/White racial binary. Rather, these are the racial identities of the individuals in question as it relates to this chapter's topic. Moreover, I would like to acknowledge that both Blackness and Whiteness can include biracial people as well as the Latinx community.
3. For more on the hidden curriculum, see Philip W. Jackson, *Life in Classrooms* (New York: Teachers College Press, 1990); and Benson R. Snyder, *The Hidden Curriculum* (Cambridge, MA: MIT Press, 1973).
4. Christopher Emdin, *For White Folks Who Teach in the Hood . . . and the Rest of Y'all Too: Reality Pedagogy and Urban Education* (Boston: Beacon Press, 2016), 177.
5. For more on how charter schools seek to replicate elite prep schools, see Emdin, *For White Folks*, 175–83.
6. For more on this subject, see Emdin, *For White Folks*.
7. Jennifer Lynn Stoever, *The Sonic Color Line: Race and the Cultural Politics of Listening* (New York: New York University Press, 2016), 2.
8. Stoever, *The Sonic Color Line*, 7.
9. Stoever, *The Sonic Color Line*, 4.
10. Stoever, *The Sonic Color Line*, 1.
11. Emdin, *For White Folks*, 9.
12. Emdin, *For White Folks*, xx.
13. Monique Morris, *Pushout: The Criminalization of Black Girls in Schools* (New York: The New Press, 2016), 3.
14. "Karen" is a slang term for a White woman who is unaware of her privilege and prejudice and who feels entitled to call the force of the state to suit her needs. Karen became popularized in 2019 and, especially, 2020 following the murder of George Floyd and the subsequent movement for Black lives.
15. Stoever, *The Sonic Color Line*, 2.
16. Zuleyka Zevallos, "Tone Policing People of Colour," *The Other Sociologist*, 17 June 2017, accessed 14 May 2020, https://othersociologist.com/2017/06/17/tone-policing-people-of-colour/.
17. Morris, *Pushout*, 4.
18. Ashleigh Wade, "When Social Media Yields More than 'Likes': Black Girls' Digital Kinship Formations," *Women, Gender, and Families of Color* 7, no. 1 (2019): 80–97.
19. Jess McHugh, "Policing Language Is Just Another Way to Silence Women," *Dame Magazine*, 6 Aug. 2018, accessed 14 May 2020, https://www.damemagazine.com/2018/08/06/policing-language-is-just-another-way-to-silence-women/.
20. McHugh, "Policing Language."

21. For more on anti-racist practices, see Ibram X. Kendi, *How to Be Anti-Racist* (New York: One World, 2019).

22. Tori Williams Douglass, "Stop Policing My Language," Tori Williams Douglass Personal Website, 28 February 2019, accessed 14 May 2020, https://www.toriglass.com/my-writing/2019/2/28/stop-policing-my-language.

23. For more on the power of swearing, see Emma Byrne, *Swearing Is Good for You: The Amazing Science of Bad Language* (New York: W. W. Norton, 2018).

24. Emdin, *For White Folks*, 175.

25. Audre Lorde, "The Master's Tools Will Never Dismantle the Master's House," in *Sister Outsider: Essays and Speeches* (Berkeley, CA: Crossing Press, 1984), 110–14.

26. Emdin, *For White Folks*, 11.

27. Marcyliena Morgan, "'Nuthin' but a G Thang': Grammar and Language Ideology in Hip Hop Identity," in *Sociocultural and Historical Contexts of African American English*, ed. Sonja L. Lanehart (Philadelphia: John Benjamins, 2001), 190.

28. Morgan, "'Nuthin' but a G Thang,'" 205.

29. Emdin, *For White Folks*, 11.

30. Byrne, *Swearing Is Good for You*.

31. Emma Byrne, "There's a Swearing Double Standard—And Women Can Change It," *Elle*, 21 March 2018, accessed 11 May 2020, https://www.elle.com/life-love/a19431418/swearing-double-standard/.

32. Byrne, "There's a Swearing Double Standard."

33. Emdin, *For White Folks*, 15.

34. Emdin, *For White Folks*, 7.

35. Emdin, *For White Folks*, 176.

36. For more on *Roth vs. United States*, see https://definitions.uslegal.com/c/contemporary-community-standards/.

OUTRO

1. Sims, Rian (@rianmicheyl). "All lives won't matter until black lives matter!" Instagram, 2 June 2020, https://www.instagram.com/p/CA9XULGAbVb/?igshid=14bq830fp6avq.

2. Mihir Zaveri, "'I Need People to Hear My Voice': Teens Protest Racism," *New York Times*, 23 June 2020, https://www.nytimes.com/2020/06/23/us/teens-protest-black-lives-matter.html.

3. Zaveri, "I Need People," 2020.

4. Harmon, Jalaiah (@jalaiah). "We are BLACK WOMEN! . . . . We have a VOICE . . . . . . We don't tear down other BLACK WOMEN! . . . . . . we have felt the pain of NOT BEING HEARD and we have decided we will deliberate about building others! . . . All too often, we women find it easier to criticize each other, instead of building each other up. With all the negativity going around let's do something positive!! Upload one picture of yourself. . . . ONLY you. Then tag as many sisters to do the same. Let's build ourselves up, instead of tearing ourselves down." Instagram, 3 June 2020, https://www.instagram.com/p/CA_2ouLDIQC/?igshid=1v4alj4us4qo.

5. Beyoncé famously did this during the 2016 Super Bowl halftime show in which she was joined by hundreds of Black women dressed in the Black Panther style, getting in formation at the onset of what would become a tumultuous period in US history in the leadup and subsequent election of Donald Trump.

SELECTED BIBLIOGRAPHY

Abril, Danielle. "Meet Dubsmash, the Video Service Stealing Some of TikTok's Thunder." *Fortune*, 14 July 2020. https://fortune.com/2020/07/14/what-is-dubsmash-tiktok-security-concerns-bans/.

Aniftos, Rania. "How 2018 Became the Year of the Dance Challenge." *Billboard*, 28 August 2018. https://www.billboard.com/articles/news/8472717/2018-year-of-the-dance-challenge.

Anzaldúa, Gloria. *Borderlands/La Frontera: The New Mestiza*. San Francisco: Aunt Lute, 1987.

Anzaldúa, Gloria. "La Prieta." In *This Bridge Called My Back: Writings by Radical Women of Color*, edited by Cherríe Moraga and Gloria Anzaldúa, 198–209. New York: Kitchen Table, Women of Color Press, 1983.

Ards, Angela. "Organizing the Hip-Hop Generation." In *It's the Joint! The Hip Hop Studies Reader*, edited by Murray Forman and Mark Anthony Neal, 311–23. New York: Routledge, 2004.

Banes, Sally. "Breaking." In *It's the Joint! The Hip Hop Studies Reader*, edited by Murray Forman and Mark Anthony Neal, 13–20. New York: Routledge, 2004.

Banes, Sally, and John F. Szwed. "'From 'Messin' Around' to 'Funky Western Civilization': The Rise and Fall of Dance Instruction Songs." In *Dancing Many Drums: Excavations in African American Dance*, edited by Thomas F. DeFrantz, 169–203. Madison: University of Wisconsin Press, 2001.

Batiste, Stephanie Leigh. "Introduction: Black Performance II: Knowing and Being." *The Black Scholar: Journal of Black Studies and Research* 49, no. 4 (2019): 1–5.

Baym, Nancy K. *Personal Connections in the Digital Age*. Cambridge, MA: Polity Press, 2010.

Bench, Harmony. *Perpetual Motion: Dance, Digital Cultures, and the Common*. Minneapolis: University of Minnesota Press, 2020.

Benjamin, Ruha. *Race after Technology: Abolitionist Tools for the New Jim Code*. Cambridge, MA: Polity Press, 2019.

Biddle, Sam, Paulo Victor Ribeiro, and Tatiana Dias. "Invisible Censorship." *The Intercept*, 16 March 2020. https://theintercept.com/2020/03/16/tiktok-app-moderators-users-discrimination/.

Blair, M. Elizabeth. "Commercialization of the Rap Music Youth Subculture." In *It's the Joint! The Hip Hop Studies Reader*, edited by Murray Forman and Mark Anthony Neal, 497–504. New York: Routledge, 2004.

Boyd, Danah M. *It's Complicated: The Social Lives of Networked Teens*. New Haven, CT: Yale University Press, 2014.

Boyd, Danah M. "Why Youth Heart Social Network Sites: The Role of Networked
    Publics in Teenage Social Life." In *Youth, Identity, and Digital Media*, edited by
    David Buckingham, 119–142. Cambridge, MA: MIT Press, 2008.
Boyd, Todd. "Check Yo Self before You Wreck Yo Self: The Death of Politics in
    Rap Music and Popular Culture." In *It's the Joint! The Hip Hop Studies
    Reader*, edited by Murray Forman and Mark Anthony Neal, 325–340.
    New York: Routledge, 2004.
Bradley, Regina. "Awkwardly Hysterical: Theorizing Black Girl Awkwardness and
    Humor in Social Media." *Comedy Studies* 6, no. 2 (2018): 148–53.
Brock, André, Jr. *Distributed Blackness: African American Cybercultures*.
    New York: New York University Press, 2020.
Brown, Jayna. *Babylon Girls: Black Women Performers and the Shaping of the Modern*.
    Durham, NC: Duke University Press, 2008.
Butler, Judith. *Bodies That Matter: On the Discursive Limits of Sex*.
    New York: Routledge, 1993.
Butler, Judith. *Gender Trouble*. New York: Routledge, 1990.
Byrne, Dara M. "Public Discourse, Community Concerns, and Civic
    Engagement: Exploring Black Social Networking Traditions on BlackPlanet.
    com." *Journal of Computer-Mediated Communication* 13, no. 1 (2007): 319–40.
Byrne, Emma. *Swearing Is Good for You: The Amazing Science of Bad Language*.
    New York: W. W. Norton, 2018.
Byrne, Emma. "There's a Swearing Double Standard—And Women Can Change It."
    Elle. 21 March 2018. https://www.elle.com/life-love/a19431418/swearing-
    double-standard/.
Caramanica, Jon. "How Hip-Hop Royalty Found a New Home on Instagram Live."
    New York Times. 7 May 2020. https://www.nytimes.com/2020/05/07/arts/
    music/hip-hop-instagram-coronavirus.html.
Chan, Stephanie. "Installs of India's Top TikTok Alternatives Grew 155% Following
    Its Ban There." *Sensor Tower*. 23 July 2020. https://sensortower.com/blog/
    tiktok-alternatives-growth-india.
Chow, Andrew R. "Lil Nas X Talks 'Old Town Road' and the Billboard Controversy."
    Time. 5 April 2019. https://time.com/5561466/lil-nas-x-old-town-road-
    billboard/.
Clark, Bryan. "The Clueless Parent's Guide to Understanding TikTok." *The Next Web*.
    31 January 2019. https://thenextweb.com/socialmedia/2019/01/31/the-
    clueless-parents-guide-to-understanding-tiktok/.
Constine, Josh. "How Dubsmash Revived Itself as #2 to TikTok." *TechCrunch*. 31
    January 2020. https://techcrunch.com/2020/01/31/dubsmash-songs/
    ?guccounter=1.
Corts, Alicia. "(Un)limited: Virtual Performance Spaces and Identity." *Theatre
    Symposium* 24 (2016): 113–28.
Cox, Aimee Meredith. *Shapeshifters: Black Girls and the Choreography of Citizenship*.
    Durham, NC: Duke University Press, 2015.
Crowe, Nic, and Simon Bradford. "'Hanging Out in Runescape': Identity, Work
    and Leisure in the Virtual Playground." *Children's Geographies* 4, no. 3
    (2006): 331–46.
Dash, Suchit, Jonas Drüppel, and Tim Specht. "Dubsmash Was Dying.
    Now Users Watch 1 Billion Videos a Month." *Fast Company*.
    13 March 2020. https://www.fastcompany.com/90476906/
    dubsmash-was-dying-now-users-watch-1-billion-videos-a-month.

DeFrantz, Thomas F. "The Black Beat Made Visible: Hip Hop Dance and Body Power." In *Of the Presence of the Body: Essays on Dance and Performance Theory*, edited by André Lepecki, 64–81. Middletown, CT: Wesleyan University Press, 2004.

Drotner, Kirsten. "Leisure Is Hard Work: Digital Practices and Future Competences." In *Youth, Identity, and Digital Media*, edited by David Buckingham, 167–184. Cambridge, MA: MIT Press, 2008.

Dubsmash. "Dubsmash Teaser Q3," dubsmash.com, July 2020.

Duncan, Fiona. "A Bunch of People, from Professors to Diplo, Consider the Tiktok Craze." *Interview Magazine*. 23 April 2020. https://www.interviewmagazine.com/culture/tik-tok-fame-videos-diplo-content-spring.

Elassar, Alaa. "TikTokers Stand in Solidarity with Black Creators to Protest Censorship." CNN. 19 May 2020. https://www.cnn.com/2020/05/19/us/tiktok-black-lives-matter-trnd/index.html.

Ellison, Nicole B., and Danah M. Boyd. "Social Network Sites: Definition, History and Scholarship." *Journal of Computer-Mediated Communication* 13, no. 1 (2007): 210–30.

Ellison, Nicole B., and Danah M. Boyd. "Sociality through Social Network Sites." In *The Oxford Handbook of Internet Studies*, edited by William H. Dutton, 151–172. Oxford: Oxford University Press, 2013.

Flores, Juan. *From Bomba to Hip-Hop: Puerto Rican Culture and Latino Identity*. New York: Columbia University Press, 2000.

Florini, Sarah. "Enclaving and Cultural Resonance in Black *Game of Thrones* Fandom." In *Fans of Color, Fandoms of Color*, edited by Abigail De Kosnik and Andre Carrington, *Transformative Works and Cultures* 29 (2019), doi.org/10.3983/twc.2019.1498.

Foster, Susan Leigh. *Choreographing Empathy: Kinesthesia in Performance*. London: Routledge, 2010.

Franko, Mark. *The Work of Dance: Labor, Movement, and Identity in the 1930s*. Middletown, CT: Wesleyan University Press, 2002.

Fraser, Nancy. "Rethinking the Public Sphere: A Contribution to the Critique of Actually Existing Democracy." In *Habermas and the Public Sphere*, edited by Craig Calhoun, 109–142. Cambridge, MA: MIT Press 1992.

Frye, Marilyn. *The Politics of Reality: Essays in Feminist Theory*. Trumansburg, NY: Crossing Press. 1983.

Gardner, Howard, and Katie Davis. *The App Generation: How Today's Youth Navigate Identity, Intimacy, and Imagination in a Digital World*. New Haven, CT: Yale University Press, 2013.

Gaunt, Kyra D. *The Games Black Girls Play: Learning the Ropes from Double-Dutch to Hip-Hop*. New York: New York University Press, 2006.

Gaunt, Kyra D. "YouTube, Twerking & You: Context Collapse and the Handheld Co-Presence of Black Girls and Miley Cyrus." *Journal of Popular Music Studies* 27, no. 3 (2015): 244–73.

Grewal, Inderpal, and Caren Kaplan. *Scattered Hegemonies: Postmodernity and Transnational Feminist Practices*. Minneapolis: University of Minnesota Press, 1994.

Halliday, Aria S. "Twerk Sumn!: Theorizing Black Girl Epistemology in the Body." *Cultural Studies* (2020).

Hamera, Judith. *Dancing Communities: Performance, Difference, and Connection in the Global City*. New York: Palgrave Macmillan, 2007.

Halpern, Jake. *Fame Junkies: The Hidden Truths behind America's Favorite Addiction*. Boston: Houghton Mifflin, 2007.

Hazzard-Gordon, Katrina. "Dance in Hip-Hop Culture." In *It's the Joint! The Hip Hop Studies Reader*, edited by Murray Forman and Mark Anthony Neal, 505–16. New York: Routledge, 2004.

Hazzard-Donald, Katrina. *The Rise of Social Dance Formations in African-American Culture*. Philadelphia: Temple University Press, 1992.

Herrera, Patricia. *Nuyorican Feminist Performance: From the Café to Hip Hop Theater*. Ann Arbor: University of Michigan Press, 2020.

hooks, bell. *Feminism Is for Everybody: Passionate Politics*. Boston: South End Press, 2000.

hooks, bell. *The Will to Change: Men, Masculinity, and Love*. New York: Washington Square Press, 2004.

Hu, Cherie. "Dubsmash Is Far from Dead—But Can It Really Survive Its Second Life?" *Forbes*. 19 February 2019. https://www.forbes.com/sites/cheriehu/2019/02/19/dubsmash-is-far-from-dead-but-can-it-really-survive-its-second-life/#4a6b493c4961.

Jeffries, Michael P. *Thug Life: Race, Gender, and the Meaning of Hip-Hop*. Chicago: University of Chicago Press, 2010.

Jennings, Kyesha. "City Girls, Hot Girls and the Re-imagining of Black Women in Hip Hop and Digital Spaces." *Global Hip Hop* 1, no. 1 (2020): 47–70.

Jennings, Rebecca. "On TikTok, Who Owns a Viral Dance?" *Vox*. 4 February 2020. https://www.vox.com/the-goods/2020/2/4/21112444/renegade-tiktok-song-dance.

Johnson, Jasmine. "b.O.s. 6.4 / In My Feelings." *ASAP/Journal*. 13 August 2018. http://asapjournal.com/b-o-s-6-4-in-my-feelings-jasmine-elizabeth-johnson/.

Johnson, Jasmine. "The #OptimisticChallenge: Decisive Black Joy." In *Black Futures*, edited by Kimberly Drew and Jenna Wortham, 152–55. New York: One World, 2020.

Johnson, Jasmine Elizabeth. "A Politics of Tenderness: Camille A. Brown and Dancers' BLACK GIRL: Linguistic Play." *The Black Scholar: Journal of Black Studies and Research* 49, no. 4 (2019): 20–34.

Kelley, Robin D. G. *Race Rebels: Culture, Politics, and the Black Working Class*. New York: Free Press, 1996.

Kendi, Ibram X. *How to Be Anti-Racist*. New York: One World, 2019.

King, Ashley. "Dubsmash Is Back, and Focused Entirely on Dance Challenges." *Digital Music News*. 21 February 2019. https://www.digitalmusicnews.com/2019/02/21/dubsmash-is-back-and-focused-entirely-on-dance-challenges/.

Kraut, Anthea. *Choreographing Copyright: Race, Gender, and Intellectual Property Rights in American Dance*. Oxford: Oxford University Press, 2017.

Lange, Patricia G. *Kids on YouTube: Technical Identities and Digital Literacies*. Walnut Creek, CA: Left Cross Press, 2014.

Lorde, Audre. "The Master's Tools Will Never Dismantle the Master's House." In *Sister Outsider: Essays and Speeches*, 110–114. Berkeley, CA: Crossing Press, 1984.

Lorenz, Taylor. "Delayed Moves, Poolside Videos and Postmates Spon: The State of Tiktok Collab Houses." *New York Times*. 21 May 2020. https://www.nytimes.com/2020/05/21/style/tiktok-collab-houses-quarantine-coronavirus.html.

Lorenz, Taylor. "Hype House and the Los Angeles TikTok Mansion Gold Rush." *New York Times*. 3 January 2020. https://www.nytimes.com/2020/01/03/style/hype-house-los-angeles-tik-tok.html.

Lorenz, Taylor. "The Original Renegade." *New York Times*. 13 February 2020. https://www.nytimes.com/2020/02/13/style/the-original-renegade.html.

Lugones, María. *Pilgrimages/Peregrinajes: Theorizing Coalition against Multiple Oppressions*. New York: Rowman & Littlefield Publishers, 2003.

Malnig, Julie, ed. *Ballroom, Boogie, Shimmy Sham, Shake: A Social and Popular Dance Reader*. Chicago: University of Illinois Press, 2009.

Martin, Florence, Chuang Wang, Teresa Petty, Weichao Wang, and Patti Willkins. "Middle School Students' Social Media Use." *Journal of Educational Technology & Society* 21, no. 1 (2018): 213–24.

McCarthy-Brown, Nyama. "The Need for Culturally Relevant Dance Education." *Journal of Dance Education* 9, no. 40 (2009): 120–25.

McHugh, Jess. "Policing Language Is Just Another Way to Silence Women." *Dame Magazine*. 6 August 2018. https://www.damemagazine.com/2018/08/06/policing-language-is-just-another-way-to-silence-women/.

Megele, Claudia. *Safeguarding Children and Young People Online: A Guide for Busy Practitioners*. Chicago: University of Chicago Press, 2016.

Miller, Jonathan. *Subsequent Productions*. New York: Viking Adult, 1986.

Minh-ha, Trinh T. "Not You/Like You: Post-Colonial Women and the Interlocking Questions of Identity and Difference." Center for Cultural Studies, University of California Santa Cruz. Inscriptions volume 3–4. 1988. Accessed 27 April 2020. https://culturalstudies.ucsc.edu/inscriptions/volume-34/trinh-t-minh-ha/.

Mitra, Jay. *Entrepreneurship, Innovation and Regional Development: An Introduction*. New York: Routledge, 2019.

Moraga, Cherríe. *A Xicana Codex of Changing Consciousness: Writings, 2000–2010*. Durham, NC: Duke University Press, 2011.

Moraga, Cherríe. "Preface." In *This Bridge Called My Back: Writings by Radical Women of Color*, edited by Gloria Anzaldúa and Cherríe Moraga, xii–xix. San Francisco: Kitchen Table Press, 1984.

Moreno, Javier, and Pablo Valdivia, "Meet Adam Martinez, the Guy behind Everyone's Viral Fave Rosa." *Buzzfeed*. 14 February 2020. https://www.buzzfeed.com/pablovaldivia/rosa-tiktok-adam-rodriguez.

Morgan, Marcyliena. "'Nuthin' but a G Thang': Grammar and Language Ideology in Hip Hop Identity." In *Sociocultural and Historical Contexts of African American English*, edited by Sonja L. Lanehart, 187–209. Amsterdam: John Benjamins Publishing, 2001.

Mosley, Della, Roberto Abreu, Ashley Ruderman and Candice Crowell. "Hashtags and Hip-Hop: Exploring the Online Performances of Hip-Hop Identified Youth Using Instagram." *Feminist Media Studies* 17, no. 2 (2017): 135–52.

Muñoz, José Esteban. *Cruising Utopia: The Then and There of Queer Futurity*. New York: New York University Press, 2009.

Muñoz, José Esteban. *Disidentifications: Queers of Color and the Performance of Politics*. Minneapolis: University of Minnesota Press, 1999.

Music Ally. "How K Camp's 'Lottery' (aka 'Renegade') Went Viral—and What Happened Next." *Music Ally*. 9 March 2020. https://musically.com/2020/03/09/k-camp-lottery-renegade-viral/.

Noble, Safiya Umoja. *Algorithms of Oppression: How Search Engines Reinforce Racism*. New York: New York University Press, 2018.

Noland, Carrie. *Agency and Embodiment: Performing Gestures/Producing Culture*. Cambridge, MA: Harvard University Press, 2009.

Patel, Sahil. "Hearst Now Has Both Seventeen and Cosmo on Up-and-Coming App Musical.ly." *Digiday*. 7 March 2018. https://digiday.com/media/seventeen-hearst-brings-cosmopolitan-musical-ly/.

Peiss, Kathy. *Cheap Amusements, Working Women, and Leisure in Turn-of-the-Century New York*. Philadelphia: Temple University Press, 1996.

Perry, Imani. *Prophets of the Hood: Politics and Poetics in Hip Hop*. Durham, NC: Duke University Press, 2004.

Pough, Gwendolyn D. *Check It While I Wreck It: Black Womanhood, Hip-Hop Culture, and the Public Sphere*. Boston: Northeastern University Press, 2004.

Price, Emmett George, III. *Hip Hop Culture*. New York: ABC-CLIO, 2006.

Quinn, Rachel Afi. "This Bridge Called the Internet: Black Lesbian Feminist Activism in Santo Domingo." In *Transatlantic Feminisms: Women and Gender Studies in Africa and the Diaspora*, edited by Cheryl R. Rodriguez, Dzodzi Tsikata, and Akosua Adomako Ampofo, 25–44. New York: Lexington Books, 2015.

Ranft, Erin. "Blogs as Alternative Spaces for African American Literature and Student Voices." *CLA Journal* 59, no. 3 (2016): 232–41.

Rickman, Aimee. *Adolescence, Girlhood, and Media Migration: US Teens' Use of Social Media to Negotiate Struggles*. New York: Springer, 2018.

Rose, Tricia. *Black Noise: Rap Music and Black Culture in Contemporary America*. Middletown, CT: Wesleyan University Press, 1994.

Rumsey, Phoebe. *Embodied Nostalgia: Early Twentieth Century Social Dance and US Musical Theatre*. PhD diss., CUNY Graduate Center. 2019.

Sandoval, Chela. *Methodology of the Oppressed*. Minneapolis: University of Minnesota Press, 2000.

Sandoval, Chela. "US Third World Feminism: The Theory and Method of the Oppositional Consciousness in the Postmodern World." *Genders* 10 (1991): 1–24.

Schloss, Joseph G. *Foundation: B-girls, B-girls and Hip-Hop Culture in New York*. Oxford: Oxford University Press, 2019.

Sensor Tower. "The Top Mobile Apps, Games, and Publishers of Q1 2018: Sensor Tower's Data Digest." *Sensor Tower*. 1 May 2018. https://sensortower.com/blog/top-apps-games-publishers-q1-2018.

Stoever, Jennifer Lynn. *The Sonic Color Line: Race and the Cultural Politics of Listening*. New York: New York University Press, 2016.

Taylor, Diana. *The Archive and Repertoire: Performing Cultural Memory in the Americas*. Durham, NC: Duke University Press, 2003.

Tomko, Linda J. *Dancing Class: Gender, Ethnicity, and Social Divides in American Dance, 1890–1920*. Bloomington: Indiana University Press, 1999.

Twersky, Carolyn. "The Hype House Just Moved Out of Their Gorgeous LA Mansion." *Seventeen*. 1 June 2020. https://www.seventeen.com/celebrity/a32731655/hype-house-moved-out-of-la-mansion/.

Turner, Edit L. B. *Communitas: The Anthropology of Collective Joy*. New York: Palgrave Macmillan, 2012.

Uhls, Yalda T., and Patricia M. Greenfield. "The Rise of Fame: An Historical Content Analysis." *Cyberpsychology: Journal of Psychological Research on Cyberspace* 5, no. 1 (2011).

Vie, Stephanie. "What's Going On?" Challenges and Opportunities for Social Media Use in the Writing Classroom." *Journal of Faculty Development* 29, no. 2 (2015): 33–44.

Wade, Ashleigh. "New Genres of Being Human: World Making through Viral Blackness." *The Black Scholar* 47, no. 3 (2017): 33–44.

Wade, Ashleigh. "When Social Media Yields More Than 'Likes': Black Girls' Digital Kinship Formations." *Women, Gender, and Families of Color* 7, no. 1 (2019): 80–97.

Walk-Morris, Tatiana. "TikTok's Digital Blackface Problem." *One Zero*. 12 February 2020. https://onezero.medium.com/tiktoks-digital-blackface-problem-409571589a8.

Wang, Sean. "A Close Look into Tik Tok." *Medium*. 15 May 2018. https://medium.com/@seanzhiyangwangsk/a-look-into-tik-toks-success-6c12ebae572c.

Ward, Tom. "The Hype House Is Changing the Face of TikTok." *Forbes*. 24 February 2020. https://www.forbes.com/sites/tomward/2020/02/24/the-hype-house-is-changing-the-face-of-tiktok/#74a32db77c1b.

Watkins, S. Craig. "Black Youth and the Ironies of Capitalism." In *It's the Joint! The Hip Hop Studies Reader*, edited by Murray Forman and Mark Anthony Neal, 557–78. New York: Routledge, 2004.

Watkins, S. Craig. *Representing: Hip Hop Culture and the Production of Black Cinema*. Chicago: University of Chicago Press, 1998.

Wicker, Jewel. "Renegade Creator Jalaiah Harmon on Reclaiming the Viral Dance." *Teen Vogue*. 15 April 2020. https://www.teenvogue.com/story/jalaiah-harmon-renegade-creator-viral-dance.

Williams, Raymond. *Culture*. London: Fontana Press, 1981.

Williams Douglass, Tori. "Stop Policing My Language." Tori Williams Douglass Personal Website. 28 February 2019. https://www.toriglass.com/my-writing/2019/2/28/stop-policing-my-language.

Zevallos, Zuleyka. "Tone Policing People of Colour." *The Other Sociologist*. 17 June 2017. https://othersociologist.com/2017/06/17/tone-policing-people-of-colour/.

AUTHOR BIO

Trevor Boffone never intended to return to the high school classroom after completing his PhD in Latinx Cultural Studies. His plan was to teach high school while also going on the market for a tenure-track job one last time. But he found a home teaching Spanish and dancing through the halls with his students. Their work went viral and Boffone hasn't looked back.

Boffone is a public intellectual who examines race, ethnicity, gender, sexuality, and community in American culture. He is the co-editor of *Encuentro: Latinx Performance for the New American Theater* (Northwestern University Press, 2019), *Teatro Latino: Nuevas obras de los Estados Unidos* (La Casita Grande, 2019), *Nerds, Goths, Geeks, and Freaks: Outsiders in Chicanx/Latinx Young Adult Literature* (University Press of Mississippi, 2020), *Shakespeare and Latinidad* (Edinburgh University Press, 2021), and *Seeking Common Ground: Latinx and Latin American Theatre and Performance* (Bloomsbury Methuen Drama, 2021).

INDEX